GEORGE C.
MARSHALL

Soldier-Statesman
of the American Century

TWAYNE'S TWENTIETH-CENTURY AMERICAN BIOGRAPHY SERIES

John Milton Cooper, Jr., General Editor

GEORGE C. MARSHALL

Soldier-Statesman of the American Century

Mark A. Stoler

TWAYNE PUBLISHERS
A part of Gale, Cengage Learning

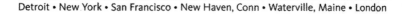

GALE
CENGAGE Learning

Detroit • New York • San Francisco • New Haven, Conn • Waterville, Maine • London

GALE
CENGAGE Learning™

Copyright © 1989 Twayne Publishers, a part of Gale, Cengage Learning
All rights reserved.
Twayne
27500 Drake Rd.
Farmington Hills, MI 48331-3535

Twayne's Twentieth-Century
American Biography Series No. 10

Book Production by Janet Zietowski.
Copyediting supervised by Barbara Sutton.
Typeset in 11/13 Goudy by Compset, Inc.

Cover design by One Plus One Studio.
Cover photograph courtesy of Culver Pictures, Inc.

Library of Congress Cataloging in Publication Data

Stoler, Mark A.
George C. Marshall : soldier-statesman of the American century.

(Twayne's twentieth-century American biography
series ; 10)
Bibliography: p.
Includes index.
1. Marshall, George C. (George Catlett), 1880–1959.
2. Generals—United States—Biography.   3. United States.
Army—Biography.   4. Statesman—United States—Biography.
5. United States—History, Military—20th century.
I. Title. II. Series.
E745.M37S75   1989   973.91′092′4   [B]   88-29474
ISBN 0-8057-7768-7
ISBN 0-8057-7785-7 (pbk.)

Printed in the United States of America
20 21 22 23 24   14 13 12 11 10

ED075

To Avrum A. and Jacob M. Miller

CONTENTS

PREFACE

During the first half of the twentieth century, the United States emerged as the most powerful and influential nation in the world. George C. Marshall's extraordinary career paralleled this rise to power. From the Philippine insurrection that followed America's first colonial venture at the turn of the century through two world wars, the cold war, and the Korean conflict, Marshall was a participant over a fifty-year period in almost every major event and issue that marked the emergence of the United States as a superpower. That emergence, and Marshall's role in it, stand as two central and interrelated themes of this book.

Between 1939 and 1951 Marshall was also a key formulator of U.S. policies, serving as World War II army chief of staff (1939–45), special presidential emissary to China (1945–47), secretary of state during the height of the cold war (1947–49), and secretary of defense during the Korean War (1950–51). He was thus one of the creators not only of America's awesome military power but also of its major foreign policies and global strategies in the contemporary world. Statesman as well as soldier, his character and accomplishments were so exceptional that he is placed in the company only of George Washington when historical parallels and superlatives are used.

Marshall's character cast a giant historical shadow. His leadership qualities, self-control, sense of honor and duty, and apparent lack of personal ambition were so extraordinary that virtually every individual with whom he worked, from President Harry S. Truman on down, felt dutybound to recount and comment on them in hushed tones of veneration. As with George Washington, the result was the creation of a historical monument and legend that, although often accurate as to personal characteristics, just as often masked rather than revealed the subject's key beliefs and historical contributions.

For Marshall the most important of these beliefs and contributions concerned power. Throughout his career he was forced to deal with the different aspects, complexities, ironies, nuances, and contradictions of power as the United States continued to amass it. While the theologian Reinhold Niebuhr

ix

was attempting to explain these to an American people unprepared for global responsibilities, Marshall, by his actions and beliefs, became the incarnation of the leader who learned to understand them and to act accordingly. Power was not limitless or divisible, appearances to the contrary notwithstanding. Its military, political, and economic aspects could not be divorced from each other. Nor could they be equated, or renounced in an effort to maintain a state of moral purity. In the imperfect world of human beings, each had to be accepted, understood, coordinated, and made to serve the goals of a rational and ethical policy. That required the creation and implementation of specific strategies that appropriately linked available means with desired ends and that reinforced rather than challenged the most cherished values of American society. Strategy, in short, realistically and properly had to serve policy, not subvert it.

Marshall consistently attempted to implement these principles. In the process he strongly supported a series of key concepts. Foremost among these was the need for a citizen rather than a professional army in a democracy, the importance of civilian control over the military, the primacy of Europe over Asia in U.S. strategy and policy, the linking of economic with military and diplomatic issues, and the acceptance of limited as well as unlimited war. His support of these concepts stands as an additional, important theme of this book.

ACKNOWLEDGMENTS

Biography is a popular and enjoyable form of historical literature. It is also a complex and difficult one to research and write, as I have painfully discovered. This is especially true with an individual like George Marshall, who was involved with so many important issues and whose character was so private and reticent. Numerous individuals have helped me to overcome these difficulties, and I am deeply indebted to them.

Foremost in this category is Marshall biographer Forrest C. Pogue, who answered my numerous questions, read and commented on the manuscript, and shared with me his valuable time and enormous knowledge. This is nothing new. For many years he has offered assistance to others no matter how numerous the requests, how busy his schedule, or how lowly the status of the requestor. Many young scholars suddenly cast adrift to do research in Washington, myself included, can attest to this fact. In numerous ways we are his grateful advisees.

Marshall papers editor Larry Bland also offered invaluable assistance by reading and commenting on the manuscript as well as answering my many questions. Equally important was his overall help and that of archivist John Jacob during my visits to the Marshall Library in Lexington, Virginia. Marshall Foundation director Gordon Beyer and former director Fred Hadsel offered encouragement and exceptional hospitality.

I am also grateful to the Foundation for permission to publish material from the George C. Marshall and Paul M. Robinett papers and to reproduce photographs from its collections; to the Yale University Library for permission to publish material from the Henry L. Stimson papers; and to Bill Mauldin and Wil-Jo Associates for permission to reproduce Mr. Mauldin's 1959 cartoon tribute to George Marshall.

Elsewhere, Twayne American Biography Series editor John Milton Cooper honored me with the request to write this volume and has consistently provided critical support, encouragement, patience, and advice. So have numerous colleagues and friends in the University of Vermont History Department, most notably Constance M. McGovern and Samuel B. Hand. I am also deeply indebted to the university for a sabbatical leave to complete this project, and to the reference and documents staffs of the Bailey-Howe Library for their important assistance. At other institutions, colleagues J. Garry Clifford, Lloyd C. Gardner, Michael J. Hogan, Warren F. Kimball, Melvyn P. Leffler, Timothy K. Nenninger, Thomas G. Paterson, William W. Stueck, Nancy Bernkopf Tucker, and Theodore A. Wilson all gave of their time and knowledge. I also owe an enormous debt to the students and faculty of the Naval War College, where I spent the 1981–82 academic year as a visiting professor in the Strategy Department, for many of the ideas developed in this volume as well as one of the most intellectually stimulating experiences of my career. Foremost in this category is Captain Marino J. Bartolomei, U.S. Navy, my co-teacher and friend.

These individuals have all provided me with invaluable information, advice, criticism, help, and support. None of them, however, bears responsibility for the quality of this work. That continues to rest solely with the author.

1

TWO WORLDS,
1880–1902

On 10 December 1953 an elderly American of commanding presence accepted the Nobel Peace Prize for "the most constructive, peaceful work we have seen in this century," the European Recovery Program. The recipient stands unique among all others who have been given this highly prestigious award. For most of his life, he had served as an army officer. Never before had the peace prize gone to a professional soldier.

In World War I he had helped to train a massive U.S. Army and planned its largest operations. During World War II he had created the greatest war machine the world had ever seen. Afterward he had played a pivotal role in its re-creation and in the formulation of U.S. global strategy and foreign policy. A few years before receiving the Nobel prize he had overseen yet another U.S. war effort, the third in his career.

Adding to the paradox a warrior receiving a peace prize was the fact that while he was being honored at the awards ceremony in Oslo, Norway, he was simultaneously being labeled a Communist dupe and a traitor by some elements within his own country and a warmonger by others. The ceremony was itself disrupted by three young men screaming "murderer" from the balcony and handing out accusatory leaflets. Ignoring the disruption, the entire audience rose to applaud and honor the man they considered primarily responsible not only for the World War II victory over nazism but also for their postwar victory over starvation and despair.[1]

Such paradoxes were nothing new for the award recipient, George Catlett Marshall. He had experienced them for many years and by 1953 had come to view them as far from remarkable. From the moment of his birth in 1880 to this triumph in Oslo, he had consistently lived in multiple, contradictory worlds and had managed to harmonize the conflicts between them. In the process, he had created an extraordinary list of accomplishments for himself and his country.

Marshall had been born and raised in two dramatically different worlds. The first was the traditional, rural environment that had existed in North America since the establishment of the English colonies. The second was the world of the industrial revolution that swept through the United States in the second half of the nineteenth century and transformed almost every aspect of life. Industry replaced agriculture as the primary economic base of society, and cities replaced farms and small towns as the organizational unit within which most people lived. In time, such alterations would make the United States the richest and most powerful country in the world. They would also profoundly affect the ways Americans lived and the ways in which they thought.

Unlike political revolutions, this industrial revolution did not take place within a brief period of time. The changes resulting from industrialization, massive ones, developed gradually over decades and affected different aspects of life in different ways at different times. Some aspects remained quite traditional well into the twentieth century. As a result, the United States in the late nineteenth century was an odd combination of two worlds: the new industrial one and the old rural one.

George Catlett Marshall, Jr., was born into this dual world on 31 December 1880, in Uniontown, Pennsylvania. His parents, Laura Bradford Marshall and George Catlett Marshall, Sr., were a prosperous, middle-class couple from old, well-established Virginia and Kentucky families. They had married in 1873 and between 1874 and 1876 had had three children: William Champe, who died at six months; Stuart Bradford; and Marie. George, Jr., was born four years later and baptized in June 1881 at the local Episcopal church.

Most of the early influences on the young George Marshall came from the older and rural rather than the new, industrial America, and many of those influences were southern. Although he was born and raised in Pennsylvania and although his father had briefly fought for the

Union in Kentucky during the Civil War, Marshall's family was overwhelmingly Virginian in terms of history and values. Its roots dated back to before the Revolution. The great Supreme Court chief justice John Marshall had been a distant relative, and the names of Marshall, Catlett, and Bradford were well known in Virginia and Kentucky history. Marshall's parents were in many ways classic products of this history, and they attempted to inculcate in their children the traditional values, morals, and manners of this region.

Although situated north of the Mason-Dixon line, Uniontown reinforced many of those traditional, rural values. It had been established in 1776 as a waystop along the old National Road across the Allegheny Mountains, only to be cut off from future rapid development in the nineteenth century when railroads replaced stagecoaches. In 1880 it was still a small town of 3,500, and it remained this way throughout most of Marshall's childhood.

On the surface, then, Marshall's early years were both traditional and rural, and in his later reminiscences about his childhood, the industrial revolution is barely mentioned. Instead one is given an idyllic image of nineteenth-century small-town America, an image that could have been taken directly out of a Mark Twain novel. Neither electricity nor automobiles existed in this image. Young George's world consisted of a five-mile radius around his large, two-story brick home at the end of Uniontown's West Main Street, though within that radius, he later recollected, "I seem to have stuck my nose in everything." That included exploration of the stream and historic Braddock trail, which ran near the house, and participation with his circle of childhood friends, who nicknamed him "Flicker," in games and sports such as baseball, sledding, and iceskating. It also included hunting, fishing, and walking with his father through the nearby fields and woods and listening to the stories of James Fenimore Cooper and Arthur Conan Doyle at his parents' feet. As he learned to read, young George developed a taste for some of the cheap penny thrillers of the era. He also developed an ability to get into trouble with his parents and older siblings and apparently received his fair share of paternal spankings for such behavior. The last of these occurred when he tried to turn a water hose on his sister, only to hit his mother by accident when she walked out the door instead.[2]

Beneath this surface of idyllic small-town America, however, the industrial revolution deeply affected Marshall and his family. Uniontown continued to exist and prosper primarily because of that revolution in the form of the iron and steel industry and the massive coal deposits in the area. Marshall's father was an industrial entrepreneur who had moved to Pennsylvania after the Civil War to make his fortune in coke. He succeeded in doing so during the 1870s and 1880s, and in 1889 he and his partners realized an enormous profit by selling most of their holdings to the growing empire of Henry Clay Frick. Not surprisingly, many of Marshall's later recollections of his childhood activities involved amateur entrepreneurship of some sort.[3]

The industrial revolution was thus the economic basis of Marshall's family and home town. Eventually the most visible signs of this revolution in the form of massive expansion and urbanization transformed Uniontown and, in Marshall's later words, "buried my youthful associations . . . under a twenty foot fill."[4] But this did not occur until after he left in 1897. Prior to that time, Uniontown remained a small, preindustrial town, and throughout his life Marshall remained most comfortable and relaxed in rural pursuits, such as gardening, that he had learned as a boy. Nevertheless, certain aspects of industrialization were already affecting Uniontown in the 1880s.

Homogeneity in the area had begun to break down as workers with foreign names and customs arrived from Europe to mine the precious ores and run the furnaces. When they launched strikes to improve their low wages and terrible working conditions, mine owners responded with strikebreakers and private police. Violence often resulted, with the state militia called in and workers killed. The unsuccessful 1892 strike against the Carnegie steelworks in Homestead, Pennsylvania, was one of the bloodiest and most famous of such episodes and one that Marshall remembered "very well" in his later years. He also remembered the retaliatory violence of the workers, particularly the secret Molly Maguires who threatened his father and assassinated his father's partner. George himself was wounded while watching one strike when a lump of coal thrown from behind a picket line hit him on the forehead and left a small blue scar.[5]

Of equal if not more impact on the young Marshall was the family's sudden loss of financial security in 1890. His father had invested the small fortune resulting from the sale to Frick in land and a hotel in the Blue Ridge Mountain resort of Luray, Virginia. George would later refer to this decision of his father as "the great mistake of his life, and much against my mother's advice." Soon after the land boom in the area collapsed, and the inn burned down. In classic boom-and-bust cycle, Marshall, Sr., lost almost overnight all he had worked for and gained in the preceding twenty years. While by no means reduced to poverty, Marshall later remembered that the family was forced "to economize very bitterly." Only his mother's landholdings provided the income to see them through this period and the tuition for his college education. Young George was humiliated by the experience and developed what his official biographer labeled "a passion for solvency which he never lost."[6]

A more indirect result of industrialization may have had the greatest impact of all on the young Marshall: the changing size and nature of the American family. In 1800 the average number of children in a family had been more than seven. By 1890 that number was down to a little more than four. The fact that George Marshall remained the youngest member of a small family is thus related to the industrial revolution. This family status played an important role in determining his relationships with his parents and siblings, as did the Victorian values that had fully developed within the American family.

Perhaps most notable in this regard was the close relationship Marshall developed with his mother, a relationship encouraged by society's mores, as well as by his status as the youngest child. She was a quiet, affectionate, and supportive woman, and her younger son seemed to hold a special place in her heart. When Stuart and Marie went off to school, only he remained at home, and he was thus to an extent raised as an only child. He later admitted that his mother had spoiled him. More important, she became his "confidante in practically all my boyish escapades and difficulties." Clearly she was the most important person in his childhood and by his own recollection a "constant and lasting influence on my life."[7]

His relationships with his father and siblings were not as close or warm. To his older brother and sister, he was primarily a younger embarrassment and annoyance, and he was not intimate with either of them. Nor was he close to his father, a man who, despite a reputation for social gregariousness, was cold and aloof at home, as well as highly critical of his younger son. That son may well have reciprocated such feelings when his father lost his fortune and thereby failed in what was then considered his primary familial task: to be the breadwinner. Marshall's recollection in later years, however, was that his father simply preferred older brother Stuart to him.[8]

Marshall's possible feelings of rejection and low self-esteem may have been reinforced by his physical awkwardness and poor performance as a student. By age ten he was quite tall, had large feet, and was made fun of by his classmates. He was also considered a slow learner, primarily because of poor preparation and attitude rather than low intelligence. His first experiences with education had been the rigid tutoring of a great-aunt when he was five, followed by enrollment in a nonchallenging school run by a local spinster. The combined impact of these two could not have been worse. "Having learned from his great aunt to hate studying," his official biographer has noted, "George was pleased to find at Miss Thompson's that it was apparently unnecessary." That pleasure was short-lived, for when he transferred to public school a few years later, he was unprepared and did poorly.[9]

Ashamed and humiliated by his academic performance and the treatment he received from his peers, distant from his father and his siblings, young Marshall responded by seeking approval and companionship elsewhere. John R. Wightman, a new, young pastor at his church who was having trouble winning local acceptance, became a close friend and a major influence. Marshall also responded by developing some protective and distinctive character traits that complemented parental values and would remain key components of his adult personality. Most notable in this regard were his shyness and reserve, his desire to excel as a means of proving his worth to his critics, and his insistence on avoiding the appearance of failure or flaw, an insistence that later became an important aspect of his leadership ability. Highly illustrative of this characteristic was his reaction when a group of young girls laughingly refused to pay for a ride on his raft despite their previous agreement to do so; he pulled a plug and sank the raft, with them still on it. "I never forgot that," he later reminisced, "because I had to do something and I had to think quickly, and what I did set me up again as the temporary master of the situation."[10]

None of this was very exceptional for an American child in the 1880s and 1890s, however, and what may be most striking about Marshall's early years is how normal and uneventful they were. One early biographer labeled his childhood "unremarkable,"[11] and it is indeed true that little substantive can be found to distinguish Marshall from his peers before 1897. At about that time, however, he decided to become a professional soldier. That decision was quite distinctive; so was the method he chose to reach his goal.

With the Civil War still recent memory, many male children in the late nineteenth century dreamed of becoming soldiers. Most of them gave up such dreams as they matured, however, for the reality of the post–Civil War army was a far cry from the images held by children—

and by most Americans since. While those images center on the gallant cavalry rescuing the wagon train from the Indians, the reality was a paltry force of 25,000 officers and men, the bulk taken from the dregs of society, which fought its last major Indian battle in 1890. Stationed on the frontier with little to do save policing, this force was both isolated from and despised by the bulk of society, and there was little opportunity for either adventure or advancement.[12]

On these grounds alone, Marshall's parents would have opposed his choice of career. His father raised additional objections as a Civil War veteran who knew the harsh reality of war at first-hand and as a realist who did not think his son could obtain an officer's commission. The problem was both political and academic. The only sure road to a commission was appointment to the U.S. Military Academy at West Point, and that required nomination by one's congressman or senator. Unfortunately Marshall's father was a Democrat, while his congressman and senators were Republicans. Moreover, Marshall's mediocre academic performance did not promise success on the competitive examination his congressman gave to those interested in attending West Point. Nor was he convinced he could pass the physical examination in the light of an injured right elbow (it had been partly dislocated in childhood and never healed properly).[13]

Faced with these obstacles as well as parental opposition, Marshall never even applied to West Point. There was, however, a possible alternative route to the army that his father could not oppose, a route steeped in southern history and tradition and one his older brother had already traveled: he could attend the Virginia Military Institute (VMI).

Situated at the southern end of the historic Shenandoah valley in Lexington, Virginia, VMI in 1897 was by no means the place to go if one desired an army career. It was a military school, but only a small percentage of its graduates held regular commissions, and the training of professional officers was not its primary aim. Rather that aim was to inculcate in its students the so-called "military virtues," most notably discipline, and to produce solid citizens who by training and values could temporarily leave civilian life and serve as officers if a national emergency arose.

This "citizen-soldier" concept dated far back into English history and the first English settlements in the New World, and it formed the basis of the American military tradition. According to that tradition, primary responsibility for the common defense rested with local, trained citizens organized into militia units, not with a professional force, which

7

could constitute a threat to civil liberties and economic well-being. Such militia units had existed in all the American colonies prior to 1776. They had played a major role in the American War for Independence, and they had been dealt with extensively in both the Constitution and early congressional legislation. Indeed, the rationale for the Second Amendment in the Bill of Rights guaranteeing citizens the right to bear arms concerns the right and responsibility of those citizens to be part of an organized and trained militia.

The militia units had never worked according to this theoretical model. In practice they were ill trained and unreliable, and their officers were often incompetent political appointments. During the Revolutionary War, they had proved useful on occasion but only when well led and used in conjunction with regulars from Washington's Continental Army. Over the next century they had gradually lost power and influence to the regular army and the special national volunteer armies that Congress established in times of emergency. Still, those volunteer armies required trained officers beyond the number produced by West Point. So did the National Guard, a group of elite state militia units that emerged after the Civil War as the general militia system collapsed. VMI and other "tin colleges" like the Citadel in South Carolina provided such potential officers in the form of a college-educated, militarily trained group of civilians capable and ready to lead armed forces when called upon.

In addition to being part of this national military tradition, VMI was also a key component in the southern military tradition. General Thomas "Stonewall" Jackson had taught there prior to his remarkable military career in the Civil War, and the school venerated his campaigns and memory. It also venerated the cadets who had been called out during May 1864 to check a Union force at nearby New Market and who had fought and died on that battlefield. In 1897 these memories were still recent history. General Scott Shipp, the school superintendent, had commanded the VMI cadets at New Market and had been wounded in the battle.

An institution so steeped in southern and national traditions appealed to the Marshall family. Stuart Marshall had attended and graduated from VMI in 1894 with a specialty in chemistry and had gone on to work in private industry. It seemed there could be no objection to young George's doing likewise, but there was, for Stuart feared his awkward and academically slow younger brother would disgrace the family name if allowed to attend, and he said so. His objections were overruled, but they were to have a profound influence on George's career, at VMI and later. He overheard Stuart's insulting comments and angrily vowed to "wipe his eye" by surpassing him. The "urging" to succeed "came from overhearing this conversation," Marshall later recalled with intense feeling, "and it had quite a psychological effect on my career."[14]

Vowing to succeed was one thing. Doing so was another, and Marshall entered VMI in the fall of 1897 with a few strikes already against him. He arrived late and weak after a bout with typhoid fever. He was a northerner in the southern heartland, his Yankee twang clearly separating him from most of his peers and placing him once again between two worlds. He was academically ill prepared, tall, awkward, and shy. According to one story, "He could not drill. He could not march. All he could do was sweat, look uncomfortable and be embarrassed whenever spoken to."[15]

Life at VMI for a first-year student, or "Rat," was brutal under the best of circumstances. Along with the rigid, spartan atmosphere of the school and the emphasis on discipline went the virtual sadism of older students who practiced a particularly severe form of hazing. By virtue of his unique characteristics, Marshall was quickly singled out, and in his first few weeks at VMI he was ordered to squat directly over an unsheathed bayonet and to remain in that position until ordered otherwise. He did so without comment or complaint, but, still weak from typhoid fever, he collapsed after twenty minutes, receiving a gash on his buttock and barely escaping serious injury. He never told the authorities what had happened. Impressed by his stoicism and silence as well as frightened by the fact that this illegal hazing prank had gotten out of hand, the upperclassmen then treated him with new-found respect.

That respect increased as "Rat" Marshall set about mastering VMI's requirements and values to fulfill his vow. He remained a mediocre student academically but by effort raised himself to nineteenth in his class of forty-seven and began to excel at what the school most valued: drill, dress, self-control, discipline, and leadership. At the end of his first year, he was appointed first corporal of cadets, the highest rank in his class. By the end of his second year, he was one of the first sergeants. By the end of his third year, he had made the football team, developed a specialty and ability in engineering, and been named first captain of the corps of cadets, a tribute, in the words of one early biographer "not to his brains but to his prowess as a precision machine."[16]

While accurate to an extent, that comment is also misleading. Marshall was far from stupid, and he excelled at much more than spit and polish. His appointment as first captain was also a tribute to his self-

9

control, his discipline, and, perhaps most important, his leadership and ability to manage men. Marshall would later claim that VMI taught him these characteristics,[17] but it is probably more accurate to state that the school nurtured what were natural strengths within him by placing such a high value on them. Driven to excel by Stuart's insults, as well as his desire for an army commission, he transformed his childhood traits so he could succeed by VMI's norms and developed additional strengths as needed. Shyness, for example, became austerity and coolness, and stoicism and hard work translated into perfection on the drill field. The result was a unique character and form of charisma, a leadership over others that must be understood in late nineteenth-century military rather than late twentieth-century civilian terms. It was marked by austerity, discipline, and distance from his peers, and it gave Marshall what he wanted most from them and from his superiors at VMI: not love but respect.

But love came too, albeit from a different source. Her name was Elizabeth Carter Coles. Nicknamed Lily, she was a beautiful, vivacious member of one of Virginia's first families who lived in Lexington with her widowed mother. She was at least four years Marshall's senior and had dated Stuart when he had been a cadet at VMI. Marshall must have later savored this unexpected and unique aspect of surpassing his sibling. He met Lily during his last year at VMI and within a few weeks they were "steadies." Ambition was now tempered by love and by an expanding social life under Lily's influence, with Marshall even risking his career by illegally leaving the school after hours, a dismissal offense known as "running the block," in order to be with her. "I was very much in love," was his explanation in later years, "and I was willing to take the chance."[18] By the mores of the era, marriage was clearly in the foreseeable future.

Men who married at that time had to be able to support a wife financially, and in the spring of 1901 Marshall did not have a job. He wanted more than ever to be an army officer, but even with his excellent record at VMI, a commission in the small U.S. Army would be difficult for a non–West Pointer to obtain.

By 1901, however, obtaining a commission was a bit easier than it had been four years earlier, for the army had quadrupled in size from 25,000 to 100,000 and officers were badly needed. The reason for this expansion was the dramatic rise of the United States to world power in the late nineteenth century, a rise symbolized and stimulated by the

Spanish-American War of 1898. Marshall received an officer's commission because of this rise to power, and his ensuing career would be inextricably interwoven with every major component of it.

U.S. ascension to world power actually preceded the Spanish-American War by many years. Between 1783 and 1853 the United States had expanded dramatically across North America to become a continental power of massive proportions. Further expansion was then temporarily checked by sectional conflict and the ensuing Civil War. Secretary of State William Henry Seward had attempted to resurrect the expansionist thrust immediately after the war, but with the notable exceptions of Alaska and Midway, he had been blocked by the politics of Reconstruction and congressional insistence on dismantling the massive armed force that had won the war for the Union. By 1880 the army was down to a paltry 25,000, and the ignored and rotting navy ranked seventeenth in the world.

The industrial revolution changed all that. Advances in transportation and communication increased U.S. contact with and interest in the rest of the world. Other technological advances increased the range and killing power of weapons, leading some Americans to question whether they could continue to pursue their traditional isolationist foreign policy regarding Europe and to rely on the Atlantic Ocean as their primary defense against potential Old World aggressors. The expansion of U.S. industry in the late nineteenth century also led to overproduction, cyclical depressions, growing labor-management violence, and a heated search for overseas markets for American goods as a solution to these problems. For many, the Census Bureau's official announcement in 1890 of the end of the frontier symbolized the end of opportunity in the United States and the need to expand overseas in search of new opportunities. The era also witnessed a revival of the American belief in a divinely inspired mission to bring the blessings of Christianity and democracy to the rest of the world and thereby to remake the world in the American image, as well as a growing social Darwinian belief that civilizations had to expand or die. The result was a revival of overseas expansionist energies that reached fruition during the 1890s.

Such expansion often involved the threat and/or use of military force, and throughout the 1890s the navy grew enormously to meet the increasing overseas interests and commitments of the United States. The army did not, however, for until 1898 none of these interests required the use of large land forces. The Spanish-American War changed that,

11

and in 1898 Congress authorized the temporary expansion of the regular army to 65,000, as well as the creation of a volunteer force of 200,000 in order to defeat the Spanish and liberate Cuba.

The war tremendously excited all VMI students, including Marshall. Upon the outbreak of hostilities, the entire corps unanimously offered its services to the government and then followed the war news with intense interest. Marshall was particularly interested, for the volunteer forces included both recent VMI graduates he knew and a Pennsylvania National Guard regiment with one company from Uniontown. That company wound up in the Philippines, and during the summer of 1899 Marshall returned to Uniontown and participated in the tumultuous homecoming parade the local heroes received. It affected him tremendously, and he later stated that this "first great emotional reaction" had "a determining effect on my choice of profession."[19]

Forty years after the event, Marshall also realized that the parade had symbolized a dramatic shift in American perceptions and activities. "Few of us had ever heard of the Philippines until that year," he noted in 1939. "We had heard of manila rope, but we did not know where Manila was." Now they did, and while the parade was "a grand American small town demonstration of pride in its young men and of wholesome enthusiasm over their achievements," in retrospect "most of us realized that it was much more than that. It reflected the introduction of America into the affairs of the world beyond the seas."[20]

This introduction both solidified Marshall's desire to become a soldier and made possible the fulfillment of that desire. After all of its previous wars, the United States had dismantled the expanded regular and volunteer forces created to fight. This time it did not. Occupation forces would remain in Cuba for four years and in the Philippines for many more. After Admiral George Dewey's great naval victory in Manila harbor, the army had been sent to occupy the city. President William McKinley had then decided to keep the entire archipelago, as well as Guam farther east and Puerto Rico in the Caribbean. Simultaneously the Congress, under his prodding, formally annexed the Hawaiian Islands. The United States had acquired an overseas colonial empire that would require army as well as naval forces to defend.

When Philippine rebels made clear that they found U.S. rule no more acceptable than Spanish rule, it became obvious that army forces would also be needed to put down an insurrection. Consequently the Congress in 1899 retained the expanded 65,000-man army, as well as 35,000 temporary volunteers. In 1901 it authorized a regular army of

100,000 with an additional 837 first and second lieutenancies to replace the temporary wartime officers. Priority for these commissions would be given first to West Point graduates, then to successful applicants from the ranks, then to former officers of volunteers, and finally to qualified civilians. Marshall would be in this last category, but all except the West Pointers were to be selected by competitive examination.[21]

Graduating at the time Congress was passing this bill, Marshall was presented with a unique opportunity to obtain a commission. His parents still opposed his choice of profession, but when General Shipp strongly supported the idea, Marshall's father swung behind his son and organized a campaign to obtain the commission. Such a campaign was necessary because Marshall would need a letter of authorization from the War Department simply to take the examination, and such a letter required political connections. Marshall, Sr., sent a constant stream of inquiries and appeals to influential friends in Washington. He sent his son to the capital to meet personally with those friends, including Attorney General Philander C. Knox. On his own initiative, the twenty-year-old George also managed to get past numerous guards and obstacles, bursting in on both the chairman of the House Military Affairs Committee and President McKinley.[22]

More important than such extraordinary boldness were the recommendations he received and his father's tireless efforts with friends and political connections. General Shipp made clear his belief that George was as qualified to be an officer "as any man who has been turned out here" and that if commissioned he would "soon take his stand much above the average West Point graduate." Marshall, Sr., made sure such recommendations went to the president and used every connection he had. As a result, the Pennsylvania senators made Marshall one of their allotted twenty-three nominees for the examination, noting, in a compliment to his father's methods as well as his own achievements, that he was "a young man of excellent connections and marked ability." The head of the examining board was informed at the time of the examination in late September that General Shipp considered Marshall "one of the fittest pieces of food for gunpowder turned out by his mill for many years."[23]

By that time there were 10,000 applications for the new lieutenancies and only 142 positions left. Marshall made sure he would have employment no matter what happened by taking a job as commandant and teacher at a military prep school in Danville, Virginia, but he had no need to worry. He achieved an 84.8 percent average on the three-day examination, one of the highest scores and more than sufficient to gain him a commission. It was not, however, a tribute to his intellectual abilities. The academic components of the exam were high-school level, and his grades of 65 in geography and law were barely passing. His 75 in English grammar was not much better. An 89 in history and 86 in math helped, but his high overall average was primarily the result of perfect grades in the heavily weighted categories of "physique" and "moral character and antecedents."[24]

How he had obtained the high average was not important. The fact was that he had and that he would soon have an army commission. His future relatively secure, he resigned his position at Danville late in the year and made plans to marry. In early January 1902, his commission as a second lieutenant was confirmed, albeit in infantry rather than artillery as he had preferred, and he was ordered to report to Washington by 13 February preparatory to being sent to the Philippines. On 11 February he and Lily were married in Lexington and the next morning took the train to Washington for a one-day honeymoon. The War Department gracefully extended that to ten days when he reported on the thirteenth and explained his situation. Afterward Lily returned to Lexington while George started his journey to the Philippines.

Marshall was about to begin the first of many overseas adventures he and his country would participate in over the next half-century. Trained as a nineteenth-century citizen-soldier yet commissioned in a twentieth-century army of empire, he was also once again between two worlds.

2

YOUNG OFFICER IN
A NEW ARMY,
1902–15

Between 1902 and 1916, the talented and ambitious George Marshall would serve in a series of junior military assignments overseas and in the United States. In the process he would develop an extraordinary reputation among his peers and superiors yet advance slowly in rank. Not until 1907 did he receive his first promotion, and not until 1916, at the age of thirty-five, did he become a captain. The responsibilities he held during these years were far beyond his rank, however, and by 1916 he was already perceived by many as destined for greatness.

During this time the newly expanded army began a major transformation. To an extent, U.S. overseas interests dictated this transformation, as they had the expansion. But equally if not more important were the military and political consequences of the industrial revolution, consequences that brought to a head a series of problems in traditional U.S. military policy and gave birth to a major reform movement within the army. While Marshall was too young and junior an officer to play a large role in this movement, he would become one of its first and finest products. Indeed many of the positions he held during this period were a direct result of army reform, and Marshall was in many ways the model of the new twentieth-century army officer.

Marshall's first assignment was, in effect, with a colonial army of occupation. President McKinley's decision to retain the Philippines after the Spanish-American War had been followed by a brutal conflict between Filipino guerrillas and the U.S. Army. In 1901 the rebel leader Emilio Aguinaldo was captured, but numerous rebel forces continued to fight. Not until April 1902 did those remaining on the main island of Luzon surrender, and not until July of that year did President Theodore Roosevelt proclaim the rebellion officially over. Even then sporadic fighting continued on other islands. Governmental powers were gradually being transferred from the army to civilians under newly appointed governor William Howard Taft, but 34,000 U.S. troops still remained in the Philippines when Marshall arrived in 1902.[1]

Marshall was too late to participate in any major battles against the guerrillas. His primary enemies would be disease, the weather, and boredom, something he learned almost immediately after his arrival in Manila. That arrival coincided with a cholera epidemic that killed at least 100,000 people. When he tried to get to his first assignment with the Thirtieth Infantry Regiment on the island of Mindoro, a quarantine kept his ship at sea and in the scorching heat for five days. The only relief was to swim, but the waters were shark infested. Marshall discovered this after he and a fellow lieutenant had gone into the water. What followed was a panicked race to the rope ladder on the side of the ship. "I never showed such strength and agility in my life as going up the side of that boat," Marshall later recollected. "That was the only cooling experience that we had, and it could hardly be called that."[1]

Then a typhoon hit the ship. It frightened the captain off the bridge, smashed the ribs of the man at the wheel, flooded the engine room, panicked the crew, and almost capsized the vessel. Marshall and his co-lieutenant had to take over the ship and force the frightened crew to work at gunpoint. They succeeded and arrived safely at Mindoro's capital of Calapan, where they immediately came face to face with one of the ironies of American colonialism: a sergeant teaching a group of Filipino children how to speak and sing in English while their rebel fathers remained in the surrounding hills. Soon after the cholera epidemic reached Mindoro. Marshall and the U.S. soldiers headquartered in Calapan were confined to barracks. That and rigid cleanliness measures probably saved their lives, but it also exacerbated their boredom and poor morale.[2]

Once the quarantine was lifted, Marshall proceeded to his assigned company in Mangarin on the opposite end of the island. He arrived to find no town and no other officer present save for a first lieutenant, who departed two weeks later. According to one of the soldiers, he "appeared very green in military affairs." He himself would later comment that "there was nothing much lower than a second lieutenant and I was about the junior second lieutenant in the army at that time." Yet in the absence of a first lieutenant or captain as well as civilian authority, he was both the commanding officer of the company and, in his own words, "virtually the governor" of southern Mindoro at that time. This situation would last for only six weeks until a new captain arrived, but it would be repeated on two additional occasions during Marshall's tour of duty in the Philippines and provide the first of what would be many command positions far beyond his rank.[3]

The twenty-one-year-old Marshall quickly established friendships with key local civilians and exerted his authority over the company by a combination of qualities that would mark his later military career. He relied heavily on subordinates, in this case two experienced sergeants, maintained discipline, and exhibited a rare resourcefulness for a person of his age and experience. Illustrative of this was his reaction when a few of his men panicked during a stream crossing. Fearing crocodiles, they broke and ran, knocking Marshall down and then stampeding over him in their haste to reach safety on the shore. He was not a commanding sight when he emerged from the stream, but instead of screaming or just standing and looking foolish, he immediately ordered his men to fall in behind him and recross the stream. After they did so, he ordered an about-face and recrossed the crocodile-infested stream again. Then he calmly inspected and dismissed them. Nothing was ever said again about the episode; there was no need to do so.[4]

In November 1903 Marshall returned to the United States via Japan and Hawaii and was assigned to Fort Reno, an army post across the river from Indian reservations in Oklahoma. Although Lily was able to join him there and although the post was within the continental United States, Fort Reno was in many ways just as isolated from American civilian society as the Philippines had been. Indeed one could argue that despite their enormous geographic distance from each other, the two assignments had much in common. Each involved policing a conquered populace (Cheyenne and Arapaho or Filipino). Each took place in a hostile climate, with the heat and terrain of the Southwest just as enervating as that of the Philippines. During a 1905 mapping expedition in Texas that he later described as "the hardest service I ever had in the army," Marshall faced temperatures of 130 degrees, lost about thirty-five pounds, and returned so physically transformed that the captain to whom he reported (later Chief of Staff Malin Craig) did not believe he could

17

be an officer.[5] Each assignment was also boring, with Marshall able to complete his daily tasks before noon. For relief in the Philippines, he had taken up horseback riding, a hobby that would be his favorite life-time recreation. At Fort Reno he returned to his old pastime of hunting.

The Philippine and Fort Reno assignments were similar in one other respect: both involved the "old army," an institution that despite its ex-pansion during the Spanish-American War remained essentially a nine-teenth-century phenomenon in a rapidly changing twentieth-century world.[6] VMI had taught Marshall the rules of this old army through its emphasis on rank and discipline, and the young, fastidious lieutenant was able to fit into it well. Like the United States, however, the army was rapidly changing, and what is most interesting about George Mar-shall as a young officer is not his admitted ability in traditional spit and polish but his excellence in the new arenas and responsibilities of army life—most notably higher education, staff work, and relations with ci-vilians. Between 1906 and 1916, Marshall revealed his extraordinary tal-ents in these areas.

The transformation of the U.S. Army had begun as a result of shocking revelations following the Spanish-American War. Despite its military victories in that conflict, the army had been wracked by scan-dals. Organization had almost totally broken down under the strain of wartime mobilization and in the process had revealed a host of serious problems. Troops destined for tropical Cuba had arrived in Florida for embarkation with winter uniforms. Supplies were inadequate and could not be effectively transported to the troops. Food turned out to be dis-eased. Transport to Cuba was insufficient, and no one seemed to possess an overall strategic plan or even basic knowledge of the enemy and the terrain the troops would be facing. Coordination between the army and navy in Cuba was abysmal, and the commanding officers of the two ser-vices seemed to spend more time fighting each other than the Spanish. U.S. soldiers and sailors performed well but under such circumstances suffered high and unnecessary casualties. More of them fell to diseased meat and unsanitary living conditions than to Spanish bullets.

Most of the blame for the army's problems was placed on the War Department and its incompetent secretary, Russell Alger, and in 1899 he was forced to resign. President McKinley replaced him with Elihu Root, a corporation lawyer with no background in military affairs but with a clear mandate to reform and reorganize the army so that it could effectively govern, as well as defend, America's new colonial empire.

Root quickly discovered that Alger's mismanagement was not the real problem. Rather it was the dated and illogical military organization that had developed within the army and the War Department and, on a deeper level, the traditional military policy of the United States.

Authority within the army flowed from two distinct and antithetical chains of command. The first was the commanding general, who was responsible to the president for military operations and discipline. The second consisted of ten permanent bureau chiefs, who were responsible for such support services as recruitment, supplies, and finances; they reported to the secretary of war and the Congress, and they possessed enormous influence on Capitol Hill as well as within the army.

An equally dual and unworkable system existed in regard to manpower mobilization. Throughout its history, the United States had theoretically relied for defense on a small professional army backed by a huge mass of citizen-soldiers organized by state within a theoretical militia model. It had done so primarily for political and philosophical reasons, fearing the concentration of power and subsequent menace to liberty embodied in a large, professional force under only federal control. So great was the fear of concentrated power among the Founding Fathers of the Constitution that they divided authority over the armed forces within their checks and balances system, making the president commander in chief but giving Congress fiscal control and leaving the states primarily responsible for the militia.

While politically astute, the system had again and again proved itself to be militarily unworkable. Under state control, the militia remained largely untrained and unreliable, with the War of 1812 providing a series of humiliating and disastrous examples of where reliance upon such a force could lead. Instead the United States had come to rely for defense on its small professional army, supplemented when necessary by national volunteers. Those volunteers had to be raised and trained at the last minute, however. And in peacetime, a jealous and penurious Congress kept careful watch over a War Department it severely distrusted and a president it often trusted even less.

During the late nineteenth century, a few army officers had examined these and related problems in detail. Foremost among them was Emory Upton, a brilliant young officer whose *The Military Policy of the United States* (1880) constituted a devastating critique of the ineffectiveness of traditional U.S. military policy and a call for drastic change. The American military system, Upton argued, had left the country totally unprepared for every war it had fought. The United States had survived these wars only because of the incompetence of its opponents and the fact that it had been granted sufficient time to mobilize and train regular forces. With rapid industrialization, however, such time might not be available in the future. Moreover, unpreparedness had resulted in much heavier casualties than necessary in previous conflicts. In the Civil War, for example, a preexisting professional force of substantial size could have ended the South's rebellion in a matter of months, saving the country hundreds of thousands of needless deaths.

Upton and other reformers called for an end to the existing militia system and its replacement by a large, conscripted, national army whose members would form a well-trained reserve once their tour of duty as regulars had ended. They also called for increased education and the creation of a centralized general staff to organize, plan for, and control this new military force. Such general staffs, mass armies of conscripts, and trained reserve forces were already coming into use throughout Europe, most notably in Germany, and Upton had been particularly impressed by the German model.[7]

In retrospect, the advent of these staffs and armies in the late nineteenth century was far from accidental, for they represented the application of the principles of mass production and scientific management from the industrial revolution to the armed forces. That industrial revolution provided not merely new implements of war. It also provided the material capacity, the professional expertise, and the organizational ability to feed, clothe, arm, train, and rapidly move huge numbers of men. That expertise and ability was centered in the general staff, a virtual corporate board of directors for the military. In effect, the armed forces of Europe were experiencing the same technological and managerial revolutions that were affecting society as a whole, and reformers like Upton wanted to bring that revolution to the U.S. armed forces.[8]

Many of Upton's ideas smacked of militarism and were grossly out of step with American values, however, and his incomplete manuscript remained buried for over twenty years after his tragic suicide in 1881. It was well known in army circles, however, and Root read and published it when he took office. By that time, American society was much more receptive to some of Upton's ideas than it had been earlier. This was not simply because of the War Department scandals during the Spanish-American War but also because army reform fit in with the general reform movement sweeping the country.

That movement was known as progressivism. Complex, diffuse, and far ranging, progressivism has always defied simple analysis. Essentially, however, it was an effort to bring rationality and order to what appeared to be the chaotic results of industrialization by an emphasis on professional expertise, efficiency, and a good dose of middle-class morality. In the political and economic spheres, this involved an expansion of governmental powers, especially federal and executive powers, in order to end corruption and make government more efficient and responsive to the people. In the military sphere, it would involve a similar expansion and centralization of power along with massive professionalization of the officer corps and an emphasis on education, training, efficiency, and military preparedness. While this military reform movement had begun long before 1900, it expanded and flourished during the ensuing progressive decades.[9]

Under Secretary Root, this effort focused on four areas: greater federal control over the militia, an end to the dual command structure and its replacement with a general staff, modest expansion and reorganization of the regular army, and the creation of a modern military education system to reward merit, encourage professionalism, and train staff officers. Knowing the Congress would never agree to abolish the state militia in favor of a national conscript army, Root settled, in the Dick Act of 1903, for some federal control over the arming, training, and officer commissioning of the "organized militia"—the state National Guard units. In the same year, Congress agreed to replace the dual command system with a general staff of forty-four officers under a single chief of staff. Meanwhile Root brought the army up to its authorized strength of 100,000, reorganized its regiments, established the Army War College, reopened the old infantry and cavalry school at Fort Leavenworth as a general service and staff college, and created a pyramid educational system running from required training courses on all posts for junior officers through Leavenworth and the War College for those likely to move up to higher command and staff duty.

It was in this new educational system, which met much opposition from older officers, that Marshall first excelled and came to prominence. After passing the required courses at Fort Reno, he applied for and received assignment to Leavenworth, by then the focal point of army education and reform, in the first-year general service course. When he arrived in August 1906, Marshall discovered that most of his classmates were older, more experienced, better prepared, and of higher rank. Indeed, immediately after his selection, Chief of Staff General J. Franklin Bell, former head of Leavenworth and a soldier deeply interested in army education, had directed that only captains and majors be chosen for the school. Marshall was thus in the last Leavenworth class to admit men of his rank.[10]

Marshall's junior status acted as a tremendous spur to his ambition. He became so determined to succeed that he overcame his old antipathy to academic study. He later stated, "I knew I would have to study harder than I had ever dreamed of studying before in my life. I just worked day and night." As a result he "finally got into the habit of study, which I never really had," but "it was the hardest work I ever did in my life."[11]

Much of this work was still the traditional rote memorization, but along with that went some major innovations. In the tactics class, for example, Major John F. Morrison was training an entire generation of officers, who would become known as "Morrison men," in the new "applicatory" style by having them solve operational problems rather than memorize formulas. Marshall was tremendously impressed by this method and teacher, later noting that Morrison "spoke a language that . . . appealed very much to our common sense" and that he "taught me all I will ever know of tactics."[12] Marshall's horizons were further broadened by the study of strategy and military history and by contact with some of the finest minds within the army—both on the staff and in the student body (Marshall's class alone would produce nine future generals). As one scholar has aptly concluded, Leavenworth during these years was the "intellectual center of the army," and Marshall was clearly affected by what an early biographer labeled the school's atmosphere of "enthusiastic intellectual renaissance."[13]

Armed with his new study habits as well as his driving ambition, Marshall excelled in this environment. To advance to the next rung on Root's new educational ladder, the staff college at Leavenworth, an officer had to rank in the top 50 percent of the one-year general service course. At the end of the year Marshall was first in his class. Along the way, he had also passed the promotion exams and become a first lieutenant.

This success brought Marshall to the attention of Chief of Staff Bell, who introduced him to additional key components of army reform. Under the Dick Act of 1903, National Guard training was to conform to federal standards. In 1907 Bell recommended Marshall to be one of five army instructors temporarily assigned to the Pennsylvania National

Guard. Although this assignment lasted only one week, it was critical to Marshall's growth and career. The twenty-six-year-old lieutenant exhibited a surprising ability to work well with guard volunteers, teaching them and getting them to excel in as well as enjoy what they did, and he was invited to return the following summer. Thus began a long, important association with the National Guard by which Marshall would gain invaluable experience, otherwise unavailable to young officers, in two key areas of the new army: working with civilians and directing maneuvers of large units. "I was able to do things there with a regiment where I wouldn't be able to get command of a company on a post," he later stated.[14]

Marshall's second year at Leavenworth, in the staff college, was less pressurized and even more intellectually stimulating than the first. As one participant later stated, "We were there in the midst of a transformation and we knew it." Freed from rote work and intellectually challenged as he had never been before, Marshall by his own later admission found his "habits of thought" being trained and "learned how to learn" at this time.[15] His studies focused on the broader aspects of strategy, tactics, staff work, and military history, and they included much material that would be invaluable in his later career.

Some of the most important of this material concerned the relationship between politics and the military. Prussian military philosopher Carl von Clausewitz had pointed out almost a hundred years earlier that war was meaningful only as an instrument of national policy. This was a difficult lesson for an officer to accept, for it meant the subordination of battlefield concerns to broader, political issues. During a presentation at the end of a 1908 student field trip to the Civil War battlefield at Gettysburg, Marshall illustrated a growing recognition and acceptance of this inextricable linkage and subordination of war to politics. General Lee had decided to invade Pennsylvania, he emphasized in that presentation, more for political than for military reasons, and political conditions at the time needed to be "closely borne in mind" when reviewing the opposing generals' moves.[16]

Perceiving political and military affairs in conjunction was also difficult for Marshall because the combination seemed to conflict with the antipolitical tradition of the U.S. Army. According to this tradition, an officer was a servant and defender of but not a participant in civilian society and its partisan politics. The basis of this belief was the constitutional principle of civilian control of the military, and in recent years it had been strongly reinforced by both the physical isolation of the army on its small posts and overseas garrisons and the growing professionalization of the officer corps.[17]

Despite this tradition, however, successful generals had been elected to high public office throughout U.S. history. Moreover, although progressivism had reinforced the distinction between civilian and military spheres by its emphasis on professional education and expertise, the movement's basic ideas had also blurred that distinction. Army reformers, for example, championed civilian managerial values and techniques within the military. Some were also quite willing to make political appeals to civilian society in pressing for reform and military preparedness. Simultaneously many civilian reformers called for a new emphasis within society on military values, such as discipline and self-sacrifice, to temper the greed and narrow self-interest that they saw at the base of America's problems. President Theodore Roosevelt was a strong proponent of this "warrior critique of the business civilization." Even the pacifist philosopher William James recognized that the country needed a "moral equivalent of war."[18]

Many army officers agreed, championing universal military training (UMT) as a way to inculcate these values and "Americanize" the new immigrants, as well as achieve military preparedness without creating a large standing army. From seeing the inculcation of those values as both positive and necessary, it was but a short step for some high-ranking officers, most notably General Leonard Wood and protégés such as Douglas MacArthur, to see inculcators like themselves as the individuals most suited to lead the nation politically.

As a product of army professionalization and reform, Marshall was profoundly aware of the strong relationship between the military and American society, and he strongly supported preparedness and UMT as the modern continuation of the citizen-soldier concept VMI had taught him. Moreover, it was at this time that he first illustrated and developed his ability to work with citizen-soldiers in the National Guard. He firmly believed, however, that political activity was antithetical to his professional responsibilities and values and that officers should have nothing to do with partisan politics. Throughout his life, he refused on principle to accept any nomination for elective posts or even to vote in any election. This lack of personal political ambition, combined with acceptance of a strong link between military and political affairs, would become one of the central themes of his career.

A lack of personal political ambition was in no way equivalent to a lack of professional ambition, however, and Marshall continued to be driven to excel. At the end of his second year at Leavenworth, his performance was again considered outstanding. Morrison rated him "one of the best minds I know," and the academic board's report on him was twice as long as that for anyone else.[19] The board unanimously selected him as one of five class members to remain as an instructor, though he would be outranked by all of his students. Chief of Staff Bell gave special permission, and in 1908 the young first lieutenant began teaching engineering and military art to army captains and majors. He was a brilliant success, exhibiting once again the exceptional talent for teaching that had first appeared with the Pennsylvania National Guard.

To be a good teacher, one must be a good student, and for the next two years Marshall continued to learn at Leavenworth. He also continued to meet and impress individuals whose paths would cross his for the next forty-five years. Included in this group were two high-ranking officers under whom he would soon serve directly, Hunter Liggett and Chief of Staff Bell, as well as future Chief of Staff Douglas MacArthur. Among his students were many of the individuals who would run the General Headquarters and First Army staffs in France during World War I. Foremost in this group was John McAuley Palmer, who would become a lifetime friend and heavily influence Marshall's views on U.S. military policy and the citizen-soldier.

Marshall's teaching method at Leavenworth was "to direct men by trying to make them see the way to go." That method seemed to work equally well with civilians as with army officers, for the Pennsylvania National Guard continued to invite Marshall back for summers, and he soon developed an extraordinary reputation in civilian as well as army circles. Bell wanted to make him assistant chief of the new General Staff Division of Militia Affairs. VMI twice asked him to be its commandant. The governor of Massachusetts and the head of the Pennsylvania Guard asked for him personally as a full-time instructor. When Marshall's tour at Leavenworth ended in 1910 and he returned from a five-month leave in Europe, General Wood, the new chief of staff, sent him to Massachusetts where he organized a school program for guard officers and drew up plans for statewide maneuvers.[20]

Marshall was probably lucky Wood sent him to Massachusetts instead of Washington, for the General Staff was under assault both within the army and by the Congress. Adjutant General Fred C. Ainsworth, the last of the powerful bureau chiefs, had launched a concerted effort to reverse the general thrust of Root's General Staff Act by keeping the chief of staff relatively powerless. Wood and Secretary of War Henry L. Stimson defeated Ainsworth and forced him to resign, but his powerful friends in Congress obtained revenge by successfully blocking all General Staff reform measures for the duration of Wood's term.

It would take many additional years and much effort before the General Staff and its chief would emerge as the locus of power within the army, effort in which Marshall would play a key role. At this time, however, he continued to excel as a teacher of both soldiers and civilians. He also continued to develop and exhibit the enormous talent for staff work that would mark his later career, most notably his ability to plan the large-scale maneuvers that army reformers were emphasizing. In 1911 he participated in major maneuvers in Texas that were one of the first to make use of modern communications. His plans in that same year for statewide National Guard maneuvers in Massachusetts were the largest militia exercises ever attempted. In 1912 he worked with General Tasker H. Bliss, a key reformer and future chief of staff, on an even larger set of maneuvers that involved regular units as well as the National Guard from New York, New Jersey, and New England.

By this time, however, Marshall had been detached from his regiment for six years and had not been overseas for nine. By congressional law, he was forced in 1912 to return to command of a single company on an isolated post. Soon after he was reassigned to the Philippines despite his request for overseas assignment anywhere else, a request based on fear of the effect of the Philippine climate on Lily's heart condition. "I am now paying the penalty for having had too many good things during the past seven years," he noted just prior to his July 1913 departure for Manila.[21]

Lily was able to go to Japan during the worst part of the year, however, and Marshall's star continued to rise during this second overseas assignment. With General Bell in charge of the Philippines Department, Marshall once again assumed responsibilities far beyond his rank and succeeded brilliantly. In maneuvers during 1914 to test Luzon's defenses against external attack, he was first appointed adjutant of a 5,000-man invading force and then made acting chief of staff and placed in de facto command because the chief of staff was ill and the commander incompetent. "Between you and myself," he boasted to brother Stuart, "I had an opportunity that rarely ever comes to a Colonel," as well as one that with a single exception "has never been heard of before being given to anyone below that rank."[22]

Similar opportunities unprecedented for a lieutenant were given to

Marshall in the following year when General Liggett became commander of Fort McKinley in Manila and then replaced Bell as commander of the Philippines Department. Aware from Leavenworth days of Marshall's talents and unwilling to see him transferred, Liggett made Marshall his personal aide and used him as a virtual executive assistant. So did General Bell in 1916 when Marshall returned to the United States and became deeply involved in setting up citizen-soldier training camps in California and Utah.

Marshall's extraordinary successes in these assignments added to his growing reputation as a prodigy despite his low rank, and out of those activities flowed a series of stories that became part of a growing Marshall legend. On one occasion he correctly wagered that an officer inspecting his company would detect three "flawed" soldiers—one unshaved, one with unbuttoned blouse, and one with no bayonet—and in the process totally miss three serious tactical blunders during the field exercises. Future Air Forces Chief Henry H. "Hap" Arnold saw Marshall examining a map and dictating precise orders under the shade of a bamboo clump during the Philippine maneuvers and informed his wife that he had just seen a future chief of staff in action. "This officer," his company commander wrote on his efficiency report, "for his years of service, age and rank, is one of the most completely equipped for military service it has been my lot to observe. . . . Should the exigencies of active service place him in exalted command I would be glad to serve under him." Another superior rated him the best leader of large bodies of troops in the army.[23]

Additional praise came from Generals Liggett and Bell. Both concluded on Marshall's efficiency reports that he was qualified to be chief of staff of a division or corps, and Bell, it is said, considered him the greatest potential wartime leader in the army. The most extraordinary praise came in 1916 when an officer who had been with Marshall during the Philippine maneuvers filled out an efficiency report on his performance in Utah. In reply to the question as to whether he would like to have Marshall serve under his command, Lieutenant Colonel Johnson Hagood replied, "Yes, but I would prefer to serve *under his command*. . . . In my opinion there are not five officers in the Army as well qualified as he to command a division in the field." The praise did not end there. Hagood concluded that

> he is a military genius and one of those rare cases of wonderful military development during peace. He is of the proper age, has had the training and experience, and possesses the ability to command large

27

bodies of troops in the field. The army and the nation sorely needs such men in the grade of General Officer at this time, and if I had the power I would nominate him to fill the next vacancy in the grade of Brigadier General in the line of the army notwithstanding the law limiting the selection to Colonels. He is my junior by over 1800 files.[24]

Despite such praise, Marshall throughout this time remained an unfulfilled and in some ways an unhappy man. Part of the problem may have been the death of his father in 1909 before most of this praise and recognition occurred. While he might boast of his accomplishments in letters to Stuart, his older brother could not provide fatherly approval. Nor did Marshall have the children that so often ameliorate worldly ambition in driven men. Lily did provide him with emotional fulfillment and release, perhaps the only emotional fulfillment and release this austere and reclusive individual had. Stories abound regarding Marshall's racing home after the day's work to be with her and of their numerous quiet evenings together at home because her heart condition precluded heavy social engagements. Despite those quiet evenings, however, the driven lieutenant was clearly working too hard. Indeed, he had succeeded by working himself to the breaking point.

In 1912–13 Marshall's body rebelled against the strain. Twice during these years he was diagnosed as having neurasthenia, a catchall medical phrase used at that time to describe everything from physical exhaustion to a nervous breakdown. Exactly where Marshall stood on this spectrum remains unclear. The first attack had included a physical collapse in the street, followed by a medical diagnosis of "acute dilation of the heart." The second attack was officially diagnosed as "subacute," but it required ten days of hospitalization in Manila, followed by four months of combined sick leave and regular leave to recuperate fully. He and Lily went to Japan, Manchuria, and Korea, and he returned with a knowledge that he must control his schedule and relax more if he was to survive. He explained in 1939, "I woke up at about thirty-three to the fact that I was working myself to death." He was also developing an unenviable reputation of being "merely a pick and shovel man." Henceforth he would try to avoid detail work as much as possible "and to relax as completely as I could manage in a pleasurable fashion." That would include horseback riding for one hour before breakfast every morning, playing tennis every afternoon, and hunting whenever possible.[25]

What probably upset Marshall more than his health was the slow pace of his career. Despite all the extraordinary praise from his superiors, he was in 1916 a thirty-five-year-old first lieutenant who, by his standards, might be going nowhere. The problem, he realized, lay with the army's promotional policies and lack of opportunity, not with him. Seniority remained the key to high rank, and there were too many people ahead of him in what was still a very small army. Moreover, his brilliance as a manager was actually beginning to hinder his advancement, for the army continued to value and reward line over staff positions. And since he was educated and able far beyond his rank, generals like Bell and Liggett found that the only way to make full use of his talents was to make him a personal aide and give him extensive powers; otherwise he would be "merely a lieutenant in a company." But assignment as an aide was not a line position and made future promotion even more difficult, thereby leading to additional aide assignments in the future and creating a vicious cycle.[26]

Marshall's recognition of the situation did nothing to relieve the frustration and sense of failure this ambitious individual felt. For the rest of his life, he would remain quite bitter about it, and in late 1915 he considered resignation. "The absolute stagnation in promotion in the infantry," he wrote to his friend General E. W. Nichols, the superintendent at VMI, "has caused me to make tentative plans for resigning as soon as business conditions improve somewhat." Even if Congress expanded the army, his prospects for advancement remained so limited that he did not feel it would be "right to waste all my best years in the vain struggle against insurmountable obstacles." Marshall admitted that the "assured and fairly fat living" provided by a future in the army without advancement was tempting "when you consider the difficulties and positive dangers of starting anew in civil life at my age." Nevertheless, "with only one life to live I feel that the acceptance of my present secured position would mean that I lacked the back bone and necessary moral courage to do the right thing."[27]

Whether Marshall was serious or just venting his frustration on a friend remains unclear. Nichols warned him to "think twice and think long" before resigning and tried to reassure him by making clear that "you are an eminent success in your present line of endeavor, highly esteemed by everyone who knows you and with a standing in the service of the very highest bar none." Besides, the Wilson administration was planning a major increase in the army, a move that would enable Marshall to be promoted to captain. Nichols concluded by advising his friend "to stick to it. If you do I am very sure in time you will be among the high ranking officers in the service."[28]

Nichols turned out to be correct on all counts. In 1916 Marshall was promoted to captain, and in the following year, totally unforeseen opportunities for his talents and ambition opened up when the United States declared war on Germany.

3

THE WORLD WAR AND AFTER,
1914–24

Although the United States in 1914 was the world's industrial giant, its diplomatic and military power still lagged far behind Europe. This situation would change dramatically during the next thirty years as the nation emerged to become the world's first superpower. To an extent that emergence was the logical, if delayed, consequence of the enormous American industrial revolution, but it was also the result of two world wars during which Europe almost destroyed itself while the United States fully asserted its power. World War I and its aftermath constituted the first act in this drama, an act in which George Marshall played an important role and became deeply involved with one of the great figures in U.S. military history.

The outbreak of a general European war in 1914 came as a surprise to most people. No such conflict had occurred since the Napoleonic Wars a hundred years earlier, and Europeans believed they were now too "civilized" to engage in another self-destructive orgy of continental-wide violence. They were wrong. By 1914 Europe was divided into two armed camps, and on 28 June the catalyst for war occurred when a Serbian nationalist assassinated the archduke and duchess of Austria-Hungary. The resulting chain reaction drew all the powers of Europe into the conflict. Within the space of a few months, the Central Powers of Germany,

31

Austria-Hungary, and Turkey were battling the Allied powers of England, France, and Russia, soon joined by Italy, Japan, and lesser powers, in a war of unprecedented magnitude and destruction.

The eventual entry of the United States into this conflict in 1917 was at least as much of a surprise to most Americans as the outbreak of the war itself. They claimed to have no interest in either the issues that had started the war or in its outcome, an attitude with deep roots in U.S. history. Throughout that history, the country had prided itself on its supposed isolation from Europe and had turned this geographic fact into a major tenet of its foreign policy and ideology. "Kindly separated by nature and a wide ocean," in Thomas Jefferson's famous 1801 words, "from the exterminating havoc of one quarter of the globe," the United States, the "chosen country," would be free to develop a liberty-loving and peaceful society that could serve as a model to the decadent Europeans of how people could and should live.[1]

What such statements and beliefs ignored were the real ties between the United States and Europe that bridged the three thousand miles of ocean. Most Americans had come from Europe, and despite the recent emphasis on new markets in the underdeveloped world, the biggest U.S. trading partners were European countries. Along with these economic ties went a traditional, legalistic, and moralistic insistence by the United States on a broad definition of the rights of neutrals in wartime. This combination had led the United States into the last general European war in 1812. In the light of America's economic growth and new status as a world power since that time, it was highly unlikely it would remain uninvolved in any long European conflict.

At first, however, few believed the war in Europe would last very long. That it did not end quickly was primarily the result of changes in warfare wrought by the industrial revolution. New weaponry and transportation, most notably the machine gun and the railroad, gave the defense an enormous advantage. As a result, most offensive operations during World War I failed, and after the initial German thrust through Belgium and northern France, the western front turned into two series of trenches running from the English Channel to the Swiss Alps. Neither side could break through the other's defenses, and each wasted millions of lives trying. The question thus became which side would be exhausted first in this brutal, unlimited, and total war of attrition.

By early 1915 both coalitions had begun extensive economic warfare as part of their efforts. That warfare would lead the United States into the war in 1917, much as it had 105 years earlier. As in 1812, British ship seizures and other violations of neutral rights tremendously angered Americans, but this time the violations of Britain's enemy angered them much more. Unable to match the size and power of the British fleet, Germany had responded to England's blockade with extensive use of a new weapon, the U-boat or submarine, which sank Allied merchant and passenger ships without warning. Like the British blockade, the submarine hurt U.S. trade; unlike the British blockade, it also cost American lives and was considered a barbaric violation of the rules of warfare. When a German U-boat sank the British passenger liner *Lusitania* without warning on 8 May 1915, killing 128 Americans and 1,070 others, the United States and Germany appeared to be at the verge of war.

War was not declared at that time or during the next twenty-three months, for the two countries were able to reach a diplomatic settlement whereby Germany temporarily bowed to U.S. insistence that it not sink unresisting merchant or passenger ships. But the crisis alerted Americans to the fact that they could easily get drawn into this war, and many came to believe that their unpreparedness for such a conflict only encouraged other powers to violate U.S. neutral rights with impunity.

Marshall and his superiors thus discovered new and substantial support among the civilian populace for expansion and reform of the armed forces. By 1916 10,000 civilians had joined former Chief of Staff General Leonard Wood's "Plattsburg" movement to train reserve officers at summer camps, and military preparedness had become a major issue in U.S. politics. With President Woodrow Wilson supporting the movement, Congress in that year appropriated funds for a navy "second to none" and passed a new National Defense Act that expanded the regular army to 175,000 and the National Guard to 400,000, established a regular army reserve, increased federal supervision of the guard, improved army-guard coordination and reserve officer training, and set up machinery for economic mobilization in wartime.

This act theoretically continued the Root reforms, but most military reformers considered it totally inadequate as both an immediate and a long-term measure. Five years would be needed to put it into effect, and even after that time, there was no guarantee it would work. Many officers insisted that no plan involving the National Guard could work, and they pressed instead for a fully federalized reserve force. Guard performance during the Mexican crisis of 1916 appeared to validate this insistence. When the administration ordered General John J. Pershing and part of the regular army into Mexico after rebel leader Pancho Villa had crossed the border and killed U.S. citizens, Mexican President Venustiano Carranza directed his army to stop what he considered a U.S. invasion. Clashes and a major war scare ensued, and over 100,000 National Guardsmen were ordered to the border to join the regular army. The result was chaos.

Then in early 1917 the German government reneged on its previous pledges. In an all-out effort to starve Britain into submission before Germany itself collapsed from exhaustion, Berlin instituted unrestricted submarine warfare on all shipping, U.S. as well as Allied. German military leaders realized that this could lead the United States into the war but believed that the small size of the U.S. Army and the difficulty of getting any forces across the submarine-infested Atlantic would preclude any effective U.S. participation. So would U.S. preoccupation with the Mexican imbroglio, a preoccupation Berlin sought to exploit by secretly offering Carranza a military alliance against the United States. When this so-called Zimmermann telegram was intercepted and published, it only increased U.S. anger. On 2 April President Wilson requested a declaration of war and a virtual crusade not merely to defeat Germany but to "make the world safe for democracy." Congress agreed on 6 April. One month later it replaced the 1916 National Defense Act with a bill to raise a mass army for this crusade by conscription.

Like most other young officers, Marshall's attention during this time had been focused on the close Mexican crisis rather than the distant one with Germany. Indeed he returned to the United States in mid-1916 with orders to join General Pershing. But General Bell had other plans for him, and during the next few months he became deeply immersed in the practical aspects of the preparedness movement. Now commanding the Western Department of the army, Bell had Marshall detailed as an aide in order to prevent his transfer to the Mexican border and then sent him to Monterey to help Brigadier General William L. Sibert set up an officer training program for 1,200 volunteers. This was no simple task. The volunteers were quite wealthy and paying their own way, and the resulting atmosphere was more conducive to a party than to military training. Relying on a combination of humor, seriousness, and previous experience with National Guard units, Marshall was able to communicate effectively with this group and win their friendship as well as their support for much more rigorous training. He then helped in setting up another camp at Fort Douglas in Utah and in late September returned to Bell's headquarters in San Francisco.[2]

With the declaration of war in April, Bell was transferred to New York to head the Eastern Department of the army. Marshall accompanied him and was soon setting up additional camps as well as organizing and supplying the massive force being conscripted and trained for service in Europe, tasks he later labeled "the most strenuous, hectic and laborious of my [wartime] experience."³ When Bell was hospitalized with influenza, Marshall was virtually in charge of the mobilization effort in the Eastern Department. His performance was once again outstanding but once again frustrating, for he wanted to go to France with the American Expeditionary Force (AEF) under General Pershing rather than simply help to organize that force from New York. His opportunity came when his old boss General Sibert was picked to head the First Division, the unit to be sent to France immediately. Sibert requested and received Marshall's transfer to his divisional staff, and on 26 June the thirty-six-year-old captain followed his superior as the second man ashore from the first convoy of U.S. troops to arrive in France.⁴

The situation they faced was far from encouraging. After almost three full years of bloody warfare, the Allies were at the verge of total exhaustion. In the East, the overthrow of the czar and establishment of a liberal provisional government in March masked the impending collapse of the Russian Army and war effort. In the West, Britain and France suffered a million casualties in their unsuccessful 1917 offensives and could no longer fully replace their stupendous losses from the remaining manpower pool. On the front, French units had mutinied in the aftermath of these failures. The Allies desperately needed American men as well as a psychological lift, and the First Division had been sent over so quickly primarily as part of an effort to bolster Allied morale.

It could do little else, for the First Division did not really exist in 1917. Nor did any of the other newly established U.S. divisions. With the regular army only 130,000 men strong these divisions had to be virtually created from the draftees who were just then being inducted. That process would take a great deal of time and effort.

Marshall received some bold illustrations of U.S. unpreparedness during his Atlantic crossing. The staff of the division had never met before, and at their first meeting on board the ship they had to be informed of the division's organization. Most of the men were new enlistees, and many had received their weapons only days before. Despairing over their "complete ignorance of their weapons or anything," Marshall was temporarily heartened to watch a crisp naval gunnery practice begin, only to discover that the crew had neither ammunition nor aim. "The only thing they succeeded in hitting was the horizon and the foreground," something he labeled "rather disastrous for morale." Arrival in

France did not improve the situation. Not only did the new artillery companies lack howitzers and mortars, but some of the men had not even heard of these weapons. And when a French general questioned a disheveled American sentry about his rifle, that individual responded by handing it over and then sitting down on a windowsill to roll a cigarette.[5]

One battalion of the First Division paraded in Paris on 4 July to raise French morale, but it would be many months before the United States could field combat-ready forces. The First Division was thus sent to Lorraine for training, with Marshall designated its chief of operations. Pershings's General Headquarters (GHQ) temporarily borrowed him to find more training areas and billets in the region for three additional new divisions scheduled to arrive but then in late July ordered him to return and plan the First Division's detailed training program. That remained his major preoccupation for the rest of the year.

Looking at U.S. unpreparedness as well as their own depleted forces, the British and French high commands argued that the Americans should be sent immediately into existing Allied units for training and used as replacements within those units. Backed by President Wilson, General Pershing fiercely resisted such "amalgamation" proposals, insisting instead that his forces constitute a separate U.S. army. It was admittedly a matter of prestige, but it was also a matter of power and influence; an independent force would give Wilson leverage at the postwar peace conference to obtain the lofty objectives he was then enunciating, and the president's one order to Pershing had been to keep the U.S. Army separate.

Possession of combat-ready forces would obviously strengthen Pershing's hand in this debate, and he thus took an avid interest in First Division training during the summer and fall of 1917. Often he would visit division headquarters on short notice, and unhappiness with General Sibert's performance quickly developed during these visits. On 3 October he made that unhappiness public by openly attacking the divisional commander in front of his subordinates. Marshall was one of those subordinates and at that time the acting divisional chief of staff with the temporary rank of major. Loyal to General Sibert and convinced this humiliation was unjustified, he quickly sprang to his commander's defense. When Pershing tried to ignore his protests and depart, Marshall exploded. He put a hand on Pershing's arm to prevent him from leaving and, according to his later recollections, "practically forced him to talk."

What followed was more a lecture than a conversation, for when Marshall was angry, according to one of his assistants, "no one else could get in a word. He overwhelmed his opponent by a torrent of facts." And the facts, he now insisted, pointed to GHQ rather than General Sibert as the source of the problem. "You know we have our troubles," Pershing replied. "Yes, I know you do, General," Marshall shot back, "but ours are immediate and every day and have to be solved before night. . . . We have made the best we can of this thing. The only thing you've gotten out was to change the names . . . and now you are criticizing us for using the names you changed." Pershing offered to "look into it," but that was insufficient for the thoroughly aroused Marshall, who figured he was already "up to my neck" and "might as well not try to float but to splash a little bit." There was no need, he replied, to "look into it. It's right here in the orders. It's a fact. It's here. That's the only thing we've gotten from you and now we are being harassed for that." Finally able to break away, Pershing reminded Marshall that he needed "to appreciate the troubles we have," only to receive the reply that "we have them every day and many a day and we have to solve every one of them by night."[6]

The other officers, including General Sibert, were horrified by what Marshall had done. Convinced he would be immediately relieved, they all said goodbye to him. But they had severely misjudged General Pershing. Marshall had won his respect by this outburst, and rather than relieve him, the AEF commander frequently consulted with him thereafter on First Division problems. By the summer of 1918 Marshall would be a temporary colonel on Pershing's own staff and within two years his personal aide. A long and vitally important relationship had begun.

Sibert, however, was finished, and in December Pershing replaced him with General Robert L. Bullard. Bullard held as high an opinion of Marshall as anyone else and was ready to make him divisional chief of staff. His outburst had cast doubt, however, on his relations with GHQ. Moreover, Marshall remained infuriated over what he considered the unfair treatment General Sibert had received and made no secret of his feelings. He later recollected, "I demonstrated to General Bullard I had no business being made chief of staff in that state of mind." Instead he remained in the subordinate role of chief of operations. This delayed his further promotion, with serious consequences, and from the episode Marshall learned, albeit the hard way, the importance of controlling his temper. "That was the lesson I got right there and I never forgot it," he later recalled. "I never made the mistake—I don't think—again."[7]

While Marshall was trying to train raw American recruits and having his confrontation with General Pershing, the Allied situation continued to deteriorate sharply. By October 1917, Britain's Flanders offensive was ending in dismal failure, with 250,000 dead. Simultaneously the Germans made devastating use of new tactics they had developed on the eastern front to break the trench deadlock. Employing these tactics against the Italians at Caporetto, they shattered the Italian lines, took 275,000 prisoners, and advanced a startling sixty miles. In November, the Bolsheviks overthrew the Provisional Government in Russia and soon withdrew that nation from the war. Germany then began to transfer major forces from the eastern to the western front and on 21 March 1918, began a highly successful series of major offensives in France. In the first five days alone, German forces advanced twenty-five miles and threatened to shatter the Allied lines. By early June those forces were back on the Marne River and threatening Paris.

In this crisis, the Allies appointed Marshal Ferdinand Foch commander in chief of all their forces. Although his powers were circumscribed, he did provide coordination and a unity of command that Marshall would remember and build upon in World War II. Along with the Foch appointment, General Pershing proved willing to offer the Allies U.S. units to help stem the German advance. Marshall's First Division, which had completed its training and moved into the line during January, was one of these units. On 28 May, in an effort to boost morale as well as illustrate American fighting prowess, it launched a successful attack that Marshall had helped plan against an exposed German position at the town of Cantigny and then beat back two German counterattacks. Soon after the Second and Third divisions participated in bitter fighting at Belleau Wood and Château-Thierry that played a key role in the successful Allied efforts to stem the German advance on Paris. By July the enemy offensive had been halted, the Allies were counterattacking, and General Foch was planning a major counteroffensive for the fall.

That counteroffensive would involve large numbers of Americans. U.S. combat strength in July stood at 600,000, and additional U.S. troops were arriving at a rate of over 250,000 a month. While willing to offer the Allies U.S. divisions on a temporary basis during the crisis, General Pershing had simultaneously been amassing his own forces. In midsummer, he declared the First U.S. Army operational.

Throughout the early weeks of the crisis, Marshall had played a pivotal role in the First Division. In addition to helping with the planning of the Cantigny operation, he had become General Bullard's virtual executive when the latter was ill with neuritis. Yet he was intensely frustrated over the fact that he could not command troops or advance in rank as rapidly as colleagues who were in the line. He had been made a temporary lieutenant colonel in January, and a grateful General Bullard in June had recommended him for promotion to full colonel, but the War Department had turned down the promotion because he remained on staff. Frustrated and bitter, Marshall on 18 June requested duty with troops on the grounds that he had been on staff duty since February 1915 and was "tired from the incessant strain of office work." General Bullard forwarded the request but refused to approve it because Marshall's "special fitness is for staff work and because I doubt that in this, whether it be teaching or practice, he has an equal in the Army to-day." The general recognized and noted, however, that "his experience and merit should find a wider field than the detailed labors of a Division Staff," and he was thus assigned to Pershing's GHQ at Chaumont.[8]

Marshall found GHQ to be a very different world from First Division headquarters. It was filled with many old friends from Leavenworth who dealt with broad issues involving entire armies and millions of men, and despite his disappointment over not being allowed to command troops, Marshall apparently enjoyed, as well as profited from, his tour of duty there. He was placed under the command of Colonel Fox Conner, the head of the operations section and the officer who would become known as the brains of the AEF. Marshall was very close to Conner, with the two often referred to as a "mutual admiration society."[9] Together they would form the core of the group that planned the two great U.S. offensives of the war—Saint Mihiel and the Meuse-Argonne.

Saint Mihiel was an exposed German salient in the U.S. sector that Conner had long planned to attack. The Allies had originally approved, but in early August General Foch, desirous of exploiting the gains made by the French and British farther north, pressed for cancellation of the project and its replacement by a combined Franco-U.S. operation in the area of the Meuse River and Argonne forest. This smacked of amalgamation to Pershing, and he refused. In early September, however, a compromise was reached. The Americans would attack Saint Mihiel on 12 September but with limited objectives and with the understanding that forces would be shifted for a major Franco-U.S. offensive in the Meuse-Argonne sector on 26 September. That meant GHQ would have to plan for both offensives simultaneously and shift forces for the second while the first was still in progress. Turning this "appalling proposition" into practical operations fell to Marshall and Colonel Walter S. Grant. Marshall admitted immediately after the war it was the "most trying mental ordeal" and "toughest nut I had to crack in France," a judgment he re-affirmed thirty-five years later.[10]

Saint Mihiel was the easy part of the assignment. It was a fairly standard operation against a German salient, the Germans were already planning to withdraw from their exposed position, and the basic plan-ning had already been done. Seven divisions were to launch coordinated attacks from opposite sides of the salient to pinch it off from the main German line. In their first major action under their own command, U.S. forces successfully did this in only two days, 12 and 13 September. They then checked German counterattacks and by 16 September had com-pleted the operation, taking 16,000 prisoners at a cost of 7,000 casualties.

The Meuse-Argonne offensive was another matter. It was a huge, complex, and extremely difficult operation, undertaken as a key part of a general Allied offensive and involving fifteen divisions against an area so critical to the Germans that they had fortified it to a depth of thirteen miles. While the Saint Mihiel operation was being planned and put into effect, Marshall would simultaneously have to plan and move forces for this operation. He had to figure out how to withdraw eleven French and Italian divisions with two corps headquarters from the front and replace them with fifteen U.S. divisions and three corps headquarters, a move-ment of 220,000 troops out of the line and 600,000 into it (400,000 from Saint Mihiel) along with 3,000 guns and 900,000 tons of supplies and ammunition. To move all these men and their equipment, Marshall had only three rail lines and three roads available to him. All movements had to be coordinated with similar French Army movements to the east and west of the Americans, thereby involving Marshall in daily diplo-macy as well as logistics, and had to be done at night so as to preserve secrecy and give the Americans both surprise and the restoration of mo-bility that Pershing had been emphasizing in the training of U.S. forces.[11]

Marshall's planning was a logistical feat of unprecedented propor-tions, and it succeeded brilliantly. On 26 September the offensive began with all forces in place and in total surprise, and it did not end until the 11 November armistice. At first the Germans were able to reinforce and hold most of their positions, but the French and British quickly launched their own offensives, fulfilling Foch's directive to give the enemy no rest and no time to regroup, and in early October Pershing successfully re-sumed the U.S. offensive. Simultaneously U.S. troops continued to pour into France in enormous numbers, enabling Pershing to build up a force of thirty-nine divisions divided into two active armies under Generals Liggett and Bullard. By late October these armies occupied approximately 25 percent of the entire Allied line and an even greater percentage of Allied combat power since they were double the size of the French divisions. They were engaged in open warfare against a German Army unable to stabilize its lines. Exhausted, outmaneuvered, in retreat, and now facing a hoard of fresh U.S. troops, Germany sued for an armistice. On 11 November the guns fell silent. Although another year passed before the Versailles Peace Treaty was signed, the war was over.

Marshall's abilities to plan and to improvise as necessary during the summer and fall of 1918 had been extraordinary, and he was soon being called "the wizard" for his accomplishments in the Meuse-Argonne campaign. General Pershing gave him full credit for this "stupendous task," and one of Marshall's early biographers echoed the sentiments of many others when he labeled it "the most magnificent staff operation of the war."[12] For his early efforts, Marshall had been promoted to the temporary rank of colonel in September. The following month he was made chief of operations for the U.S. First Army under Chief of Staff General Hugh Drum and recommended by Pershing for promotion to brigadier general; in November he was appointed a corps chief of staff.

Still under forty, Marshall had emerged as one of General Pershing's chief tactical advisers and most extraordinary officers. "In both tactics and logistics," his official biographer has noted, "he had developed a competence probably unexcelled by any other officer of his age in the Army."[13] He had also developed an unexcelled competence and reputation for his diplomatic ability to arrange and operate within Allied commands. Fox Conner later told a young protégé named Dwight Eisenhower to get an assignment with Marshall if it all possible, for in the future "we will have to fight beside allies and George Marshall knows more about the techniques of arranging allied commands than any man I know. He is nothing short of a genius."[14]

Pershing clearly recognized Marshall's brilliance and after the armistice sought to retain him in whatever capacity he could. During early 1919 this involved a series of tasks: training units for occupation duties in Germany, planning how to invade Germany if the peace negotiations collapsed, working on Pershing's final report, lecturing to other officers and visiting congressmen, and cutting red tape whenever possible. In April the AEF commander asked Marshall to be one of his postwar aides. This was the same position he had held under Generals Liggett and Bell, and Pershing clearly had in mind for him once again to serve not as a secretary but as a personal adviser and executive who could act in his name.

Yet despite the Allied victory, the high esteem in which he was held by his superiors, and the new position as Pershing's aide, Marshall was far from pleased as the war ended. Once again he had assumed staff responsibilities far beyond his rank, had succeeded brilliantly, and as a result had been retained on staff and been deprived command over troops. That translated into slow promotion, which gnawed at the ambitious officer. During the war, he had watched numerous peers and subordinates in the field surpass him in rank. General Pershing had recommended him for promotion to brigadier general during the fall, but with the armistice, Congress froze promotions and thus failed to act favorably on the request. In 1920 he reverted to the rank of major (actually captain for one day) and then advanced so slowly that he would not see that first general's star for another sixteen years. For the rest of his life, he remained bitter over this lack of rapid advancement and cast at least part of the blame on his numerous assignments as an aide. Perhaps for this reason, he seldom detailed an officer to serve as his own aide after he achieved high rank.[15]

Yet serving as an aide to high-ranking generals continued to offer Marshall distinct opportunities otherwise unavailable no matter how rapid his advancement might have been. Most notable in this regard under Generals Liggett and Bell had been the ability to deal with large bodies of troops and the issues posed in their command and organization. Marshall had also been able to interact with civilians involved with military affairs and to meet and learn from high-ranking individuals in both the military and political spheres. All of these opportunities and more would now be available as aide to America's great hero and highest-ranking officer, General John J. Pershing.

Already commander of the AEF, Pershing would soon be given the rank of "General of the Armies" and in 1921 become army chief of staff. In the next few years Marshall would thus be introduced to the highest level of military and political leadership and would receive an education in politico-military affairs unavailable in any other position. He would also develop an extremely close relationship with General Pershing, a relationship that went beyond the professional to the mentor-student and father-son level.

Despite the twenty-year difference in their ages, Pershing and Marshall had numerous similarities in terms of history and personality. Each had been a mediocre student academically but had received top cadet rank (Pershing at West Point, Marshall at VMI) and had later shown a marked aptitude and fondness for teaching. Each had exhibited unusual managerial as well as battlefield ability, a requirement for command in modern warfare. Both possessed strong egos and were highly ambitious, and both were known for a cool, almost frigid professionalism that masked and controlled a sometimes violent temper. Both had also found their ambitions thwarted by the army's slow promotion system, with Pershing's situation as a young officer even worse than Marshall's; not until the age of forty-one had he obtained the rank of captain in the regular army.

The two men had equally important differences. In addition to great seniority in age and rank, Pershing was much more aggressive and out-going. A former cavalry officer, he fought hard and lived with a unique exuberance. He also possessed a series of seemingly contradictory char-acter traits. Although he was a commanding and stubborn personality of the old spit-and-polish type, he nevertheless highly valued education and, as Marshall discovered in 1917, showed an enormous and unex-pected capacity to accept criticism. Moreover, while he was coldly professional and austere at work, Pershing was intensely emotional in private and behaved boyishly when he relaxed. And in 1919 he was in need of a close aide with whom he could relax as well as work. Four years earlier, in 1915, his wife and three of his four children had died in a fire. The Mexican Revolution and World War I had kept him busy since then, but as he admitted in tears to close friend Charles G. Dawes, "Even this war can't get it out of my mind."[16]

This combination of personality traits was perhaps a bit unnerving to the new aide. Never did he meet another man, Marshall later con-fided, "who could listen to as severe criticisms, particularly personal crit-icisms, just as though it was about a man in another country. He never held it against you personally." He often accepted the advice that came with the criticism, albeit after a struggle. Marshall once wrote three sep-arate memorandums in an unsuccessful effort to convince Pershing to agree on an issue with an antagonist and then bluntly warned him that "just because you hate the guts" of the antagonist, "you're setting yourself up . . . to do something you know damn well is wrong." With a disgusted "have it your own way," Pershing acquiesced.[17]

Marshall was equally surprised and impressed by Pershing's ability to be coldly professional at work yet relaxed, social, and youthful at night, and then equally professional the next morning. Marshall's own father had been cold and austere, and he himself had shown an emotional rigidity and marked inability to relax until forced to do so by his neurasthenia. Pershing, on the other hand, seemed able to lead two separate lives. Once he left the office, he enjoyed staying up late, talking about his youth, laughing, drinking, and joking. His behavior was infectious and seemed to humanize the austere and aloof Marshall. "We would always be laughing at some joke when we drove up from the train in Washington," he later recalled, but once they entered the office, "it was just business as though we hadn't been together before."[18]

To say Pershing became a surrogate father would probably be an overstatement. Yet he clearly did become Marshall's mentor, protector, supporter, and booster, and a powerful and influential one at that. Marshall became the individual Pershing could trust with any assignment and a virtual alter ego. A strong bond of personal affection developed between the two over the next five years, and it continued until Pershing's death in 1948. They corresponded extensively and trusted each other with numerous personal matters. Marshall asked Pershing to be the best man at his second marriage, for example, and Pershing asked his former aide to help edit his memoirs and be co-executor of his papers, as well as "take charge of arrangements" in the event of his death. Throughout World War II Marshall continued to pay the AEF commander regular visits at Walter Reed Hospital despite the enormous burdens he then carried as chief of staff and the fact that Pershing's memory was failing. "No words," Marshall admitted in 1924, "can express the regret and loss I feel at the termination of my service with you. Few ever in life have such opportunities and almost none, I believe, such a delightful association as was mine with you."[19]

That association was, of course, professional as well as personal, and it enabled Marshall to broaden his horizons immensely. He accompanied Pershing on his parades and tours through the Allied capitals and major cities of the United States in 1919 and thereby came into contact with numerous important political figures. Some of these, such as Winston Churchill, he would meet again twenty years later. He also became deeply involved in one of the most important politico-military issues of the postwar era: congressional legislation to establish the size and nature of the army.

If President Wilson had had his way, this would have been a relatively easy and unimportant issue. At the Paris Peace Conference he had sought to remake international politics under U.S. leadership by substituting the rule of law, as embodied in the League of Nations, for the rule of force. But his ideas had been severely compromised at Paris, and the Senate then rejected U.S. membership in the league. It did not reject America's great power status, however, something that remained quite independent of the league. Indeed U.S. power and influence had enormously increased during the war, and with the failure of Wilson's dream, the formulation of an extensive new defense policy became mandatory. No one expected the AEF to be maintained, but a return to the pre-1917 situation was equally unthinkable.

For Marshall as well as most other army officers, World War I had provided a shocking example of the costs of unpreparedness. A full year had been required after the congressional declaration of war against Germany before the United States could field a trained army and undertake an offensive, and casualties had been higher than necessary because of the lack of peacetime training. Moreover, U.S. war production had never achieved its potential during the conflict. As a result the AEF had had to rely on Britain and France for many of its essentials, including guns, ammunition, and airplanes. The "one great lesson" Marshall drew from this experience, and emphasized in his final report, was that the "unprepared nation is helpless in a great war unless it can depend upon other nations to shield it while it prepares."[20]

In theory, most Americans agreed on the need to be militarily prepared in the future. The issue in 1919 and 1920 was what form preparedness should take. One school of thought, represented by Colonel Palmer of Pershing's staff, held that a small, regular army should be established to deal with small emergencies and to train the National Guard and reserves so that they would be prepared in time of war. Another group, led by Chief of Staff General Peyton C. March, placed little faith in this modern militia. Instead it hearkened back to ideas expressed in the early nineteenth century by Secretary of War John C. Calhoun, as well as more recently by Emory Upton and other army reformers, to provide for a peacetime army sufficiently large and expandable to absorb draftees into its own structure in times of war. For this purpose, the regular army would have to stand at 500,000, a larger force than the one envisaged for militia training.

A bill to establish such a large regular army was introduced in 1919, and it quickly aroused criticism from within the military itself, as well as from the National Guard and Congress. In an extraordinary congressional hearing, Colonel Palmer attacked it as "not in harmony with the genius of American institutions" and instead pressed for a small regular army to act as "core and mentor" to the militia. An impressed Senator

James Wadsworth asked that Palmer be assigned to the committee to help write a new bill. At the end of October General Pershing supported Palmer's concept before the committee by calling for an army of 275,000 to 300,000 to train the National Guard and reserves, the strengthening of the General Staff, and the implementation of UMT for all able-bodied male citizens.[21]

Marshall firmly believed in Palmer's ideas and was deeply involved in Pershing's recommendations. The citizen-soldier concept had been central to the VMI tradition when he had been a cadet there, and his numerous prewar experiences with the National Guard and the Platts-burg camps had convinced him that the concept was both workable and appropriate for a democratic society. These beliefs were reinforced by his close friendship with and respect for Palmer, a friendship and respect dating back to their days together at Leavenworth and now strengthened by their World War I service together at GHQ. During the summer of 1919, Marshall and Conner briefed Pershing extensively over a six-week period prior to his committee appearance and played a major role in formulating his recommendations. They also accompanied him to the hearings, thereby giving Marshall his first taste of civil-military relations at this level.[22]

The result of the committee hearings was the National Defense Act of 1920, which set the postwar army at 280,000 and created the machin-ery for a theoretical expansion to 2.3 million in time of emergency by the National Guard and an organized reserve force to be officered through college and summer training programs. Filling the ranks of that reserve force would be a more difficult matter, however, for the act did not include UMT. This was the heart of any citizen-soldier program, and without it the army could not fulfill the role Palmer, Marshall, and Pershing had wanted it to have as a trainer. Instead it reverted to the skeleton combat force March had wanted but with insufficient man-power. Congressional budget cuts in the 1920s made the situation worse. The result was the very unpreparedness Marshall and his colleagues had worked so hard to prevent.

An additional negative consequence of this episode was that it proved to be the final straw in a long-simmering conflict between Per-shing and March, a conflict that now exploded publicly and appeared with all its bitterness in both men's memoirs. Marshall was horrified by the ensuing spectacle. Even in retirement he refused to comment on it in any depth, stating that he was "not an umpire on such things. I leave that to the columnists." The controversy probably played a major role in his decision not to publish the World War I memoirs he was writing at this time, as well as his later efforts to destroy those memoirs and refusal in later years to write any autobiography. Among the major Allied figures to survive World War II, he was one of the few not to write a memoir.[23]

During 1919 and 1920 Marshall was depressed to see Pershing temporarily succumb to presidential ambitions. Whether military men should become involved in politics was an issue that had previously split the officer corps, and both men clearly stood on the negative side of the argument. They both maintained a firm policy of not even voting, and in retrospect they symbolized the apolitical viewpoint within the army as clearly as Wood and MacArthur symbolized the opposite. In 1919, however, Pershing apparently got carried away with the talk of his becoming president, and indicated he would accept the Republican nomination if offered. When it was not, he belatedly stated that he would not consider being a presidential candidate. Marshall opposed his chief's mini-campaign from the start, arguing that involvement in politics would cut down his prestige unless he was nominated "almost by acclamation," and the entire episode probably reinforced his own insistence on avoiding political ambition at all costs.[24]

With the end of the presidential boomlet and the struggle over the National Defense Act, Pershing in 1921 became chief of staff. Immediately he reorganized the staff to resemble the "G" organization he had used in France: G-1 for personnel; G-2 for intelligence: G-3 for operations and training; G-4 for supply; and the War Plans Division for strategic planning and to furnish the wartime staff for any future commanding general. This was essentially the structure that Marshall would inherit in 1939. In the meantime, as Pershing's aide, he familiarized himself with all aspects of general staff work and participated in civil-military relations at the highest levels, including the White House and Congress. In the process, he developed friendships and contacts with several important individuals in politics and business, most notably Charles G. Dawes and Bernard Baruch. With Pershing often away from Washington for extended periods, he also prepared reports, carried out special assignments, served on numerous boards, kept his chief informed of events in Washington, and gradually assumed more and more responsibilities. During Pershing's 1923–24 six-month stay in Europe, Marshall virtually ran the chief of staff's office.[25]

Marshall was also able to establish some semblance of a normal personal life. While he and Lily had been reunited upon his return to the United States, he had been forced to travel so much in 1919 and 1920 that she had remained with her mother in Lexington. Now she joined him in Washington. So did his mother, who spent part of each year in the capital, and ten-year-old Rose Page, a neighbor's daughter who tapped Marshall's love for children and was virtually adopted by the childless couple. She became Marshall's walking and riding companion, as well as a regular visitor, and she chose Marshall to be her godfather.[26]

Along with these joys of family life, Marshall prospered under a relatively normal work schedule that allowed him sufficient time for daily exercise. He went horseback riding every morning, swam and played tennis before dinner, and according to Lily was "hard as nails and black as an Indian. I've never seen him looking better."[27]

With his experiences as Pershing's aide under his belt, Marshall by 1923 was probably one of the most knowledgeable, as well as talented, officers in the army. According to most of his superiors, he possessed all the characteristics and experience necessary to be a general officer and a future chief of staff. But none of this had done anything for his rank. With the end of the war he reverted to the rank of major. In 1923 he was made a lieutenant colonel, but promotion beyond that was out of the question in the light of his position, the army's seniority rules, and Congress's continued shrinking of the armed forces. Marshall was about to enter some very depressing times. So was the army and the country as a whole.

George C. Marshall, Sr. (1845–
1909), father of George Marshall.
George C. Marshall Research Library

Laura Bradford Marshall (1846–
1928), mother of George Marshall.
George C. Marshall Research Library

Sister Marie, brother Stuart, and George C. Marshall, Jr., as children, 1884.
George C. Marshall Research Library

Marshall as a cadet at the Virginia
Military Institute, early 1900.
George C. Marshall Research Library

Lieutenant George C. Marshall at Fort
Leavenworth, circa 1908.
George C. Marshall Research Library

Elizabeth ("Lily") Carter Coles
Marshall, Marshall's first wife,
circa 1908.
George C. Marshall Research Library

General John J. Pershing, commander of the American Expeditionary Forces, with his aide Colonel George C. Marshall (temporary wartime rank), France, 1919.
National Archives

Assistant Commandant Marshall with instructors from the tactics and weapons sections of the Infantry School, Fort Benning, Georgia, 1930–31. First row (*left to right*): Morrison C. Stayer, Joseph W. Stilwell, George C. Marshall, William F. Freehoff, and Edwin Forrest Harding. Second row (*left to right*): Howard J. Liston, Omar N. Bradley, Emil W. Leard, and Freemont B. Hodson.   *George C. Marshall Research Library*

Katherine Boyce Tupper Marshall, Marshall's second wife, Chicago, 1934. *George C. Marshall Research Library*

Colonel Marshall describing troop movements of the Illinois National Guard at Camp Grant, September, 1935.
Illinois Guardsman

Brigadier General Marshall with wife Katherine on a fishing trip along the Metolius River in Oregon, 1938.
U.S. Army Signal Corps photograph

4

FRUSTRATION, GRIEF, AND TRIUMPH, 1924–39

While the United States' military strength declined during the 1920s, its economic power continued to increase until 1929, when the country entered the worst depression in its history. Lasting more than a decade, that depression would precipitate a further withdrawal of the United States from commitments overseas, as well as plunge the nation into one of the most profound economic and psychological crises in its history. It would also lead to a revolutionary transformation of the economy and government in the process of achieving recovery.

George Marshall's life during these same years developed in some strikingly parallel ways. Like the country, his power and prestige grew in the early 1920s as Pershing's aide despite the lack of official high position. After 1923, however, he suffered a professional and personal depression that was as scarring to him as the Great Depression was to the United States as a whole. Like his country, however, Marshall was revived and transformed during the 1930s, and by 1939 he had reemerged in the position for which he was so perfectly fitted: chief of staff.

In 1924 Marshall faced a dismal choice. General Pershing was retiring, and Marshall had come to the end of his allowable time in Washington. Given his reputation and status, he had some voice regarding a new assignment. Given his rank and the state of the army, none of the choices looked very good.

Although the National Defense Act of 1920 had theoretically established a new and comprehensive military organization in which Marshall could find numerous tasks to fit his talents, the act had not included the UMT necessary for the creation of a viable citizen-soldier army. Marshall might argue that "the machinery is ready, with the foreman and general managers in place," but that machinery required workers for proper functioning, and without UMT those workers were not forthcoming.[1] As a result, the regular army gradually reverted to a small, skeleton force of professionals with insufficient manpower to fulfill its functions and maintain its viability.

Congressional budget cuts worsened matters. The existing citizen-soldier training centers were abolished and the regular army dramatically decreased in size. Although the 1920 act had called for a force of 280,000, limited appropriations brought that number down to 147,000 by 1922 and fewer than 132,000 by 1923. This was barely larger than the 100,000-man limit placed on defeated Germany in the Versailles Treaty. Additional cuts came with the Great Depression, and by 1932 the army contained fewer than 120,000 enlisted men. Air power would be expanded during the second half of the decade but largely at the expense of ground forces. Within an army so shrunken by budget cuts, there appeared to be no place where Marshall could use his talents.

Congress thought it had good reason for these cuts. World War I was over, Germany defeated, and the League of Nations functioning even without U.S. membership. Japanese-American antagonism in the Pacific threatened for a while to erupt into a full-scale naval race and possibly war, but the signing of the Four, Five and Nine Power treaties at the Washington Conference of 1921–22 ended these threats and ushered in a decade of naval arms limitation and peaceful relations among the great powers of the Pacific. By 1925 those peaceful relations extended fully to Europe. Germany in the Locarno Pact appeared to accept the Versailles judgment and was welcomed back into the family of nations. In 1928 sixty-two nations signed the Kellogg-Briand Pact outlawing war as an instrument of national policy, and additional naval arms limitation agreements soon followed.

In the aftermath of World War II, historians and politicians would join military men in referring to these nonenforceable agreements derisively as the "parchment peace" and in excoriating Congress and the public for leaving the United States so militarily unprepared for the Axis threat of the 1930s. Recent scholars have challenged these conclusions, however, by noting how secure the nation actually was during the 1920s and by insisting that military policy during that decade can and should be separated from policy during the 1930s. Prior to the Great Depression and Adolf Hitler's ascension to power in Germany during 1933, the world balance of power and treaty system left the United States with no dangerous adversary in the world and thus no reason to maintain a large armed force. Moreover, congressional budget cuts forced the army and navy to make the most of what they had, and this led them to great experimentation that left the country in the forefront of military research and innovation in key areas.[2]

This revisionist argument is both convincing and long overdue. However, one must note that in a democracy, there is often a lag between a change in reality and a change in the public perception of that reality, a lag that would hinder U.S. defense preparations during the threatening 1930s. Marshall and Palmer knew this. They also knew there was no external threat in the 1920s to justify a large defense force. That is exactly why they championed UMT, which would allow the country to remain secure and prepared for a future emergency while maintaining a small force in the nonthreatening present. "If we fail in the development of a citizen army," Marshall warned in 1923, "we will be impotent in the first year of a major war." Without UMT such a citizen army could not be created. The country thus sank into serious unpreparedness, and the tiny regular army lost contact with the populace. As Marshall later noted, the officer corps also came close to losing completely its ability to organize and maneuver large bodies of troops.[3]

Faced with this situation and Pershing's forthcoming retirement, as well as his own need for a new station and keen interest in the Far East, Marshall requested and received assignment to the Fifteenth Regiment stationed in Tientsin, China. Here he would come face to face with the limits of the postwar army. He would also come face to face with the limits of U.S. power in that part of the world, limits he would encounter again later in his career.

In the aftermath of the Boxer uprising of 1900, all the imperialist powers with interests in China had demanded and received the right to station troops near Peking so as to protect their nationals and interests. Seeing itself as the protector not only of its own interests but also those of China against the rapacious Europeans, the United States at first had not used this right. Instead it had enunciated its famous Open Door policy of preserving the territorial and administrative integrity of China

51

against hostile powers. In 1912, however, in the aftermath of a nationalist revolution under Dr. Sun Yat-sen that overthrew the Manchu dynasty but proved incapable of consolidating its own power, U.S. Army forces joined those of the other powers in the commercial center of Tientsin just south of Peking.

When Marshall arrived in China in September 1924, the central government was no more than a convenient fiction. Real power resided in a series of provincial warlords who were in constant conflict, and in the south there loomed the growing power of Chiang Kai-shek, Sun's successor as head of the Nationalist movement. The job of the Fifteenth Regiment and the other non-Chinese forces around Tientsin was to protect the lives and interests of their citizens in the area and make sure none of these conflicts spilled into the foreign concessions within the city.

That was far from easy in the light of the forces available and the situation. Three warlord armies clashed around Peking in the fall of 1924, and when one of those armies broke apart under a sudden shift in alliances and the combined assault of the other two, the 1,000 men of the Fifteenth Regiment were expected to help keep the armed remnants of that collapsed force as well as the victors, a total of over 100,000 men, from destroying Tientsin. They succeeded, with Marshall receiving special commendation for his "unusual tact, patience, and foresight," but so intolerable was the overall situation that in early 1926 the general in charge of all U.S. Army forces in China proposed that his threatened command be strengthened or totally withdrawn. Washington did neither, and the regiment remained exposed at Tientsin, trying to defend U.S. interests with a thoroughly insufficient force.[4]

Some reinforcements were added a few years later, but they were nowhere near enough. Whether any size force would have been sufficient is an open question. In a state of chaos and seething with anti-Western and revolutionary sentiment, China by its size and nature defied Western efforts at control. Military power in this situation was incapable of accomplishing the objectives of U.S. policy.

To what extent Marshall learned this lesson during his tour of duty in China remains unclear. As executive officer of the Fifteenth Regiment and temporary commander on a few occasions, he clearly saw the chaos he was expected to handle. Moreover, he quickly learned to speak Chinese, becoming sufficiently fluent in six months to translate testimony in court, and thereby gained access not available to many other Westerners. Nevertheless, as a U.S. army officer, he lived in a rarefied atmosphere divorced from most of the realities of Chinese life. His major concern was the care of his troops, and his vantage point remained that of a privileged outsider with a vested interest in the status quo. Moreover, he left before Chiang had succeeded in setting up his government in Nanking and does not appear to have formed any strong opinion of the Nationalist leader beyond suspicion of his "radicalism" that most other Westerners in China shared at that time, as well as a belief that any verbal support of him by Western politicians would only encourage additional antiforeign outbursts.

Yet Marshall clearly understood the precariousness of the Western position in China, and he developed some insight into the complexities of the situation. "We are in the midst of a Chinese civil war," he bluntly informed Pershing in September 1925, and an astute "strong man," he noted a few months later, could "make foreign influence an extremely difficult, if not perilous affair inland." By June he was warning that riots in Shanghai were a "forerunner of definite demands" for removal or modification of the unequal treaties between China and the West. "How the Powers should deal with China," he admitted to Pershing in late 1926, "is a question almost impossible to answer. There has been so much of wrongdoing on both sides . . . ; there is so much of bitter hatred in the hearts of these people and so much of important business interests involved, that a normal solution can never be found." All he could do was hope "that sufficient tact and wisdom will be displayed by foreigners to avoid violent phases during the trying period that is approaching."[5]

Despite these problems, life in China was quite pleasant for Marshall. The assignment was highly coveted within the army, servants were plentiful, and morale among the troops was quite high. Lily had accompanied him, and with a commanding officer who, for a change, severely limited his duties and authority, he had more time to spend with her than he had had for many years. There was also time to develop some lasting friendships, most notably with Majors E. Forrest Harding and Joseph Stilwell. Marshall clearly enjoyed his new routine, as well as the ability to be with troops instead of in a staff position. "I am more and more pleased with my choice of station and duty," he wrote in mid-1925. "It suits me perfectly, and the most disagreeable duty here is preferable to desk duty." Near the end of his tour, he concluded that his assignment in China had been "delightful, interesting and several times, exciting. Politically it is the most interesting problem in the world today, and the most dangerous. From a military point of view, the service here has been more instructive than any where else in the army these days."[6]

The problem lay in the last two words. It must have been frustrating to be back training sergeants and corporals after the experiences of the last ten years. Moreover, Marshall's temper still was not completely under control, and he had a reputation for excitability, abruptness, and being something of a martinet. Only around Lily and children did he seem to become relaxed.

Additional frustration occurred in 1927 when he returned from China to lecture at the Army War College in Washington. Marshall had always enjoyed teaching, but this assignment was too limiting for him and he later admitted that "at a War College desk I thought I would explode."[7] But he had few choices in the army of 1927. Besides, Lily liked the atmosphere in Washington.

In August Lily underwent a serious operation for a diseased thyroid gland that was aggravating her heart condition. She came through it in good shape and was told on 15 September that she could leave the hospital the next day. But when she sat down to write the good news to her mother, she collapsed and died.

Marshall was called out of a War College lecture he had just begun to receive the news by telephone. His reserve evaporated under the impact of this shock, and in grief his head fell onto his arm on the desk. The guard who had accompanied him asked if there was anything he could do. "No, Mr. Throckmorton," Marshall replied, "I just had word that my wife, who was to join me here today, has just died." Later that day a subordinate who had been called to his quarters found him "white as a sheet." "Make all the arrangements for funeral," he wrote from his desk. "Don't ask me any questions."[8]

The blow was devastating. Lily had been the center of his life and virtually his only emotional release. Now she was gone and he was alone. "Rosie, I'm so lonely, so *lonely*," he confided to Rose Page in a voice near breaking.[9] A year later his mother died, soon followed by Lily's mother.

"No one knows better than I what such bereavement means," Pershing wrote from Paris after Lily's death, "and my heart goes out to you very fully at this crisis in your life." A week later, Marshall responded that the thought of what Pershing had endured in 1915 had given him "heart and hope." Nevertheless, he admitted,

> Twenty six years of most intimate companionship, something I have known ever since I was a mere boy, leaves me lost in my best efforts to adjust myself to future prospects in life. If I had been given to club

life or other intimacies with men outside of athletic diversions, or if
there was a campaign on or other pressing duty demanding a concentrated effort, then I think I could do better.[10]

But he had no such intimacies, campaigns, or duties in 1927. Nor did
he have children or close friends to fill the emotional void in his life or
high professional status and a promising future to fall back on. At forty-
seven, an age when most men can begin to see the rewards of their
labors, Marshall's life appeared to have hit bottom with no way up.

Marshall was not the type of man to wallow in depression. "I will
find a way," he had told Pershing, and he did.[11] Expectedly that way was
hard work, and luckily for him and the country a position opened at this
time that could provide ample scope for his energies and talents: assistant
commandant of the Infantry School at Fort Benning, Georgia. This
school was responsible for training company-grade infantry officers in
small unit tactics and with providing refresher courses for more senior
officers, as well as officers of the National Guard and the reserves. Marshall was intensely interested in such training and had decided opinions
as to what should be taught and how. Since the commandant was in
charge of the entire base and had previously worked with Marshall, the
new and restless assistant was given a virtual free hand with both the
curriculum and the teaching methods. He had longed for such authority
and scope in a place where he could make a difference, and he plunged
into the assignment with enthusiasm.

The first result was the restoration of his broken spirit. "The change
to Benning," he admitted a few years later, "was magical," for it "caught
me at my most restless moment, and gave me hundreds of interests, an
unlimited field of activity, delightful associates, and all outdoors to play
in."[12] Along with this restoration came a revolution at Fort Benning.
Marshall thoroughly restructured the curriculum and the teaching methods so as to emphasize what he had learned first at Leavenworth, then
with the National Guard, and finally in World War I: the need for simplicity in plans and orders, the ability to innovate and deal with the
unexpected, and training in warfare of movement. These were the key
lessons of war as he saw them, and he believed them especially suitable
for the American character and a citizen-soldier army. They were also a
bit heretical in 1928, especially in the light of army tradition and the
World War I experience, and tremendous effort was required to break the
instructors and students out of the old ways of thinking and acting. Mar-

shall thus emphasized originality and improvisation rather than the standard approach. He banned written lectures, often provided either poor maps or no maps for his problems and maneuvers so as to duplicate the confusion of a real battlefield, and constantly emphasized thoughtful and original responses to the unexpected. "The art of war has no traffic with rules," a textbook written under his administration at Benning began, "for the infinitely varied circumstances and conditions of combat never produce the same situation twice."[13]

The result was the "spirit of Benning," and the virtual creation of the American World War II military character and high command. Simplicity, innovativeness, and mobility would be the hallmarks of the U.S. Army of 1941-45, and the leadership of that army would consist overwhelmingly of "Marshall's men" from Fort Benning. In all, 200 future generals passed through the school during his years there, 150 as students and 50 as instructors. The latter category, which included names such as Joseph Stilwell and Omar Bradley, Marshall labeled "the most brilliant, interesting and thoroughly competent collection of men I have ever been associated with."[14]

Marshall was clearly a driven man during these years and often not much fun to be around. He remained something of a martinet and overly paternalistic, to the extent that he was nicknamed "Uncle George." Obsessed with his work, he was constantly talking and asking questions about tactics, even at social events. Usually an impressive individual with an overwhelming air of confidence and authority, he could also be a stuffed shirt and prudish bore. He never told off-color stories and could wither with a stare anyone who did or who otherwise violated his Victorian moral code. In line with that code, he stopped drinking at Benning because he believed it was improper for the assistant commandant to consume alcohol during prohibition.

Physically Marshall remained trim and fit—just under six feet in height with deep-set blue eyes and sandy, graying hair. He also managed to quit cigarettes around this time after many years of chain smoking. But a facial tic acquired during World War I was getting worse. More worrisome, he developed a thyroid disturbance that produced an irregular pulse and may have played a role in his excitability and temper. His emotional health was also questionable. For companionship he had long visits from sister Marie and goddaughter Rose Page, as well as the presence of friends like Majors Harding and Stilwell from China days, but essentially Marshall remained a lonely, private man still in the grip of personal tragedy. His house was filled with photographs of his wife, and he admitted to Rose that he dreaded returning to it alone. Only with children did he seem to unwind.[15] And for all his energy and accomplishments at Fort Benning, he was still a lieutenant colonel as he entered his fifties.

All of that would change in the next few years. One evening in 1929 at a friend's dinner party in nearby Columbus, Marshall was introduced to Katherine Boyce Tupper Brown, a forty-seven-year-old former actress and widow from Baltimore. "You are a rather unusual Army officer," she quipped before dinner; "I have never known one to refuse a cocktail before." He asked how many officers she knew. "Not many," she had to reply, and for the rest of the evening they bantered back and forth. Then he asked to drive her to where she was staying, the home of a Mrs. Blanchard, but instead drove around the town for an hour. "After two years haven't you learned your way around Columbus?" she finally asked. "Extremely well," he replied, "or I could not have stayed off the block where Mrs. Blanchard lives!"[16]

He monopolized her time for the duration of her brief stay in Columbus, corresponded with her during the summer, and saw her again when she came back to Columbus in the spring of 1930. He then went to her summer home on Fire Island, New York, to meet her three children and win their approval, something on which she had insisted. In midsummer he informed Pershing that they would marry on 15 October. They did, with his former boss and mentor serving as best man and attracting a crowd that outnumbered the invited guests.

With school in session, they skipped the honeymoon and returned to Benning immediately, where the new Mrs. Marshall received a crash course in the social responsibilities of an officer's wife. Those responsibilities were extensive, and while she soon mastered them, some of the early episodes were both harsh and humorous. The commandant's reception in their honor, for example, took place the day they arrived and required her to meet and greet a thousand people on a receiving line. Marshall stood at her left, whispering names and key facts about each individual so that she could make appropriate comments. Halfway through this ordeal, she was in a daze, and when Marshall whispered "triplets," she graciously thanked the woman in front of her for the gift of "your lovely triplets." Somehow she managed to survive the rest of the evening, only to be informed on the following day that she was expected to host a reception in the afternoon for a hundred people. After two years of learning such social requirements at Benning, she concluded in her memoirs, "I was a fair Army wife."[17]

Katherine Marshall clearly provided her new husband with the emotional stability and outlet a man of his temperament needed. She also provided him with a ready-made family: three teenage children from her first marriage. Previously childless, Marshall now achieved additional emotional fulfillment as a stepfather, a role into which he fit easily and comfortably. Molly, the eldest, became his riding companion and close friend; Clifton and especially Allen, the youngest, were the sons he had never had.

Career changes soon gave Marshall additional fulfillment, both personal and professional. In June 1932 he was sent to Fort Screven, Georgia, to do what he loved most: command troops—in this case a battalion from the Eighth Infantry Regiment. A year later he was placed in command of the entire regiment, promoted to colonel effective 1 September, and transferred to Fort Moultrie, South Carolina. Here his performance was once again outstanding and once again illustrated his intense interest in the welfare of his men. The worst of the depression had hit by this time, and Congress had cut not only army size but also army pay. Fearful that his men would not be able to feed their families, he instituted (and participated in) the "lunch pail" system whereby a soldier's entire family could receive the same meal he did for fifteen cents a day.[18]

Ironically, however, Marshall wound up spending much of his time at Forts Screven and Moultrie with civilian rather than military issues and people. Given his prewar experiences with the National Guard and his views on the citizen-soldier army, he was well aware of the close connection between military and civilian societies and the need to strengthen ties between the two. He had stated in 1923 that the training of citizen-soldiers required "a thoroughly sympathetic and comprehensive understanding of the civilian viewpoint," and even without UMT he continued to believe in the importance of such understanding and contact.[19] At Forts Benning, Screven, and Moultrie he made concerted efforts to be involved and interact with the neighboring civilian community, something that pleasantly surprised citizens used to commanders who preferred to remain isolated. He also became deeply involved in 1933 with a key project of President Franklin D. Roosevelt's New Deal recovery program: the Civilian Conservation Corps (CCC).

The CCC placed thousands of unemployed young men from cities in rural camps where they were paid to reforest eroded areas and pursue other conservation work. In addition to offering federally funded work relief to the unemployed, this program provided the nation with badly needed environmental programs while giving the country's urban youth valuable training in a healthy, outdoor environment. The army was involved from the start in organizing the new CCC members into self-sustaining companies, and this role was soon enlarged to include the organization and operation of the camps, as well as the movement of 250,000 men into them. All of this the army successfully did, processing 275,000 men by 1 July and organizing them into 133 companies and camps.[20]

Marshall was deeply interested and involved in this work at Forts Screven and Moultrie, and he often expressed great pride in the camps and their personnel. In a sense, the members of the CCC became a replacement for the citizen-soldiers he had wanted to train, and although they could not defend the country, they clearly could illustrate the old VMI and progressive belief in the positive effects of military discipline on the nation's youth. "From the first," according to his wife, the otherwise politically conservative Marshall was "fascinated by the opportunities he felt it [the CCC] afforded to build up the minds and bodies of the youth of this country and also to lessen the hardship of the depression." He called the CCC "the greatest social experiment outside of Russia" and wished he could have been its national director.[21]

As an officer, Marshall was also fascinated by the challenge and the new methods required in training youth who were not members of the army and could not be subjected to traditional army discipline. The fact that so much of this work involved the out-of-doors added to his enthusiasm; according to one assistant, he "ate, breathed and digested" CCC problems. CCC work, he concluded, was "a splendid experience for the War Department and the army" and the "best antidote for mental stagnation that an Army officer in my position can have.[22]

Unfortunately, however, successful work with civilians did not lead to promotion. Rather, like staff work, it led simply to additional civilian assignments, and in October 1933 Chief of Staff General Douglas MacArthur recommended Marshall to be senior instructor for the troubled Illinois National Guard in Chicago. Marshall was deeply upset, for at fifty-three he was running out of time in his efforts to achieve high rank, and the Illinois position led nowhere. He appealed to General MacArthur but without success. The War Department considered the position "a critical one" in the light of the labor unrest and unemployment in Illinois, and the chief of staff had submitted Marshall's name as his only recommendation because he had "no superior among infantry colonels."[23]

The thought of using the guard against civilians made the unwanted assignment worse, especially considering the negative reaction to MacArthur's use of force the previous year against the Bonus Marchers. So did the Chicago location and the need to live in an apartment, something that may have depressed the nature-loving Marshall as much as the assignment itself. "Those first months in Chicago I shall never forget," Mrs. Marshall later wrote. "George had a grey, drawn look which I had never seen before, and have seldom seen since."[24] Despite MacArthur's praise that he had no superior at his rank, Marshall appeared once again to have reached a professional dead end.

Within a few months, however, he had shaken off his depression and recaptured his enthusiasm. He also began to produce impressive results with the guard. Moreover, the assignment in the long run proved helpful to his career, for he was able to extend his knowledge, contacts, and reputation within civilian society. He worked closely, for example, with Major General Roy D. Keehn, an influential attorney and member of the Democratic party as well as the guard commander in Illinois, even accompanying him to appearances before state legislative committees to request additional funds. He reestablished close contact with Major General Frank R. McCoy, an old and powerful friend with extensive diplomatic-military experience who moved into the same apartment house across the hall, and with Charles G. Dawes, the influential banker and former budget director and vice-president he had met as Pershing's aide. Dawes introduced him to Chicago's business and professional leaders and arranged for him to speak before numerous civic organizations.[25]

As his official biographer has noted, Marshall spent so much time with civilians between 1927 and 1937 that "he became familiar with the civilian point of view in a way rare among professional military men." A member of his staff later recollected that "he had a feeling for civilians that few Army officers . . . have had. . . . He didn't have to adjust to civilians—they were a natural part of his environment. . . . I think he regarded civilians and military as part of a whole."[26] Such experiences and beliefs go a long way toward explaining Marshall's extraordinary success in civil as well as military assignments between 1939 and 1951.

All of this lay in the future, however. In 1934 Marshall was a colonel, and his frustration over this fact continued. "I have had the discouraging experience of seeing the man I relieved in France as G-3 of the army, promoted [to brigadier general] years ago, and my assistant as G-3 of the army similarly advanced six years ago," he bitterly wrote to Pershing late that year in an appeal for his assistance when a few brigadier generalships became vacant. "I want one of them," he bluntly informed his former chief. "As I will soon be 54 I must get started if I am to go anywhere in the Army."[27]

Marshall's request for Pershing's aid was actually quite limited, for he was "determined not to exert political influence in my effort to be recognized," and he believed that soliciting letters from senior officers would not work. All he wanted was help in getting the secretary of war to read his efficiency reports since 1915. Pershing and other supporters did that and more, but to little avail, for while poor efficiency reports could block promotion, good ones could not secure advancement outside the seniority system save under extraordinary circumstances—usually a combination of war and high-level pressure. Even Pershing's influence was ineffective against this system during the 1930s. By 1936, however, Marshall was finally high enough on the seniority list to receive what almost everyone realized was a long overdue promotion to brigadier general. Along with that promotion came assignment to Vancouver Barracks, Washington, just north of Portland, Oregon, to command the Fifth Brigade of the Third Division and supervise CCC camps in the district.[28]

Katherine Marshall later described this assignment as "two of the happiest years of our life." He was back in command of troops and working with the CCC, two tasks he enjoyed above all others. Both kept him out-of-doors, by their nature and by his insistence on going into the field to see how his men were doing and how he could help them, and he quickly fell in love with the dramatic Oregon countryside. So did Mrs. Marshall, and in the summer the two would often drive away in late afternoon with fishing gear and fry pan, catch and eat their dinner outdoors, and return at twilight.[29]

Marshall also established close relationships once again with the civilian community. The governor of Oregon, Charles H. Martin, was a retired general and friend who provided him with important contacts and numerous speaking engagements that helped hone his oratorical skills. As a brigadier general he also had high visibility with the press, visibility that was increased when three Soviet flyers on the first successful polar flight suddenly landed at Vancouver Barracks instead of San Francisco and, along with the press and the diplomats, became house guests of the Marshalls.[30]

During this assignment Marshall was able to overcome a serious health problem that had suddenly reemerged. Just prior to the departure from Chicago, his thyroid had flared up again to produce a high and irregular pulse. In early 1937 he underwent surgery in San Francisco and had one diseased lobe of the thyroid successfully removed. After the surgery he added more exercise to his daily regimen, watched his pulse carefully, and squelched rumors of ill health that could have easily destroyed any future advancement.[31]

In the aftermath of this episode Marshall's irritability and temper decreased markedly. Whether that was the result of the operation, or of his new regimen, promotion, and pleasant assignment on top of the surgery, is not clear. What is clear is that there was a difference in his behavior as well as his health. Friends noticed, according to one biographer, "that the old nervous intensity had been replaced by an unfamiliar calmness." Another saw in this episode the beginning of "the emergence of the calm Olympian mask which he was later to present to the world."[32] After years of effort, he had finally succeeded in bringing his most visible emotions under the control he so desired.

The idyllic life the Marshalls were leading at Vancouver Barracks was cut short in the summer of 1938 when he was ordered to Washington to head the War Plans Division (WPD) of the General Staff. This order "came as a distinct blow to both of us," Katherine Marshall later stated, for her husband clearly preferred troop to staff duty. "I loathe a desk," he admitted to Pershing at this time.[33] Equally if not more important, he believed that continued troop duty was now mandatory if he was to make major general and obtain the highest rung on the army's professional ladder: the chief of staff position that would open in the following year when General Malin Craig's term expired.

Unknown to Marshall, however, numerous individuals within the War Department were already thinking of his rise to the chief's position by an alternative route. Deputy Chief of Staff General Stanley D. Embick, for example, saw Marshall moving from WPD to his own post as soon as he took over a scheduled corps command later in the year and from there into the chief's office without the need for further troop command or promotion. Secretary of War Harry H. Woodring liked the idea because he was searching for an alternative chief of staff nominee to the front-running General Hugh A. Drum. So did General Craig and Assistant Secretary of War Louis A. Johnson, who had been impressed by Marshall during a recent visit to Vancouver Barracks. In October Johnson forced the issue and after only three months as chief of WPD Marshall was promoted to the deputy chief of staff slot Embick had just vacated.[34]

Marshall was now only one step away from the chief of staff position, but it appeared to be a huge step and one from which he was separated by impassable barriers. Within the army hierarchy he was still quite junior, with twenty-one major generals and eleven brigadier generals senior to him. Equally if not more important, Marshall had entered a political minefield within the War Department, a minefield that had already come close to destroying Chief of Staff Craig. "Thank God, George, you have come to hold up my trembling hands," Craig said in 1938. "I shall never forgive Washington," his wife told Mrs. Marshall; "they have crucified my husband."[35]

The main problem was the intense conflict between Secretary Woodring and Assistant Secretary Johnson. As he did in many other bureaucracies, Roosevelt had appointed to the top two positions within the War Department men who disagreed vehemently in terms of policies, were of different temperaments, and could not work together. To make matters worse, Johnson felt he had been promised Woodring's job by FDR, but Woodring had no intention of resigning. By the time Marshall arrived, there was a virtual state of war between the two that politicized all issues within the department and forced the chief of staff to walk an impossible political tightrope. Indeed one of the great ironies of Marshall's appointment as deputy was that both men saw him as a potential ally against the other, while Craig saw him as his own salvation.

Behind this personal conflict stood a much broader and unresolved issue: how the United States should respond to the expansionist moves of Nazi Germany, fascist Italy, and a militarist Japan. The War Department's split on this issue, between the cautious, isolationist Woodring and the aggressive, interventionist Johnson, mirrored the split in American society and further paralyzed the department.

Throughout the decade Americans had watched with growing concern as Germany, Italy, and Japan destroyed the treaty structure of the 1920s. As early as 1931 the Japanese Army had seized Manchuria. Two years later Tokyo withdrew from the League of Nations. So did Germany under its new leader, Adolf Hitler, who also denounced the Versailles Treaty and began to rearm. In 1935 Italian dictator Benito Mussolini made war on Ethiopia. In the following year Hitler occupied and rearmed the demilitarized Rhineland, while both powers aided the fascist forces of General Francisco Franco in the Spanish Civil War. In 1937 Japan invaded China proper, and all three countries allied as the so-called Axis powers. In 1938 Hitler annexed Austria and began to make demands regarding the Sudetenland in western Czechoslovakia. War fever spread.

Anglo-French appeasement of Hitler at Munich would end the war scare in the fall of 1938 but only temporarily.

While most Americans found Axis aggression highly offensive, a clear majority insisted that the United States had no business getting involved in these issues and that it could remain isolated from any war that broke out. Convinced by this time that their participation in World War I had been a mistake that would be repeated unless preventive measures were taken, Congress between 1935 and 1937 passed a series of neutrality acts designed to avert such a repetition. Loans, commerce in arms and ammunition, any trade on U.S. ships, and U.S. travel on belligerent ships were prohibited in the event of war. Trade would be limited to noncontraband goods paid for in advance and carried on belligerent ships via the so-called cash-and-carry principle. Opponents of these policies insisted that they were unworkable and counterproductive. The United States, the internationalists maintained, could not and should not attempt to isolate itself from the world crisis, for Axis success would constitute a mortal threat to American values and security. British and French resistance to the Axis should therefore be supported.

President Roosevelt's sympathies lay with the internationalists, but he was intent on maintaining his congressional coalition for the domestic New Deal program, and he therefore refused to challenge the isolationist sentiment in Congress. In 1937 he had suggested a possible "quarantine" of aggressor states but had quickly backed off when strong isolationist opposition surfaced. In 1938 he shifted to a seemingly less controversial proposal: rearmament so as to be able to defend U.S. neutrality should war break out. This was, in a sense, the old preparedness argument and one with which the War Department concurred. For many isolationists, however, Roosevelt's request for a military buildup illustrated his desire to become involved in the world crisis; granting that request would provide him with the tools to do so.

Within the executive branch, an additional argument raged over the type of rearmament that should take place. Roosevelt supported a dramatic first move—the massive expansion of U.S. aircraft production—in order to counter German air power, impress the Axis with U.S. potential and resolve, and create a sufficient aircraft surplus to supply Britain and France. Isolationists opposed this proposal. So did many within the War Department who thought less of air power than did the president.

Throughout the interwar years, an intense battle had raged within the department and the country as a whole over what to do with the

Army Air Corps. Led by such colorful figures as Colonel William "Billy" Mitchell, proponents of air power had maintained that strategic bombing of cities could by itself win wars by destroying the enemy's industrial ability and psychological will to resist and had called for the creation of a large air force independent of the army to fulfill this task and virtually to replace traditional land and naval forces. Critics had disagreed strongly with these conclusions, emphasizing instead the tactical and subordinate role of air power in support of ground troops and the development of a balanced armed force within a single staff and department. These individuals found little of value in Roosevelt's proposal and favored a more gradual and balanced rearmament program.

Rearmament was thus a military, political, and foreign policy issue that further split the War Department, as well as the country as a whole. Marshall's dramatic entry into this debate occurred on 14 November 1938, when he accompanied Craig to a high-level White House meeting during which President Roosevelt outlined his plan to ask Congress for funds to build 10,000 airplanes a year but not funds to provide crews for those planes or build up ground forces. Marshall was only beginning to learn about air power at this time, having just completed a cross-country air tour during which he had sympathetically listened to air corps complaints, but the president's plan was unbalanced and made little, if any, military sense. Yet no one at the meeting was willing to say so. To the contrary, they all supported Roosevelt, until he asked the silent Marshall, "Don't you think so, George?" Marshall did not. He was also offended at the first name reference, which he found "a misrepresentation of our intimacy," and not afraid to speak out. "Mr. President, I am sorry" he replied, "but I don't agree with that at all."[36]

Marshall later remembered that "that ended the conference. The president gave me a very startled look, and when I went out they all bade me good-bye and said that my tour in Washington was over."[37] As with Pershing in 1917, however, Marshall's bluntness impressed rather than alienated his superior. Here was someone who would tell Roosevelt the truth rather than what he thought the president wanted to hear.

In the next few months, Marshall also impressed Roosevelt's closest adviser, Harry Hopkins, with whom he was working on the aircraft procurement program. Marshall had become aware of just how much of Hopkins's relief funds from the Works Progress Administration had been and could be spent on War Department projects, as well as how important Hopkins was as a conduit to the president. He quickly gained Hopkins's sympathy and support—for himself as well as for the rebuilding of the army, and after the war he concluded that Hopkins had played the key role in his appointment as chief of staff.[38]

He also continued to impress Woodring and Johnson, each of whom still saw him as a potential ally against the other, as well as others with whom he came into contact. Moreover, he was not as junior as he may have appeared; recent army practice required a chief of staff to be young enough to complete a four-year term before reaching sixty-four, and of the thirty-three generals above him on the seniority list, twenty nine could not do so. That changed Marshall's rank to fifth, and of the five, only General Hugh A. Drum, Pershing's former chief of staff, had equally good credentials. But Drum's publicity campaign on his own behalf backfired by alienating President Roosevelt. "Drum, Drum," one magazine quoted the president as saying, "I wish he would stop beating his own drum." Marshall's refusal to launch a similar campaign, a refusal based as much on an astute understanding of his strengths and weaknesses in this situation as his values and modesty, stood in sharp contrast and probably helped him. So did General Pershing's support.[39]

In April 1939 Roosevelt decided in favor of Marshall. Without informing the secretary of war or anyone else, the president called the deputy chief to the White House study on Sunday afternoon, 23 April, to give him the news. Marshall told Roosevelt that he "wanted the right to say what I think and it would often be unpleasing." Roosevelt already knew that from the 1938 episode and responded affirmatively. "You said yes pleasantly," Marshall warned, "but it may be unpleasant." On 27 April the appointment was announced. Marshall would become acting chief of staff on 1 July when Craig would begin his final leave, and officially take over on 1 September.[40]

The final ascent had been extraordinarily rapid. Chief of staff was the highest rank in the army, a rank that carried with it the four stars of a full general. Just prior to the appointment, Marshall had had only one star. Three years earlier, he had had no stars. As recently as 1933, he had been a lieutenant colonel. Finally, however, all the praise and predictions, all the positive assessments by his superiors, had had their impact. At age fifty-nine Marshall had satisfied his ambition and reached the top of his profession.

What remained to be seen was how he would perform at the top. In a sense, all of his previous work had been training for this position. And yet he was quite unprepared for the tasks facing him in 1939. For despite his notable skills as a staff officer and tactician and his extensive experience with civilians, Marshall had little if any background in strategic planning, the uses of air power, the nuances of presidential and congressional relationships, or international relations. In a sense, his work in Washington during the eleven months between his October 1938 arrival and his September 1939 official induction as chief of staff constituted a crash course in these issues, culminating in a highly successful diplomatic mission to Brazil to counter Axis influence.[41]

Even if he had possessed background in these issues, however, Marshall would have been unprepared to be chief of staff in the summer of 1939. So would anyone else, for a global war of unprecedented proportions was about to begin.

5

PREPARING FOR THE UNPREPARABLE
1939–41

The morning of 1 September 1939, was a long and eventful one for George Marshall. It began at 3 A.M. with a telephone call informing him of the German invasion of Poland and ended more than eight hours later with a special White House conference to discuss the European crisis. In between he was promoted to the permanent major generalship just vacated by the retiring General Craig and sworn in as army chief of staff with the temporary rank of four-star general. "My day of induction into office was momentous, with the starting of what appears to be a World War," he noted a few days later. "You know, I think you timed your affairs very beautifully," he wrote Craig on 19 September, "because you certainly left me on a hot spot."[1]

It was indeed a hot spot, for as Marshall's induction day coincided with the beginning of World War II, so his first two years as chief of staff coincided with stunning Axis military victories and the subsequent need to prepare the United States for possible armed conflict. This was an enormously difficult task—much more difficult than the one he and the country had faced during World War I. Warfare had become more complex and total during the intervening twenty years, and mobilization now required a breadth of vision that could encompass the entire globe geographically and every aspect of the nation's resources conceptually. The task was complicated by the sharp split within the country over whether to intervene in the war and by the competing interests of potential U.S. allies in the world conflict.

While many of his past experiences would prove helpful in this crisis, nothing in Marshall's previous training had specifically prepared him for dealing with such issues. Nothing could have. The situation was unprecedented, and to deal with it effectively he had to move beyond many of the concepts and boundaries he had lived with throughout his life. So did most other Americans. Like them, Marshall's thought patterns would be dramatically transformed during these years, and while he would later rate them his most difficult during the war, they were also the most important in expanding his horizons beyond the previous confines of his profession.

Marshall's most pressing task during the early months of the war was to win presidential and congressional approval for an expansion of the regular army. A small buildup had taken place during the later 1930s, but the army in November 1939 contained fewer than 175,000 men in nine understrength divisions and ranked only nineteenth in the world.[2] As deputy chief of staff, Marshall earlier in the year had developed a program to add approximately 25,000 men, as well as equipment, to this force so as to be able to field five combat-strength divisions, and he had requested Pershing's aid in winning presidential support. The old AEF commander had complied, but neither Roosevelt nor the Congress had agreed. Isolationists still saw any rearmament as giving the president tools to involve the United States in a needless war, while FDR still favored his unbalanced airplane procurement program and did not wish to antagonize his opponents further at this time by requesting an increase in ground strength.[3]

The outbreak of war in September hardly altered this situation. Roosevelt did proclaim a state of limited national emergency and authorize a modest increase in the army and the National Guard. He also requested and received congressional repeal of the arms embargo so that Britain and France could purchase war material on a cash-and-carry basis. When Marshall requested funds to equip the additional forces Roosevelt had authorized, however, he met with sharp congressional opposition.

Marshall tried to counter this opposition in public speeches and radio addresses, as well as congressional testimony. The U.S. "might be compared at this hour to a very young giant in a position of tremendous power," he prophetically stated in mid-October, "possessing all those generous youthful qualities of virility, idealism and directness of purpose, untempered by the wisdom of years." Such wisdom, he insisted, required recognition of the fact that the army was not prepared to defend the country, that enormous time would be needed to get it prepared, and that the effort would have to begin immediately. Consistently he reminded his audiences of past American unpreparedness and its costs. In the last war, he told a House committee, allies had given the AEF time "while it found itself." This luxury might not be available again, and the United States "must be prepared to stand on our own two feet." It was not so prepared, he bluntly told the American Historical Association at year's end. "If Europe blazes in the late spring or summer," he warned a House committee in February, "we must put our house in order before the sparks reach the Western Hemisphere."[4]

The committee's response to this warning was to cut the armed forces budget by nearly 10 percent in April. Marshall then asked Bernard Baruch, the influential financier and World War I industrial czar he had met while an aide to Pershing, for help. A special dinner meeting with about a dozen key senators was arranged, and so effective was Marshall in making his case at that meeting that Baruch later labeled it a "turning point" in convincing preparedness critics in the Senate.[5]

Convincing Roosevelt was another matter. The president was by no means opposed to preparedness, but his concept remained centered on airplanes rather than a balanced force, and at this stage he by no means had confidence in Marshall or his judgments. Treasury Secretary Henry Morgenthau did, and on his advice Marshall in mid-May prepared a full program for presentation to the president and Congress. By that time Hitler had already invaded Denmark, Norway, and the low countries. Marshall's program called for the creation of a balanced force of 1¼ million men by the end of 1941 and carried a price tag of $650 million. "I don't scare easily," Morgenthau said, and "I am not scared yet." "It makes me dizzy," Marshall replied. "It makes me dizzy," Morgenthau shot back, "if we don't get it."[6]

Roosevelt remained unconvinced, however, and at a 13 May meeting he breezily dismissed both the proposal and any further arguments. Desperate and enraged, Marshall decided it was time to follow the treasury secretary's advice to "stand right up" to the president "and tell him what you think. . . . There are too few people who do it and he likes it." Whether Roosevelt truly liked what followed is debatable. Asking for "three minutes," Marshall let go with a torrent of facts and warnings. "If you don't do something," he concluded, "and do it right away . . . ,

I don't know what is going to happen to this country. . . . *you have got to do something and you've got to do it today.*" Under the impact of this barrage, Roosevelt agreed to some of Marshall's requests on the spot and a few days later asked Congress for more than $1 billion in defense expenditures for a balanced force. Two weeks later he requested another billion. By the end of May army funding requests stood at more than $2.5 billion, an amount equal to the total army budget for the previous five years.[7] Congress would soon approve these requests, and much more.

The presidential and congressional shift on defense expenditures was by no means solely the result of Marshall's persuasiveness. On 14 May Hitler's armies broke through the French lines at Sedan and in one week reached the channel coast. By month's end the British were evacuating their army from the beaches of Dunkirk, and the Germans turned south against the French. Italy then entered the war as Germany's ally. Paris surrendered to the Germans on 14 June, France itself a week later. In only six weeks Hitler had successfully completed what the kaiser's armies had been unable to do in four bloody years of trench warfare. German forces were now on the Atlantic coast, and only England stood between them and total victory.

Hitler's victories staggered Americans and forced them to rethink some of their major assumptions about the world. Most notably it called into question their supposed lack of interest in the European balance of power and reliance on the Atlantic Ocean for defense. Nazi victories and the advent of air power made that ocean look very small and vulnerable, especially the 1,600-mile narrows section between the eastern bulge of Brazil and the West African colony of the now-defeated French. Many Americans also began to realize that U.S. security throughout the nineteenth century had actually been based on the balance of power, for that balance had precluded the rise of a single, hostile nation dominant on land and sea that could threaten the Western Hemisphere. U.S. security was thus linked to the security of the key nineteenth-century balancer, Great Britain, and the first line of U.S. defense had been and remained British sea power rather than the Atlantic Ocean.

If Britain were defeated, U.S. security would be endangered by a Germany supreme on land and sea. Able to draw upon all the resources of Europe, it could dominate or attack the Western Hemisphere at will. At best in this situation, the United States would have to become a garrison state with an enormous army and navy. Nor would Germany be the only enemy. With the other nations of Europe defeated, the United States would have no support in the Far East, and Japan would clearly

71

seek to eliminate U.S. power from that part of the world and achieve dominance. Already the Japanese were taking advantage of Europe's distress to extend their influence into Southeast Asia and the Pacific, and in September they warned the United States against interference by joining with Germany and Italy in the Tripartite Pact.

Such facts and conclusions necessitated the initiation of some bold and innovative policies. A large army and navy would have to be created as soon as possible and a global rather than simply a regional strategy decided upon. Within that strategy, the United States in its own interests would have to provide substantial military assistance to Great Britain and any other countries willing and able to fight Germany and the other Axis powers. It might also have to become a belligerent itself and act decisively before all its potential allies were defeated.

Few Americans thought the entire matter through this clearly in 1940. Rather it dawned on them in segments and virtually on the level of instinct rather than thought. Most telling in this regard was the sudden willingness of the previously parsimonious Congress to appropriate billions of dollars for defense without any clear idea of how the money should be used. Moreover, numerous citizens disagreed entirely with the growing interventionist sentiment. Organizing in the America First Committee, they continued to insist that no vital U.S. interests were at stake in this war and that the country could and should continue its historic isolationist policy toward European wars.

As army chief, Marshall stood at the center of this controversy. Both viewpoints were represented in his staff, the administration, and the Congress, and both affected individual perceptions regarding the type of preparedness the country should undertake. This was not simply a matter of agreeing with one side or the other in the argument. Even if Marshall supported the internationalist assessment, for example, questions remained regarding priorities. Did aid to Britain take precedence over the buildup of U.S. forces? Should those forces be primarily air, naval, or ground? Where should they be concentrated? Marshall would be forced to grapple with these and related questions for the next eighteen months.

So would his new civilian superior as secretary of war, an individual whose appointment was one of the first results of the 1940 German victories. The Woodring-Johnson feud had almost paralyzed the War Department for many months, and in the light of the present crisis, it could not be allowed to continue. Nor did the internationalist Roosevelt want a continuation of cautious, isolationist leadership in the War and Navy departments at this moment of crisis or a partisan debate in this presidential election year over questions of national security. He therefore created a bipartisan cabinet in June by choosing two internationalist Republicans, Frank Knox and Henry Stimson, to be his new secretaries of navy and war, respectively.

These may have been two of the best cabinet appointments Roosevelt ever made. Knox had been a newspaper editor and the 1936 Republican nominee for vice-president, and he proved to be a highly capable wartime naval secretary until his death in 1944. Stimson's extraordinary career of public service spanned the century. Secretary of war under President Taft, a colonel in France during World War I, special emissary to Nicaragua and governor-general of the Philippines in the 1920s, and secretary of state under President Hoover from 1929 to 1932, he was by 1940 a senior statesman of seventy-two who commanded great respect in all quarters. Like Marshall, he had no political ambitions. Indeed the two possessed similar characters and values and had known and respected each other since World War I. During the 1920s, Stimson had even suggested Marshall as his own aide in the Philippines and as constabulary chief to his successor, positions Marshall had gracefully declined. Now they would work together, and their collaboration would be one of the closest and most important in Washington during the war. The door between their offices was always open, and although they disagreed at times, they divided tasks admirably and complemented each other perfectly.[8]

The same could not be said of Marshall's relations with his commander in chief. A year earlier Roosevelt had ordered the army and navy chiefs to report directly to him rather than through the service secretaries, thereby making Marshall in theory his senior military adviser. That did not, however, make him one of the president's intimate, trusted, or followed advisers. To the contrary, their views of what was required in this crisis were poles apart. So were their temperaments and methods of operation.

The logical and orderly Marshall objected to the president's haphazard decision-making processes and chaotic administrative procedures. He also objected to Roosevelt's informality and quickly made clear that their relationship was not on a first-name basis. This was not merely a matter of Victorian propriety. Marshall realized he would have to maintain his distance from this extraordinarily powerful man if he was to keep his independence and integrity. Consequently he insisted on being called "General Marshall" rather than "George" when others were present, and worked as much as possible with Hopkins rather than the president. He also made a point of refusing to laugh at Roosevelt's jokes, visit his Hyde Park home, or drop in at the White House "casually and informally" as the president desired.[9]

Marshall also disagreed with the president on numerous, specific policies. In the spring and summer of 1940, he found Roosevelt too cautious on asking Congress for army appropriations, too anxious to aid Britain, and too much oriented toward the navy at the expense of the army. The three positions were related. Roosevelt had been assistant secretary of the navy during World War I and retained a strong affection for that service, a fact over which Marshall jokingly chided FDR when he once asked the president to cease referring in meetings to the army as "they" and the navy as "us."[10] Beyond the emotional ties, Roosevelt had clearly imbibed naval strategic and geopolitical doctrine as espoused fifty years earlier by Alfred Thayer Mahan, as well as more recent theories regarding strategic air power. These led him to emphasize the importance of air and naval over ground forces, to see U.S. security closely linked to the British fleet, and to consider both aid to Britain and the buildup of sea and air power as cheap, effective, and politically safe substitutes for a large army.

Marshall found such presidential thinking dangerously misguided. While he would strongly support air corps expansion and grant it complete autonomy by 1941 within the War Department, he insisted that air power was no substitute for ground forces. Nor were naval power and material aid to Britain. Each was an important component of U.S. security, but a large, well-trained, and well-equipped army remained vital. The United States did not have anything resembling such a force in June 1940, and Marshall and his advisers considered its creation the most important task the nation faced. Roosevelt, however, still refused to commit himself fully to this goal, though the army at this time ranked only eighteenth in the world, just ahead of Bulgaria's.[11] Indeed, his insistence on aiding Britain hindered Marshall's efforts to develop a larger and more effective army by depriving the army chief of scarce war materials. Moreover, Britain's position in the summer and fall of 1940 was so precarious that many doubted its ability to survive and felt that any aid to London would be completely wasted.

Publicly Marshall refused to make statements contrary to presidential policies. Privately, however, he consistently disagreed with Roosevelt's caution regarding the buildup of the U.S. Army and lack of caution over aid to Britain, especially in regard to scarce and desperately needed aircraft. He did not oppose aid per se at this time, but he first wanted to make sure that Britain would survive and that sending aid would not hinder the development of U.S. forces.[12] So did the Congress. In late June it forbade the sale of any further war material unless Marshall and naval chief Admiral Harold R. Stark certified that it was not "essential" for U.S. defense. Undeterred, FDR asked for such certification for fifty over-age naval destroyers as well as for arms, ammunition, and aircraft.

The fact that the United States would receive ninety-nine-year leases on British bases in the Caribbean and the Atlantic in return for the fifty destroyers enabled Stark to give such certification on the grounds of a net strategic gain for the United States, and in early September the famous destroyer-bases deal was announced. Marshall could not do the same. "If we were required to mobilize after having released guns necessary for this mobilization and were found to be short," a staff member warned him, "everyone who was a party to the deal might hope to be hanging from a lamp post." In June the army chief had relented to the extent of certifying as surplus numerous World War I era arms, thereby enabling the British to purchase them via cash and carry, but by month's end he had begun to demand evidence of British ability to survive before he would approve additional aid and rejected a presidential proposal to send scarce bombers to England. When Roosevelt resurrected this proposal in September, Marshall bluntly informed him that there were only forty-nine such bombers fit for duty in the continental United States. The president's head shot back, according to Morgenthau, "as if someone had hit him in the chest."[13]

By November, however, Marshall had become convinced from reports from army observers he had sent to London that Britain could and would survive, and he relented to the extent of allowing some of the bombers to be "tested" in England, a stretching of the truth he later considered his only duplicity with Congress.[14] Simultaneously he pressed for greater emphasis on a U.S. buildup. That pressure was often quite indirect as well as effective, and it illustrated his growing political acumen and influence.

In the spring of 1940, for example, Marshall refused to lend his official support to a movement led by Grenville Clark and other private citizens to create the first peacetime draft in American history. This refusal was based on his fear that official support could actually hurt both the movement and the army by precipitating an antimilitarist backlash in Congress, as well as disrupting preexisting mobilization plans. Privately, however, he authorized members of his staff to help draft the bill, and once it was introduced and received support in Congress, he strongly endorsed it before the Senate Military Affairs Committee. He also took the opportunity to ask for enormous sums to arm and equip the draftees so as to be able to create an effective army of 1.5 million to 2 million men by mid-1942. By September Congress had agreed to these appropriations as well as the draft and the calling up of the National Guard and reserves, moves that enabled the army to reach 800,000 men by year's end. "For the first time in our history," Marshall informed the American people during a 16 September radio address, "we are beginning in time of peace to prepare against the possibility of war." Whether the task could be completed remained an open question, however. "For almost twenty years we had all of the time and almost none of the money," he noted in midsummer; "today we have all of the money and no time."[15]

During this time period, Marshall's influence with the House and Senate grew enormously. Whereas presidential proposals were attacked as partisan and manipulative, almost anything suggested or supported by the chief of staff came to be seen as in the national interest. "Let General Marshall, and only General Marshall, do all the testifying in connection with the Bill you are about to send up for additional appropriations for the Army," Morgenthau had advised Roosevelt as early as 15 May. The president followed that advice. Indeed Marshall made seven trips to the capitol between 29 May and 5 June. In the six-month period running from April through September, he spent twenty-one days testifying in fifteen separate hearings.[16]

Marshall's extraordinary influence with Congress was the result of a host of factors. He later noted three of them: his lack of "ulterior motive," the beginning of congressional trust in his judgment, and, most important, the fact that his advocacy of certain measures could remove partisan labels. "If Republicans could assure their constituency that they were doing it on my suggestion, and not on Mr. Roosevelt's suggestion," he explained in 1956, "they could go ahead and back the thing." In addition to these factors, Marshall had experience with legislative bodies dating back to his service under Pershing in the 1920s and with the Illinois National Guard during the 1930s, experience that now proved valuable. He also possessed enormous experience with civilians in general, understood the civilian mentality, and as chief of staff consistently tried to project a nonmilitarist and nonconfrontational image. Particularly illustrative in this regard was his insistence before Pearl Harbor that he and his subordinates appear in civilian rather than military clothes, his cooperative attitude with congressional investigating committees, and his refusal to challenge the law requiring him to certify goods as nonessential before sale to Britain though he believed it unconstitutional.[17]

In congressional hearings, Marshall was able to project an effective image of cool professionalism, thorough mastery of the facts, truthfulness, and nonpartisanship. Partially this image was an accurate reflection of his character and personality. He was, simply put, all that he seemed to be. He was also charismatic, and his aura of authority, leadership, and control extended beyond the military realm. A newsboy seeing Marshall enter his office building in civilian clothes might not recognize who he was, according to one story, but he would definitely know *what* he was: lawful authority.[18]

Marshall exuded a combination of self-discipline, knowledge, total honesty, and frankness that seemed to mesmerize as well as astound and reassure congressmen. "He has the presence of a great man," House Speaker Sam Rayburn stated. And while by no means a spellbinding orator when using a prepared text, he could overwhelm an audience when delivering impromptu remarks with his knowledge of detail and his passionate belief in what he was saying. One staff member who had heard Woodrow Wilson, William Jennings Bryan, and both Roosevelts concluded that "none of them could hold a candle to General Marshall when he wanted to make people do things."[19]

Marshall's refusal to avoid ugly facts, such as the impossibility of ever returning to pre-1939 policies no matter what the outcome of the war, only added to his image. "He would tell the truth even if it hurt his cause," Rayburn remembered. "Congress always respected him" for this and "would give him things they would give no one else." That respect was reinforced by his rejection of additional funds for unrequested projects as counterproductive emotional "enthusiasms" that could not be allowed to interfere with calm and rational planning. The "flag-waving days of warfare are gone," he bluntly asserted in this regard. "The successful Army of today is composed of specialists, thoroughly trained . . . , and above all, organized into a perfect team. Today, it is imperative that cold factual analysis prevail over enthusiastic emotional outbursts. Sentiment must submit to common sense."[20]

While Marshall clearly believed what he said, his image with the Congress was also the result of a conscious strategy. He deliberately avoided discussion of all political issues that could be considered partisan, for example, and consistently phrased his arguments in terms of managerial objectivity and nonpartisan national security. "I have but one purpose, one mission," he consistently emphasized, "and that is to produce the most efficient Army in the world." He was even able to skirt the isolationist-internationalist debate by arguing that this army was necessary for continental and hemispheric defense and deterring aggressors rather than for overseas duty. As one subordinate noted, he possessed "an uncanny eye for the political angle of every problem."[21]

To believe that the personality Marshall projected before Congress was totally natural is naive. While clearly based on everyday characteristics and values, that image was as much a conscious creation as his command image before troops. As he had throughout his life, he was once again projecting an appearance of full control, understanding, and calm that did not and could not truly exist but that had to be reassuring to a Congress nearly hysterical over the events occurring in Europe. "Marshall is the most accomplished actor in the Army," one official who worked closely with him noted. "Everybody thinks MacArthur is, but he's not. The difference between them is that you always *know* MacArthur is acting!"[22]

While Marshall continued to create his army, Prime Minister Winston S. Churchill informed Roosevelt in late 1940 that Britain was fast running out of funds with which to purchase U.S. war material. With his political flank recently secured by reelection for an unprecedented third term, the president reacted by boldly proposing that Congress grant him the authority to lend or lease war material to any nation whose defense he deemed essential to U.S. security. Marshall welcomed and supported this Lend-Lease bill. As important as aiding Britain, it would enable the United States to expand its industrial plant capacity, thereby fulfilling both nations' future military needs and allowing him to create a long-range plan for military procurement. It would also encourage America's friends and warn potential foes that "we mean business." Clearly, however, it was a belligerent act that, he said later, made war with Germany "a probability—better than a possibility."[23] Consequently it highlighted the need for strategic plans to govern the use of U.S. forces in the event of the country's entry into the war.

During the early decades of the century, army and navy planners had devised a series of contingency "color" plans to cover the possibility of war with specific powers. Attention during the interwar years had focused on the Orange plan for war with Japan, but during the spring of

1939 five new Rainbow plans had been ordered to cover the possibility of war against an Axis coalition of "colors." Rainbows 1, 3, and 4 were to be based on the United States fighting that coalition by itself and devoting its primary military effort to continental and hemispheric defense (1 and 4), or offensive operations against Japan in the Pacific (3). Rainbows 2 and 5 assumed that Britain and France were allies and that the United States would either devote its primary military effort to an offensive against Japan (2) or else assume a defensive posture in the Pacific and concentrate forces for an invasion of Africa or Europe (5).

Attention in 1939 and 1940 centered on the two plans for unilateral hemispheric defense, Rainbows 1 and 4, but by the end of 1940 it was obvious that the changed military situation required a new strategy. In November Admiral Stark took the lead by forcefully asserting that if the United States entered the war, the only sound strategy would be a revised version of Rainbow 5—to assume a defensive posture against the relatively weak Japan and to concentrate with Britain in the Atlantic-European theater in order to defeat the more powerful and threatening Germany—and he recommended staff conversations with the British to reach accord on this.

Stark actually updated a long-held if seldom-expressed consensus among American strategists that in any war against a European-Asian coalition, the United States should concentrate against the more dangerous European foe. Consequently Marshall agreed with the essentials of the naval chief's assessments and conclusions. So did the president. By March 1941, secret Anglo-American staff conversations in Washington had resulted in ABC-1, a military understanding to assume a defensive posture in the Pacific and concentrate on the defeat of Germany first if Britain and the United States found themselves allied in a war against the Axis powers. A revised version of Rainbow 5 subsequently became the basic war plan of the United States. With good reason, one historian has labeled this Germany-first approach "the most important single strategic concept" of World War II.[24] It not only allowed for future concentration against the more powerful Axis enemy but also provided a common and sound strategic principle to unify the most important members of the Grand Alliance and thus a solid framework for coalition strategy making throughout the war.

While Marshall would eventually play a major role in the formulation and implementation of this strategy, the initiative in 1940 and early 1941 lay primarily in the hands of Stark and the navy. At this time

Marshall was preoccupied with the formation of the army and aid to Britain and possessed virtually no experience in strategic planning. Equally important his staff was badly split on the implications, if not the substance, of Stark's approach. Planning with Britain in the event of U.S. entry into the war was admittedly quite different from planning to enter that conflict. Nevertheless, Stark's logic and conclusions raised the question of whether, in its own interests, the United States should enter the war. That question became critical in April and May when German offensives against British shipping in the Atlantic as well as British armies in North Africa and the Balkans seemed to threaten London's ability to continue the struggle.

While some of Marshall's advisers clearly accepted the internationalist view that U.S. security required British survival and that that survival now necessitated U.S. entry, others disagreed vehemently. Unlike their naval counterparts, army planners had for centuries thought in continental rather than global terms, and throughout the 1930s this led many of them to adopt an isolationist viewpoint and emphasize hemispheric security. That emphasis was reinforced by the lack of military preparedness for any major overseas ventures and by the perceived Nazi threat in Latin America. Marshall's diplomatic mission to Brazil in the spring of 1939 to counter pro-Axis sentiment had made him very much aware of this threat, and throughout 1940–41 he remained intensely concerned with securing Latin America against German influence and/or possible invasion. The isolationist viewpoint within the army was also reinforced by strong anti-British sentiment. "We cannot afford," a planning paper warned in early 1941, "nor do we need, to entrust our national future to British direction. . . . Never absent from British minds are their postwar interests, commercial and military. We should likewise safeguard our own eventual interests."[25]

Yet U.S. security was clearly linked to British survival, and that survival now seemed to be in danger. By April Marshall could no longer avoid these strategic issues and simply let the navy take the lead. While the immediate issue was whether to convoy British merchant ships in the western Atlantic, beyond lay the question of using U.S. expeditionary forces to occupy overseas bases in the Atlantic and on the West African coast and actual belligerency. Whatever his lack of background and the splits within his own staff, Marshall had to begin making major strategic recommendations with profound political repercussions.

The full depth of Marshall's ensuing dilemmas emerged on 16 April when he asked members of his staff for advice prior to meeting with the president. "Should we recommend a war status?" he asked. "What do we think should be done?" It was now mandatory, he insisted, to "begin the education of the President as to the true strategic situation" and to tell him whether an immediate decision was necessary, as well as "what he has to work with." Colonel Joseph McNarney summarized the interventionist point of view by noting that "we do have a Navy in being and can do something. If we wait, we will end up alone, and internal disturbances may bring on communism. I may be called a fire-eater, but something must be done." He was countered by Major General Stanley Embick, the former deputy chief of staff who had played a role in Marshall's rise and whom Marshall had now called back to Washington to act as senior military adviser to himself and the president. Emphasizing U.S. unpreparedness as well as his hostility to British strategy and leadership, he recommended continued nonintervention. [26]

Marshall essentially adopted a middle-of-the-road position at this time. While he agreed with McNarney on the importance of British aid and survival, he felt that his forces were by no means prepared for overseas activity and that the president was dangerously overcommitting the country. Consequently he counseled caution and argued against the use of the emerging U.S. Army outside the Western Hemisphere. Partially as a result of such warnings, Roosevelt dropped his plans for invasion and occupation of Dakar in French West Africa and the Azores Islands in the Atlantic and agreed instead to examine possible troop movements into Brazil. Simultaneously, however, he ordered the occupation of Greenland in April and Iceland by marines in July, gradually extended U.S. naval commitments in the Atlantic, and maintained a hard line against Japanese expansion in the Far East. In May China was added to the list of Lend-Lease recipients. In July all Japanese assets in the United States were frozen.

By that time the immediate crisis regarding Britain had temporarily eased, for on 22 June Hitler shifted his attention to the east by launching a massive attack against the Soviet Union. In the long run, this attack would change the entire complexion of the war and provide one of the keys to eventual victory over Germany. At the time, however, it was perceived as providing Britain and the United States with a temporary respite against major German offensives in the west, for few believed the Soviets could survive more than six weeks against the German onslaught. Nevertheless, all agreed that Russia had to be given aid as long as its forces fought the Germans. This meant another competitor for the still-scarce American war materials and thus a further dispersion of the American mobilization effort.

In late July Roosevelt suddenly ordered Marshall and his other key advisers to join him for a secret rendezvous off the coast of Newfoundland with Churchill and his staff. While the conference would become famous for the Atlantic Charter that the two men issued enunciating a set of Wilsonian war aims, the main topics discussed were military in nature. Supported by his own chiefs of staff, Churchill insisted that large ground forces would not be needed to defeat Germany and pressed for full-scale U.S. belligerency, a combined Anglo-American invasion of North Africa, a strong Anglo-American diplomatic front against further Japanese expansion in the Far East, and the sending of a U.S. naval squadron to Singapore as a show of combined resolve against Tokyo. Marshall and Stark were appalled by these suggestions and succeeded in postponing action on most of them. Clearly, however, Churchill had planted additional dispersionary ideas in Roosevelt's mind, ideas Marshall would have difficulty overcoming.[27]

Marshall had long felt that the only way to halt such dispersions and mobilize in a sound manner was to have an overall plan, and by the summer of 1941 he was far from alone. Most of the president's key advisers favored the creation of such a plan, and even Roosevelt agreed in early summer by ordering the armed forces to produce an estimate of the "over-all production requirements required to defeat our potential enemies." Completed by the planners and signed by Marshall and Stark in early September, the resulting "Victory Program" went far beyond the issue of production. U.S. security, it bluntly stated, could be achieved only through the defeat of the Axis, and such defeat would require U.S. entry into the war and concentration against Germany, as well as the arming and supplying of Allied forces. Moreover, it warned, while naval and air forces could contribute to victory, by themselves such forces "seldom, if ever, win important wars. It should be recognized as an almost invariable rule that only land armies can finally win wars." In a separate army estimate, Major Albert C. Wedemeyer of Marshall's staff therefore called for the creation of an army of 8.75 million men, organized into 215 ground divisions and a huge air force, to be used for a massive invasion of Europe no later than mid-1943.[28] A few weeks after he signed this estimate, Marshall oversaw the largest and most successful army maneuvers to date in Louisiana, maneuvers in which a colonel named Dwight D. Eisenhower excelled and came to his attention.

The Victory Program and the Louisiana maneuvers were impressive and in a sense the capstones of Marshall's many achievements over the previous eighteen months. During that time he had overseen the passage of the first peacetime draft in the United States, the expansion of the army from fewer than 200,000 to a balanced force of over 1.4 million men, the establishment of excellent relations with the navy and the Congress, the distribution of war material to potential allies around the globe, army-navy and Anglo-American agreement on a sound global strategy in the event of U.S. entry into the war, and the creation of a total military procurement program. In the process he had become one of the most important and respected men in Washington and the individual most responsible for the unprecedented state of preparedness in which the United States found itself on the eve of its entrance into World War II.

Yet the armed forces were far from fully prepared, and Marshall was far from universally admired or pleased with the situation. The late fall of 1941 was, in fact, one of the most frustrating and miserable times in his career.

One problem was Congress, where Marshall's influence was reaching its limits. While he may have had no political ambitions or partisan connections, he was chief of staff to a very controversial president and an officer who pressed for controversial programs. Overall he remained highly effective and desired, testifying in 1941 at eighteen separate hearings.[29] Inevitably, however, he began to be attacked by some as Roosevelt's tool and as much a manipulator and conspirator as the president. This was most notable in the summer of 1941 when he strongly supported an extension of the draft. Many considered this a betrayal of his 1940 promises, and he found himself viciously attacked in Congress, the press, and even within the army as OHIO ("Over the Hill in October") became a much-publicized piece of inductee graffiti. Nearly a quarter of his mail at this time contained personal abuse or threats of violence against himself or the president. "I am being called—a Benedict Arnold, a skunk, Hitler Marshall, a stooge, Traitor, etc, etc.," he confided to friends, and "am getting knocks from every side." But he continued to insist that "the national interest is imperiled" and that an emergency existed "whether or not the Congress declares it," and in the end he was successful—albeit by the slimmest of margins; Congress in August agreed to extend the draft by a single vote, 203–202.[30]

Compounding his problems with Congress were his promotion policies. Throughout the 1939–41 expansion of the army, Marshall had developed a system to create, train, and officer new divisions at a rapid rate, and he took an intense personal interest in this process. Often he visited his forces to check on their progress. He also insisted on replacing old and/or ineffective officers who could not meet his standards with young, competent, and aggressive commanders. Roosevelt and the Congress gave him the power to do this by severely modifying the old seniority system, and he proceeded with a ruthless efficiency. Only one of the 1939 senior generals would survive his purge and command troops in battle during World War II. His "little black book" of officers' names with notations became one of the most feared items in the army, and he lost many old friends. To make matters worse, he soon discovered that many, if not most, of the National Guard officers could not meet the standards he had set for high command. Those officers had friends in Congress, and by the fall Marshall was feeling the pressure from them, as well as the isolationists. "I am taking a rather heavy political beating these days," he confided to his stepdaughter, Molly, in early December.[31]

Marshall's relations with the president were not much better. While Roosevelt's respect for him was clearly growing, the president still refused to heed much of his advice and continued to overcommit U.S. forces and production. In August FDR insisted that scarce airplanes be sent to the Soviet Union even if they had to be taken from the air corps. In September he refused to accept the Victory Program. Impressed by Churchill's peripheral ideas and their promise of minimal casualties, frightened by the slim margin on the draft vote, and perhaps still believing that the United States could avoid full-scale belligerency, he expressed to Stimson his displeasure over the assumption "that we must invade and crush Germany" and instead resurrected the possibility of an invasion of French West Africa while simultaneously toying with the idea of reducing army size.[32] Marshall and Stimson were able to shelve these ideas temporarily in early October, but soon after the United States became fully involved in an undeclared naval war with German submarines in the Atlantic.

An equally serious situation developed in the Far East. During the summer, Marshall and his planners had reevaluated their Pacific strategy and concluded that an air power build up in the Philippines could make the islands defensible and perhaps deter further Japanese aggression. A new U.S. command had therefore been created under General MacArthur, the islands' defense forces chief and former U.S. army chief of staff, who had been recalled to active duty. Immediately a conflict erupted over supplies to be sent to this command as opposed to the Soviet Union. Meanwhile, Japanese-U.S. relations continued to deteriorate and reached the crisis stage by November, before the Philippine buildup was complete.

Still unprepared and desperate to avoid war in the Pacific with one brewing in the Atlantic, Marshall and Stark pressed for a temporary diplomatic agreement with Tokyo, a ninety-day modus vivendi similar in terms to what Japan was proposing, so that they could complete their buildup. Their suggestion smacked of appeasement, however, and it was rejected by Roosevelt and Secretary of State Cordell Hull. Instead Hull responded to the last Japanese diplomatic offer on 26 November with a ten-point moralistic statement. "I have washed my hands of it," he told Stimson, "and it is now in the hands of you and Knox—the Army and the Navy."[33]

Actually Hull had dumped the problem into the overworked hands of Marshall, Stark, and their staffs. Knowing from intercepted Japanese diplomatic cables (Magic) that without a political settlement by 29 November "things are automatically going to happen," they sent out warnings to all their Pacific commanders but incorrectly assumed that the blow would fall on the Philippines. Although they had previously considered an attack on Pearl Harbor possible, their preoccupations as well as defective intelligence assessments blinded them to the Japanese capacity to attack and destroy the U.S. fleet in Hawaii simultaneously.[34]

One reason for this blindness was the fact that Marshall and his staff had been forced to deal with so many issues and crises that they were approaching a state of physical and mental exhaustion. "If I lose this job perhaps I can get in a six ball juggling act, if there are any vaudeville shows left," he had sardonically commented in June. "Each day I think I have reached the peak of difficulties and pressures," he wrote to Molly on 20 October, "but last week was the worst of all, a combination of Russian affairs, the Japanese situation, supplies to England, the political pressures, developments in relation to National Guard and some Regular officers over relief from command, the development of the next period of training for the Army, the approaching hearings on the Lease-Loan, etc. etc. do not give me many peaceful hours."[35]

Early in his tenure as chief of staff, Marshall had responded to the growing pressures with a rigid daily schedule which provided him with some relief. Awake before 6:30, he was in his office by 7:30 and worked there with a ruthless efficiency that terrified his subordinates, who were expected to enter on schedule, sit down without speaking or saluting, give him a clear and brief presentation, answer questions, offer contrary opinions when appropriate, and then leave; failure to do so, especially failure to meet his "obsession for brevity and conciseness," could result in a devastatingly icy stare or on rare occasions an explosion of the old Marshall temper. At noon he returned to the chief of staff residence at Fort Myer, Virginia, for a small but relaxing lunch with Mrs. Marshall, followed by a brief nap and a return to his office. Firmly believing that no one had an original thought after 3 P.M., he would try to leave by 4 or 5 P.M. and thereafter "completely detach myself from Army affairs" so as to clear his mind for the next day. In the early morning and/or late afternoon each day he went horseback riding, sometimes with Molly or Rose Page. He claimed this did him "a world of good" and enabled him to "keep things in focus and shed almost all worries." He also swam in the Fort Myer pool. Evenings sometimes involved social events but much more often a walk with Mrs. Marshall, a post movie, or a picnic dinner and canoeing on the Potomac, followed by bed at 9 P.M.[36]

By late 1940, even this schedule had to be modified under the increasing pressures of work, and Marshall virtually gave up entertaining, accepting invitations, maintaining old contacts and friendships, or even answering the telephone at night. There were exceptions, most notably the enfeebled General Pershing whom he managed to visit regularly at Walter Reed Hospital, but overall he attempted to isolate himself as a means of maintaining his strength and clarity, as well as avoiding requests from friends for favors. That isolation was increased by the marriages and departure of Molly and Allen, followed soon after by Rose Page's departure.

Marshall's reserve, aloofness, and austerity increased noticeably at this time. "He is the most self-contained individual I have ever encountered," one subordinate noted in early 1941. "Apparently he has no confidants." That was an overstatement. More important than ever was Katherine Marshall, whose "one great objective" now became to make their residence "a sanctuary for my husband where he could rest and relax and gather strength." Together they lived in semiseclusion at Fort Myer and sought to escape the Washington area entirely during summer weekends by retreating to Dodona Manor, a 200-year-old estate in Leesburg, Virginia, that she had purchased to be their eventual home.[37]

Those retreats were all too rare, however, and by the fall of 1941, Marshall was exhausted. To make matters worse, in late October Katherine was hospitalized after slipping and breaking four ribs. On 1 December Marshall made secret preliminary plans to check both of them into the Army-Navy hospital at Hot Springs National Park, Arkansas, for a ten to fourteen-day rest. On 5 December he sardonically informed his daughter-in-law Madge that Katherine was steadily improving at home "and now manages a walk as far as the cemetery, which has an unpleasant implication but is our frequent daily objective in search of peace of mind. As a matter of fact, after some of the stormy days and weeks here, a cemetery would be pretty nice."[38]

The 7 December Japanese attack on Pearl Harbor ended all plans for a rest. Marshall, who had only recently returned from a week-long inspection trip, had a late breakfast that Sunday morning and then went for his usual horseback ride. He returned at 10 A.M. to find an urgent telephone call awaiting him from his Far Eastern intelligence officer. Hurriedly showering, he went to his office and was handed a recently intercepted Japanese Magic cable rejecting Secretary of State Hull's 26 November statement and terminating the negotiations. The fact that this message was scheduled to be delivered officially to Hull by the Japanese ambassador at 1 P.M. Washington time, dawn in the Pacific, aroused War Department suspicions, and Marshall immediately penned an additional warning to the Pacific commands. Due to a series of communication problems, however, the warning was sent by commercial telegraph and, unknown to Marshall, did not reach the army commander at Pearl Harbor until too late. More than 2,400 Americans died as Japanese aircraft achieved complete surprise and decimated the U.S. battleship fleet. That evening Marshall returned home "grim and grey" and said nothing to his wife "except that he was tired and was going to bed."[39]

Marshall's personal responsibility for the Pearl Harbor disaster has long been a subject of dispute. A series of investigations during and after the war blamed the local commanders, Rear Admiral Husband E. Kimmel and Lieutenant General Walter C. Short, but also found Stark and Marshall at fault for not noting and correcting their subordinates' omissions. Marshall accepted this judgment, albeit with the caveat that he was "not a bookkeeping machine." Most scholars have agreed and, rather than casting individual blame, have pointed out the limits of cryptographic information, structural inadequacies in the military, and the role of the "fog of war" in this situation.[40]

Some critics disagree, however. A few blame Marshall for rigid thinking and behavior, a rigidity supposedly illustrated by the image of him on horseback on the morning of 7 December instead of at home or in his office when the critical intelligence message arrived. They tend to ignore the fact that, despite the ensuing delays, he was the only official with access to this message, from the president on down, who sent any warning to the Pacific commanders. Other critics accuse him of participation in a Rooseveltian conspiracy to encourage and allow the attack as a means of manipulating the United States into war. Why Marshall would agree to such a conspiracy when he wanted to avoid war with Japan at all costs, how such a plot could have remained secret, how he could have participated in the light of his values and beliefs, and what sense it made to start a war by destroying one's battleship fleet, are some of the many questions this now-discredited thesis cannot adequately answer. Nevertheless, adherents of the conspiracy view continue to find "new evidence" to reiterate their charges and to win a popular audience.[41]

Historical conspiracy theories are appealing because they often make sense of past events that appear incomprehensible in the light of present knowledge. They usually do so, however, by gross oversimplification and a false projection of contemporary knowledge and thought patterns onto individuals in the past who simply did not possess them. This is certainly true in regard to Pearl Harbor. Japanese plans are clear in hindsight. Despite Magic, they were far from clear to the exhausted men who faced multiple crises and had their eyes fixed on the Philippines. While many scholars now admit that U.S. policy in regard to Japan was badly flawed, most continue to dismiss the conspiracy theory as simplistic, paranoid, and unable to withstand detailed historical scrutiny.[42]

Disastrous as it was, the Pearl Harbor attack did settle once and for all the isolationist-internationalist debate and the question of whether the United States should enter the war. On 8 December, in response to President Roosevelt's request, Congress declared that a state of war existed with Japan. Three days later Hitler solved a strategic nightmare for Marshall—war with Japan but not Germany when war plans called for a Germany-first strategy—by declaring war on the United States. Congress reciprocated on 12 December, formally entering World War II and linking the European and Far Eastern conflicts. For George Marshall and the rest of the nation, the ordeal of trying to prepare had finally ended. Now would come the ordeal of battle.

6

THE STRUGGLE FOR A UNIFIED GLOBAL STRATEGY, 1941–43

Official entry into World War II transformed Marshall's position in Washington as dramatically as it transformed the international status of the United States. Although highly respected throughout 1940–41, before Pearl Harbor he had been an advocate for a specific cause—military preparedness. And while he had attempted to keep that cause as nonpartisan as possible, inevitably he had become associated with the Roosevelt administration and its foreign policies. After 7 December, however, the debate over foreign policy was over. No longer would Marshall have to operate within or be limited by that debate. Now he was the completely nonpartisan army chief, a man with enormous powers and responsibilities who had to be supported in whatever request he might make if the United States was to emerge triumphant from this global conflict. That did not mean his work ceased being political. War, as always, remained inextricably interwoven with politics, but the politico-military environment and issues now changed dramatically.

For two years after Pearl Harbor, one such issue would dominate Marshall's time and energies: the search for a unified global strategy for the United States and its allies. To arrive at such a strategy was no simple task. Never before had a war been fought on so many fronts and over such large areas. The battlefield was the entire globe and the problems of organization and coordination unprecedented. These problems were political as well as military in nature, for interservice and interallied rivalries were so intense that they threatened to preclude any effective cooperation.

Marshall would play a pivotal role in overcoming these difficulties. He would be primarily responsible for the establishment and smooth functioning of the Anglo-American coordinating machinery, as well as for the development and eventual acceptance of the key strategic concept for Allied victory over Germany. In obtaining these achievements, he would participate during 1942-43 in eleven different international conferences and enter into negotiations with every major political and military leader of the Grand Alliance. While he might claim in 1939 that he was "no diplomat,"[1] by late 1943 he had clearly become the irreplaceable global statesman as well as the key military strategist and manager of that alliance.

Interallied coordination was by no means a new problem in 1941. Throughout history coalitions had illustrated a notorious inability to work together against common foes. Napoleon had once quipped that he would never lose against a coalition, and while he had eventually been proved incorrect, the rest of Europe had required four different alliances and fifteen bloody years before they could present him with an effective united front. Such time was not available in World War II. Only an immediate coordination of Allied resources could check the Axis initiative of 1941-42 and set the stage for eventual victory.

Aware of this fact and fearful that Pearl Harbor might lead the United States into a disastrous abandonment of the Germany-first strategy adopted less than a year earlier, Prime Minister Churchill and his advisers traveled to Washington immediately after the Japanese attack for the Arcadia summit conference. Their fears proved groundless, for Roosevelt and his senior military advisers remained firmly wedded to the Germany-first approach. How Germany was to be defeated remained an open question, however, especially since the Allies still lacked a detailed strategy and coordinating machinery. Arcadia provided the United States and Britain with an opportunity to address these deficiencies.

Marshall's emphasis throughout the conference was on the coordinating machinery. His experiences during World War I had convinced him of the importance of interallied as well as interservice cooperation, and from 1939 through 1941 he had championed such cooperation whenever possible. Now he proposed that it be achieved at an unprecedented level. Under the innocuous-sounding military principle of unity of command, the army chief suggested that the ground, naval, and air forces of all the Allied powers in the Southwest Pacific and Southeast Asia be placed under a single commander, and he clearly hoped that acceptance of this proposal would establish a precedent for other theaters.

Marshall's suggestion was staggering. Never before had the forces of two or more major powers been so fused, and never in U.S. history had such army-navy coordination been achieved. Indeed rivalry between the armed services was often as intense as national rivalries, a fact Churchill neatly illustrated when he belligerently asked Marshall what an army officer could know about handling a ship. "What the devil does a naval officer know about handling a tank?" Marshall replied. His point was not to make tank drivers of sailors but to get unified control of the Allied armed forces so as to be able to plan logically and defeat the common enemy.[2]

Under the impact of Marshall's persuasive reasoning, as well as Japan's assault and knowledge by all conference participants of the baneful effects of both service and national rivalries upon previous war efforts, the proposal quickly won naval, presidential, and British acceptance. British General Sir Archibald Wavell was placed in charge of all Allied forces in the so-called ABDA (Australian-British-Dutch-American) command, and a key precedent was thereby established for the entire Anglo-American war effort; henceforth all British and U.S. forces in a specific theater, naval and air as well as ground, would be placed under a single commander.

Who that commander would report to posed additional organizational difficulties. Marshall supported a British proposal to overcome them by setting up another revolutionary and unprecedented structure, the Anglo-American Combined Chiefs of Staff (CCS), to plan combined global strategy and direct the unified Anglo-American forces around the world. Composed of the army, navy, and air chiefs of staff of the two nations, this body was to meet in continuous session in Washington. There the British Joint Staff Mission headed by General Sir John Dill, former chief of the imperial general staff and a friend of Marshall since their first meeting in August 1941, would represent the British chiefs of staff at all times save during actual strategic conferences, when the British chiefs would attend in person. The CCS would be the supreme allied command of World War II. On Marshall's insistence, they would control the allocation of war production as well as the strategic deployment of Anglo-American forces and would report directly to Churchill and Roosevelt.

Acceptance of this proposal necessitated a major change in the U.S. chiefs of staff structure so as to parallel the British organization. The British Chiefs of Staff Committee (COS) was composed of the army, navy, and air chiefs and the personal representative of the prime minister. The U.S. Joint Board was similar in function to this committee but contained no air or presidential representative. During Arcadia, Marshall had General Henry H. Arnold, chief of the already-autonomous Army Air Forces but still his subordinate, join the army and navy chiefs on an equal basis in a new body, the Joint Chiefs of Staff (JCS). Naval fears of being outvoted were assuaged by the presence of two separate naval chiefs, Chief of Naval Operations (CNO) Admiral Stark and newly appointed commander in chief of the U.S. fleet, Admiral Ernest J. King. When King assumed both titles in March, Marshall moved to fill Stark's chair with a second admiral who would serve as chairman of the JCS and special representative to the president, a "chief of staff to the commander in chief." Under his constant prodding, Roosevelt finally agreed in July to appoint former CNO and Ambassador Admiral William D. Leahy to this post.

Out of these moves would emerge the present-day JCS organization, the centerpiece of the contemporary U.S. military establishment. Leahy's post would become chairman of the JCS when that body received formal legislative sanction in 1947. Throughout World War II, however, it existed without charter and solely at presidential discretion. And despite Marshall's objections, Roosevelt insisted on using Leahy essentially as his messenger to the JCS rather than as a true adviser and chairman of that body.[3] Partially as a result, Marshall rather than Leahy emerged as the group's leader and as its spokesman and senior adviser to the president. He also became its executive on European matters, with King assuming a similar role for the Pacific.

Meanwhile additional interservice planning committees were established to support the Joint Chiefs, while the army General Staff was thoroughly reorganized in March by Marshall's direction and executive order so as to support a global war effort, relieve the chief of some of the enormous burdens he had assumed since 1939, and remove the "deadwood" that at least one official labeled a fire hazard. The changes were more dramatic than any that had occurred since Elihu Root's reforms forty years earlier, and they wound up reducing the number of individuals with direct access to the chief from sixty-one to six. Traditional sections were either eliminated or dramatically cut back in size and power, and the three new "super commands" of Army Ground Forces, Army Air Forces, and Services of Supply were established. In addition, the old General Headquarters and War Plans Division were replaced by a new Operations Division to plan strategy, staff the interservice and interallied committees, and serve as Marshall's "Washington Command Post." To head this new division, Marshall chose the brigadier general he had only recently promoted and recalled to Washington, Dwight D. Eisenhower.[4]

Marshall had assumed a dominant role at Arcadia. According to one subordinate, he was the only officer at the conference with an original thought.[5] His growing power and influence did not yet extend to the strategic realm, however, where the better-organized and -prepared British dominated the discussions and won U.S. acquiescence in, if not agreement to, their "closing the ring" plan for victory in Europe.

Contrary to popular opinion, that plan did not call for a major invasion of the "soft underbelly" of southern Europe and was not aimed at checking Soviet advances into the Balkans. Rather it was a strategy of attrition centering on the use of Allied sea and air instead of land power to bring about a German collapse in the future at minimal cost in Western lives. Blockade, strategic bombing, commando raids, and support of resistance movements were all emphasized in this strategy as means of weakening Germany but not suffering heavy losses, with Western land offensives limited to peripheral objectives in the Mediterranean. Here Hitler's Italian and Balkan allies could be defeated and knocked out of the war, thereby weakening the German empire and perhaps triggering a chain reaction similar to the one that had precipitated German surrender in 1918.

Roosevelt was strongly attracted to this British peripheral, or "indirect," strategy, especially as expounded by the eloquent and overwhelming Churchill during their private sessions at the White House where the prime minister was staying as a special guest. Marshall's reaction was much more negative. He and his advisers saw the British approach as both militarily defective and politically manipulative, and they left Arcadia determined to replace it with a strategy of their own design.

Army objections to British plans were numerous. Accustomed to working with an abundance of manpower and material, the United States had historically relied on a direct rather than an indirect strategy whereby victory was achieved not by peripheral activities but by a concentration of superior force for the decisive defeat of the enemy army.

To ignore this objective as the British seemed determined to do, army planners maintained, was to invite military stalemate at best in a long, indecisive war. From their viewpoint, German collapse had taken place in 1918 not because of any satellite collapse caused by peripheral activities but because the Allied armies had concentrated and decisively beaten the Germans on the western front. Indeed, British peripheral activities in that conflict, including those Churchill had championed between 1914 and 1918, had weakened and delayed Allied concentration, and thereby final victory.

Delay in 1918 had not precluded that victory. It might very well do so in 1941–42, for another ally, the Soviet Union, now required immediate assistance in the form of concentrated assaults on Germany to relieve the pressure on its hard-pressed armies. Without such assistance, the Soviet Union might very well collapse, thereby giving Germany control of the entire European continent and precluding any possibility of eventual Allied victory.

There was also a Pacific war and public opinion to consider. Japan would not stand still while the United States and Britain pursued extensive and time-consuming Mediterranean campaigns, and despite the validity of the Germany-first strategy, the United States could not remain on the defensive indefinitely in the Pacific and still hope to achieve eventual victory in that theater. Nor would the American people tolerate a long, indecisive war in the European theater or continued defeats in the Pacific. Despite official agreement on a Germany-first strategy, most Americans saw Japan as their primary enemy and demanded immediate revenge for the Pearl Harbor attack. A slow, peripheral strategy in the Mediterranean would increase such demands and might force the U.S. government to abandon Germany-first.

British insistence on repeating their World War I errors in the light of these facts, Marshall's planners maintained, could only be the result of one or more of four factors: British defeatism in the aftermath of their previous experiences with the German Army: a fear of repeating the World War I stalemate and slaughter in the trenches; Churchill's personal desire to vindicate his World War I approach; and a general British desire to reap postwar political benefits in the Mediterranean by manipulating U.S. troops for British imperial purposes. "Perfidious Albion," they maintained, was once again planning to maximize its political benefits at someone else's expense, even if it meant putting the outcome of the war in doubt.

Months before Pearl Harbor, U.S. military planners had suggested an alternative strategic approach in the European theater. In the Victory Program of September 1941, they had bluntly stated "that only land armies can finally win wars" and had proposed the building of a massive army of 8.75 million men to be used by 1943 in Central Europe, an area designated "our principal theater of war." Citing the probability of negative public reaction, President Roosevelt had disagreed at that time and even suggested decreasing army size.[6] Even after Pearl Harbor, he had recoiled against the massive casualties that would be suffered in such a strategy and had found solace in Churchill's indirect approach, with its emphasis on a relatively easy invasion of French North Africa as well as the use of air and naval rather than massive land power.

Marshall found this humiliating as well as dangerous. *He* was supposed to be the key military adviser to the commander in chief. Yet it was Churchill who was staying at the White House as an honored guest and filling the president's ear with peripheral notions—notions that were militarily unsound and harmful to the war effort, to the size and position of the U.S. Army in that effort, and to future U.S. interests. Particularly galling to Marshall was the fact that at this time in the war, Roosevelt was not even sending him copies of correspondence with Churchill. After Arcadia, he knew the contents of that correspondence only because Churchill forwarded it to Field Marshall Dill, who then chose to show it to him.[7]

British peripheral concepts were not Marshall's only strategic worry. On the other side of the globe, continued Japanese successes in the aftermath of Pearl Harbor were leading to desperate requests from the navy, General MacArthur, and Pacific allies for reinforcements to stem Tokyo's advance. So extensive were these requests that they threatened the official U.S. commitment to Germany-first, a commitment many saw as irrelevant because of the speed and decisiveness of Japanese victories. The first three months after Pearl Harbor witnessed the destruction of British, Dutch, and U.S. naval forces in the Southwest Pacific, the subsequent wreckage of ABDA defensive efforts, the conquest of the supposedly impregnable British fortress of Singapore, and the invasion of the Philippines, the Dutch East Indies, and Burma as well as Malaya. By May Allied resistance had ceased in all of these areas, and the Japanese appeared capable of moving on to conquer Australia, New Zealand, and India.

The picture in the Atlantic and Mediterranean theaters was just as somber. Now free to attack U.S. shipping at will, German U-boats scored impressively against the unprepared Americans and thereby threatened the Atlantic lifeline to Britain. The Axis also gained temporary naval superiority in the Mediterranean at this time and launched a major offensive in Libya under the legendary General Erwin Rommel, an offensive that by mid-year would take them to within sixty miles of Alexandria and striking distance of the Suez Canal.

Only on the eastern front was there some optimistic news, for Soviet forces in December had effectively checked the German Army for the first time in front of Moscow and launched a major counteroffensive. By February, however, that offensive had ground to an inconclusive halt, and the Germans quickly regained the strategic initiative. In the spring, instead of again attacking Moscow, they rapidly moved south toward Stalingrad on the Volga River and the Caucasus oil fields. The nightmare of Soviet collapse and a junction of the German forces in the Caucasus, Rommel's Afrika Korps driving through Suez, and Japanese troops coming through India now loomed as a distinct possibility. So did Allied loss of naval control in all oceans and the possible additional collapse of China. In effect, the thoroughly dispersed and dispirited Allies were on the brink of total defeat.

In the midst of this unprecedented crisis, Marshall and his planners proposed a bold strategic shift to stop the dispersion of Allied forces, overthrow the indirect British approach that they believed reinforced this dispersion, and regain the strategic initiative: immediate concentration of all available forces in England for a cross-channel invasion of northern France in late 1942 or early 1943. In March Eisenhower and his Operations Division subordinates presented this plan to Marshall as the only way to check the present Allied dispersion, keep the Soviet Union in the war by diverting German forces from the East, and eventually confront and defeat the German armies. Marshall immediately accepted the plan and, supported by Arnold, Stimson, and Hopkins, began to press it on Admiral King and Roosevelt.

The irascible King proved difficult to convince. His naval forces were taking a terrible beating in the Pacific, and throughout February and March he had been bombarding the War Department and the White House with requests for reinforcements and a virtual Pacific-first-strategy. Static defense was impossible, he argued, and the United States could not allow the "white man's countries" of Australia and New Zealand to be overrun by Japan "because of the repercussions among the non-white races of the world."[8] By the end of March, however, Marshall had obtained the naval chief's support for his cross-channel strategy by a combination of personal diplomacy, promises to maintain sufficient reinforcements in the Southwest Pacific to hold Australia and New Zealand, and the logic of his argument; only by concentrating in Britain and crossing the channel could the United States relieve the pressure on the Russians and achieve the quick and decisive victory over Germany that was the necessary prerequisite to redeployment of all U.S. forces to the Pacific at a relatively early date.

The president proved relatively easy to convince, primarily because of his desire to have U.S. forces in combat in the European theater during 1942. At Arcadia he had favored Churchill's North African invasion, Operation Gymnast, for this purpose, but by early March Allied defeats had postponed the operation indefinitely at the very moment Marshall was presenting him with the cross-channel alternative. That alternative had the further advantage of providing the Soviets with the very operation they had been demanding, an operation Roosevelt could also use to block a proposed Anglo-Soviet postwar territorial settlement that he opposed. Stimson thus found the president "strongly and favorably impressed" as well as "keenly interested" in the cross-channel concept, and by 25 March he had given tentative approval to both the plan and a special mission to London to win immediate British approval. On 1 April he formally accepted the revised army plan and dispatched Marshall and Hopkins to London.[9]

Formally entitled "Operations in Western Europe," the plan became so closely associated with the army chief of staff that it was soon nicknamed the "Marshall Memorandum." It called for an immediate concentration of Anglo-American forces in Britain (Operation Bolero) for a massive cross-channel attack of forty-eight divisions in the spring of 1943 (Operation Roundup) or a smaller assault of five to ten available divisions in the fall of 1942 (Operation Sledgehammer) should Germany become critically weakened in the West or the Soviet position in the East become desperate. In London Marshall found the British surprisingly agreeable, and in the space of a few days his plan received formal approval as the combined Anglo-American strategy for 1942–43.[10]

Beneath the surface accord, however, were numerous British doubts. Essentially London had accepted Marshall's proposals not out of any belief in their viability but for fear rejection would lead the United States to turn to the Pacific. Acceptance would permanently bind the United States to Germany-first by concentrating massive forces in the United Kingdom. The British thus had no objections to Bolero.

Roundup was another matter. So was Sledgehammer, an extremely risky operation for 1942 that would have to be composed primarily of British troops and that might well end in disaster.

Marshall's planners had labeled this operation a possible "sacrifice for the common good" because of its potential to save the Soviet Union by diverting German troops even if the invading force was destroyed on the beaches. To be willing to accept such a possibility was quite courageous and noble, but with U.S. forces not scheduled to arrive in great numbers until 1943, the planners were being courageous and noble with British, not U.S., troops. This the British found outrageous, and in the privacy of their diaries and internal memorandums they assailed both Marshall and his plan. General Sir Alan Brooke, chief of the imperial general staff, was singularly unimpressed with the plan and its author, and while he later revised his estimates of Marshall, at this time he thought the army chief a strategic fool.[11]

Yet neither Brooke nor Churchill was willing to speak up for fear of driving the Americans to the Pacific. They thus agreed to Marshall's plan but almost immediately began working on Roosevelt to shift back to North Africa. "We must never let Gymnast pass from our minds," the prime minister informed the president in May, and in June he again traveled to the United States with his military advisers to bring Allied strategy back to the Mediterranean. By this time Roosevelt and Marshall had already met with visiting Soviet Foreign Minister Vyacheslav Molotov on the issue. Despite Marshall's objections, the president had virtually promised the Russian, in a public communiqué, a 1942 cross-channel invasion.[12] Now Churchill was arriving to negate that misconceived promise.

Marshall managed to thwart the prime minister on this occasion with a combination of carefully reasoned memorandums, material aid, and some blunt talk. Gymnast, he argued, would in no way aid the Soviets and would so disperse Allied forces as to preclude cross-channel operations in 1943 as well as 1942; Sledgehammer thus remained the only logical operation for 1942. When the British garrison at Tobruk unexpectedly fell to Rommel's most recent advance, Marshall graciously offered to send the British forces at Suez new tanks and guns. But when Churchill and Roosevelt suddenly mentioned after midnight one evening the possibility of sending U.S. troops into the Middle East, he angrily replied that this would be "an overthrow of everything they had been planning for" and walked out with the comment that he would not even discuss the issue "at that time of night in any way." Only Marshall would have dared to respond in this manner; the fact that Roosevelt and Churchill let him do so speaks volumes about his stature by this time with the two Allied leaders. Soon after this evening session, the conference adjourned without any clear decision save to continue with Bolero planning for the time being.[13]

Churchill did not give up so easily. He knew that Roosevelt wanted action in 1942, that London held a veto over Sledgehammer by virtue of the fact that it would be primarily a British operation, and that the president would agree to launch Gymnast if Sledgehammer was out of the question. By early July the prime minister was formally stating that Sledgehammer could not succeed or divert any German forces from the East, that he would not sanction the operation, and that Anglo-American forces should launch Gymnast instead in 1942. "This has all along been in harmony with your ideas," he told Roosevelt. In fact it is your commanding idea. Here is the true second front of 1942."[14]

Marshall was incensed. Disagreeing vehemently with such reasoning and convinced the British were guilty of manipulation and breach of faith, he pushed for a "showdown" by suggesting to Admiral King that they threaten a Pacific-first strategy if London vetoed Sledgehammer and insisted on Gymnast. King concurred, and on 10 July the two formally proposed such a policy shift to Roosevelt. If the United States were forced to engage "in any other operation than forceful, unswerving adherence to full Bolero plans," they advised the president, "we should turn to the Pacific and strike decisively against Japan; in other words, assume a defensive attitude against Germany . . . ; and use all available means in the Pacific."[15]

What Marshall and King were proposing was nothing less than the complete overthrow of the Germany-first approach, the foundation of Allied strategy. Roosevelt was appalled. "My first impression," he bluntly informed them, "is that it is exactly what Germany hoped the United States would do following Pearl Harbor." He rejected their proposal and ordered them to meet with him and prepare to depart for another strategic conference in London, accompanied by Hopkins, during which they would have to agree to Gymnast if the British rejected Sledgehammer. For emphasis he signed their directive "Commander-in-Chief" instead of "President."[16]

The extent to which Marshall and King were serious remains unclear. Roosevelt concluded that their proposal was merely a bluff designed to scare the British into agreeing to Sledgehammer, "something of a red herring," he informed Marshall, "the purpose for which he thoroughly understood."[17] After the war, Marshall, King, and Stimson all agreed. At the time, however, they argued that while the Pacific-first alternative should be used to threaten the British into agreeing to Sledge-hammer, it should also be implemented if London continued to insist on Gymnast. This conclusion stemmed from their belief that Gymnast would not aid the Soviets in any way and would preclude cross-channel operations until 1944 at the earliest. Invading North Africa would thus be equivalent to giving up on the Soviet front, and with it any hope of victory over Germany. In such situation, it was better to concentrate on the one opponent who still could be beaten while simultaneously satis-fying the demands of public opinion, the navy, General MacArthur, and Pacific and Asian allies for action against Japan.

Such logic and conclusions had appeared in most of the army's cross-channel planning papers in reference to possible British refusal to invade northern France. By July they had been reinforced by Chinese threats of a separate peace without massive U.S. aid and by public and naval pressure for more Pacific action to check the Japanese and take advantage of the recent and critical naval victory at Midway. A week before his famous "showdown" memorandum, Marshall had therefore agreed to launch the Guadalcanal campaign in the South Pacific. Now he appeared to be willing to go much further.

Roosevelt was not. He refused to sanction the Pacific-first proposal as a real possibility or as a bluff, and he even suggested altering the record so that later historians would not conclude Washington had considered abandoning the British. He also ordered Marshall and King to agree to Gymnast in London if the British rejected Sledgehammer and with Hop-kins's help quickly swept away their delaying efforts and arguments against the North African operation.[18] Rechristened Torch, that opera-tion was launched in November under the command of General Eisenhower.

On no other issue in the war did Marshall and his president disagree so fundamentally or vociferously, and at no other time during the war was the army chief so humiliated. Roosevelt had followed the advice of a British prime minister, not that offered by his own chief military ad-viser, and the prime minister had quickly turned Marshall's April victory into a stinging defeat. The fundamental flaw in Marshall's plan had been its inability to guarantee Roosevelt an offensive in 1942, an offensive the president felt mandatory for political and diplomatic reasons. Those rea-sons were not narrowly partisan. Roosevelt bravely accepted an invasion date after the November elections, thereby guaranteeing serious congressional losses for his party, but he did insist that public as well as Soviet morale required an assault sometime during the year. As Marshall later stated, one of the fundamental lessons he learned in the war was that a democracy must have a successful offensive every year. "We failed to see that the leader in a democracy must keep the people entertained. That may sound like the wrong word, but it conveys the thought. . . . People demand action."[19]

Beyond the personal blow, Churchill's triumph had destroyed Marshall's efforts to create a coherent, unified strategy. And as he had feared, the result was massive dispersion of U.S. forces and a lack of unity even within the JCS. With Torch approved and Bolero as good as dead, Admiral King felt justified in accelerating his Pacific war, an acceleration made almost inevitable by the sharp Japanese response at Guadalcanal. Marshall and Roosevelt found themselves forced to approve major reinforcements to hold the island, as well as additional support for Chiang Kai-shek in China and MacArthur's recently launched New Guinea campaign. By year's end, the United States had more forces committed to the Pacific than the Atlantic, and within the Joint Chiefs' planning network, arguments raged as to the future direction of U.S. strategy.

In early January Marshall was forced to inform the president that there was no united front within the JCS on cross-channel operations for 1943. As a result of such disarray, Churchill and his chiefs of staff were able to dominate the strategic conference later that month in Casablanca and win approval for their proposals. Although the conference became famous for Roosevelt's "unconditional surrender" statement, its major significance at the time was this British strategic victory. While the CCS did approve a combined bomber offensive against Germany and continuation of the Bolero buildup, the focus of Anglo-American activities for 1943 would remain in the Mediterranean, with the conquest of Sicily (Operation Husky) under Eisenhower's command as top priority. "We came, we listened, and we were conquered" was the bitter comment of one of Marshall's planners.[20]

Marshall was not one to dwell on defeats. Even before Casablanca, he had begun to assess the reasons for his failure and to reformulate a united front with Admiral King around the concept of a cross-channel attack, albeit in 1944 rather than 1943. That concept remained valid, Marshall's planners insisted, primarily because of the reasons given in 1942 and because the Soviet Union had not collapsed as they had feared it would without the Sledgehammer diversion. To the contrary, Soviet forces had scored a stupendous victory in late 1942–early 1943 by isolating and forcing the surrender of an entire German army in Stalingrad. In mid-1943 those forces scored an equally important if lesser-known victory by destroying a German offensive at Kursk and launching a major counteroffensive of their own.

Continued Soviet successes meant that cross-channel operations and victory in Europe were still possible and that the planners' 1942 arguments retained their validity. Moreover, the Soviets were still demanding a second front to ensure their continued participation in the war. Without the establishment of such a front, they implied, a separate Russo-German peace would be negotiated. That would make victory over Germany impossible. Even if such a peace did not ensue, Marshall's planners warned, Western refusal to cross the channel would poison future Soviet-U.S. relations and lead to Soviet refusal to fight Japan. It would also mean no large Anglo-American army in Europe to bargain for Western goals at the peace conference or prevent total military domination of Europe by a hostile Soviet Union.[21]

The events of 1942 had so scattered U.S. forces in the Mediterranean and the Pacific, however, that no cross-channel assault could be launched before 1944. Moreover, to shut down the offensives launched in the Mediterranean and the Pacific was not feasible militarily or politically. The British would not accede to any closure in the former theater, while the navy, the American people, and U.S. allies in Asia and the Pacific would not tolerate closure in the latter. Any cross-channel plan for 1944 would have to include continuation in those two theaters while simultaneously limiting them sufficiently to allow a buildup in the United Kingdom for a 1944 cross-channel attack.

Marshall and his planners soon came up with such a proposal, one that Admiral King could accept. By its terms, the JCS would agree to further Mediterranean operations in 1943 as proposed by the British but only if they were clearly limited and subordinated to a 1944 cross-channel attack and to ongoing operations against Japan. Germany-first would thus be retained but in a modified form whereby Pacific offensives would also take place and receive a higher priority than in the past.

Marshall realized that winning British agreement to such a strategy would not be easy. Heated debates would ensue, and outarguing the British would require much better coordination with the navy and the president, as well as more detailed preparation for strategic conferences than the Americans had previously shown. Consequently he championed an expansion and reform of the joint army-navy planning structure in early

1943 and paid detailed attention to ensuring prior presidential support for the united front being forged by the JCS and their planners. So did Stimson, who according to Marshall was so ardent in his support of the cross-channel concept "that he literally included it in his prayers every night."[22] In a series of meetings with Roosevelt, both men consistently emphasized the arguments being presented by the planners and the need for a united American front on future strategy. Within the JCS, potential as well as already existing army-navy disagreements were settled in advance, and a virtual battle plan was adopted for meeting the British and retaining a unified American position.

Underlying these preparations were growing fear and anger within planning circles regarding British objectives and duplicity, feelings that dated back to the old fear of manipulation and that had been heavily reinforced by the events of 1942. In its most virulent form, these feelings approached paranoia, with a devious and thoroughly untrustworthy Churchill plotting with his chiefs of staff to deceive Roosevelt so that the president would approve the politically inspired British instead of the "purely military" U.S. strategy.

Marshall knew better. So did his British colleagues who were well aware of their own bungling. As one of those individuals later commented, "Some Americans are curiously liable to suspect that they are going to be 'outsmarted' by the subtle British—perhaps because we sometimes do such stupid things that they cannot take them at face value but suspect them of being part of some dark design." On one occasion the results were quite humorous: British air chief Sir Charles Portal had to inform an embarrassed Marshall that his staff was objecting not to a British policy but to its own position paper as accepted by the British to avoid objections.[23]

One must also realize that U.S. strategy was just as political as British strategy. The difference was that it fitted U.S. rather than British political concerns and that its approval required recognition of this fact and the creation of a united front around it. As Marshall informed a Senate subcommittee in early 1943, "the thought of political matters was necessarily always in the minds" of the Joint Chiefs, and they were "not naive" regarding British "united front methods and ideas."[24]

Marshall's efforts first showed success during the spring of 1943. At the Trident strategic conference held in Washington during May, the Americans agreed to further action in the Mediterranean to knock Italy out of the war but only if offensives in what Marshall labeled this "vacuum" were strictly limited so as to ensure a 1944 cross-channel assault with a specific target date of 1 May, if seven Mediterranean divisions were transferred to England for this purpose, and if the British also agreed to an acceleration of the war against Japan. Marshall arranged and managed the American presentations at the conference, and after intense off-the-record arguments he succeeded in wringing agreement from his British counterparts.[25]

Churchill proved more difficult. Deeply upset over the refusal to sanction the actual invasion of Italy, he openly objected to the CCS agreement negotiated by Marshall. This time, however, Roosevelt fully supported Marshall. Surprised and upset, Churchill acquiesced only on condition that the army chief accompany him to Algiers for a meeting with Eisenhower and the other Mediterranean commanders. Here he clearly hoped to convince Marshall, and with him the president, of the wisdom of invading Italy. Tired and feeling "traded around like a piece of baggage," Marshall traveled with the prime minister to Algiers and there withstood a massive Churchillian verbal barrage. His only concession was the same one he had made at Trident: to accept General Eisenhower's recommendations regarding the Italian mainland after completion of the Sicilian operation.[26]

Quick success in Sicily during July led Marshall as well as Eisenhower to support an invasion of Italy as the quickest and best way to knock that country out of the war, but Churchill now pressed for more. With Mussolini deposed late that month and Italian occupation forces throughout the eastern Mediterranean dispirited and collapsing, the prime minister and his chiefs of staff unilaterally delayed the departure of seven divisions to the United Kingdom and pressed for a revision in Allied strategy so as to allow for exploitation of the fluid situation in the Mediterranean. Roosevelt seemed attracted to the opportunities unfolding, and by August Marshall faced an apparent repeat performance of 1942.

This time, however, the army chief emerged triumphant. In the revised JCS committee structure, he and his subordinates were able to maintain a united army-navy front, and in private conversations he and Stimson were able to bring the president back to the cross-channel concept. British strategy, Marshall warned Roosevelt, was based "on the speculation that a political and economic collapse, without a military invasion," could be brought about in German- and Italian-occupied territories; if incorrect, that approach would result in a protracted European war, which would result in public clamor for greater effort in the Pacific. Stimson further warned Roosevelt that the indirect British approach, which he labeled "pinprick warfare," not only would not work but would violate pledges to the Soviet Union and create serious problems with Stalin in the postwar world. If left in British hands, the cross-channel attack would never take place, for the "shadows" of the World War I trenches as well as Dunkirk "still hang too heavily over the imagination" of Churchill and other British leaders. The time had come, the secretary insisted, for Roosevelt to assume responsibility for and leadership of the 1944 cross-channel attack by pressing for Marshall to be given command of the operation.[27]

Roosevelt agreed and swung totally behind his advisers. At the ensuing Quadrant conference in Quebec during August, the British faced an even stiffer united American front than they had in May, and the meetings became so explosive that the CCS were forced once again into off-the-record conversations; when a ballistics experiment was conducted during one of these private sessions, those outside concluded that the British and U.S. military leaders had finally begun to shoot each other. Meanwhile, at Hyde Park, Churchill found the president solidly behind both Marshall's ideas and his appointment as cross-channel commander. Faced with this united front and growing U.S. military preponderance within the alliance, the prime minister acceded to most of the U.S. demands: Operation Overlord to be launched across the Channel on 1 May 1944, with a U.S. commander everyone expected to be Marshall; transfer of seven divisions from the Mediterranean to Overlord by 1 November; an invasion of the Italian mainland in September only within this context and only up to Rome; and Pacific offensives designed to defeat Japan within one year of German surrender.[28]

In early September Anglo-American forces under Eisenhower successfully invaded southern Italy and forced that government to surrender, but they were stopped south of Rome by German reinforcements. Incredibly Churchill now forced another round in the debate. Still intent on reaping some benefits in the eastern Mediterranean from Italy's surrender as well as ensuring success for Allied operations on the Italian leg, he requested retention of landing craft and troops in the Mediterranean, and thus a delay in Overlord, in order to support the Italian campaign, to encourage Turkey to enter the war, and to take Rhodes and other Aegean islands before the Germans could move into the vacuum created by the surrendering Italians.

Once again Marshall and his colleagues were incensed. This time, however, the issue was trilateral rather than bilateral. Influenced by recently improved relations with the Soviets and the importance of these issues to them as well as by the constant warnings of Marshall and Stimson, Roosevelt decided to postpone the final decision for the planned summit conference with Soviet leader Josef Stalin at Tehran in late November. At that conference Stalin would be asked to choose either immediate and expanded Mediterranean action with a delayed Overlord or Overlord on time with Mediterranean activity limited to Italy. No one knew which way he would go. Although the Soviet leader had been demanding cross-channel operations for years, he had recently appeared more interested in immediate relief via the Mediterranean.

At the preliminary Anglo-American conference in Cairo, Roosevelt refused even to discuss European strategy. Instead he invited Chinese leader Chiang Kai-shek and his military advisers to the meeting, thereby ensuring that it would focus on the war against Japan and frustrating the British to no end. Churchill was furious and took his anger out on Marshall, keeping the army chief up until 2 A.M. one morning with demands for action against Rhodes. For a brief moment Marshall's old temper and defiance flared as he shot back that "not one American soldier is going to die on that God damned beach."[29] All eyes now turned to Tehran for the final decision on European strategy.

The irony of Stalin's determining a two-year Anglo-American debate at Tehran was compounded by a further irony: Marshall, the most vociferous proponent for the cross-channel concept, missed the first and critical meeting. With no plenary session on the first full day of the conference, he and Arnold decided to go sightseeing in the Iranian capital and were unavailable when the meeting was suddenly rescheduled. Roosevelt thus entered the session with only Admiral King and Harry Hopkins to advise him. But Marshall had done his homework and en route to Cairo-Tehran had reemphasized to the president all the reasons for supporting Overlord. Roosevelt carefully reiterated to Stalin the salient points Marshall had been emphasizing and made clear his own preference for cross-channel operations.[30]

The Soviet leader came down solidly behind Overlord on schedule instead of the Mediterranean, as well as a supporting invasion of southern France with forces currently in Italy. He also promised a coordinated offensive on the eastern front in conjunction with Overlord and Soviet entry into the war against Japan after Germany had been defeated. Once he did so, Churchill was outvoted. The prime minister would fight heatedly for two more days at Tehran, but Stalin and Roosevelt were unmovable. So were Marshall and his Soviet counterpart, Marshall Kliment Voroshilov, during the military conferences at Tehran, and in the end the British were forced to admit defeat. Overlord would be launched in May 1944 and would form the basis of a coordinated, worldwide Allied strategy.[31]

The long debate was finally over. After two full years of controversy and more than ninety days of meetings, the Allies had adopted a unified, coordinated strategy for the defeat of the Axis. Much of the credit belonged to Marshall. It was he who had championed the concepts of interservice and interallied planning as well as unity of command in the field, concepts that had resulted in the JCS and CCS organizations and unified commands in all theaters. He was also the individual who had first proposed formally the cross-channel concept in early 1942 and had fought doggedly for it against repeated opposition from the British, the navy, and his own president. He had survived early defeats, learned his lessons from them, and returned to the battle with a deeper understanding of all the complex factors involved in creating a coalition strategy.

Foremost among those factors had been the political ones. Strategy, he had clearly learned, was inseparable from politics, and political factors could exercise "a determining influence on military operations."[32] Those factors were both domestic and international. A democracy required yearly victories, an alliance a coordinated approach made difficult by the competing interests of the partners, and a nation interservice and civil-military coordination if it wished to gain approval for its plans within a coalition.

As he learned these lessons, Marshall had functioned more and more in the political realm and had become as much a diplomat and politician as a soldier and manager. In the JCS and CCS he had emerged as first among equals. In the White House he was clearly by year's end the president's trusted military counselor. In Allied capitals he possessed enormous influence and respect. Even Churchill noted that the individual he had perceived "as a rugged soldier and a magnificent organiser" was also "a statesman with a penetrating and commanding view of the whole scene," and by 1943 he made it a practice to have dinner with him at the beginning of every Anglo-American conference.[33]

So successful and important had Marshall become in interservice, civil-military, and Allied coordination that some began to question whether he could be transferred to the Overlord command without disastrous consequences for the U.S. and Allied war effort. Foremost among those raising the question was the president of the United States.

Roosevelt's concern stemmed from statements by Marshall's JCS colleagues, by General Pershing, and by members of Congress that he was irreplaceable in Washington and that the Overlord command was, in effect, a demotion to a single theater. The president attempted to deflect such charges by expanding the Overlord command so as to include the Mediterranean, but Churchill balked at this subordination of all British forces to a single American while Roosevelt could figure out no sound arrangement whereby Marshall could function as both chief of staff and Overlord commander. Still, his respect for the army chief had become so enormous, and his desire to make him "the Pershing of the second World War" so great, that he was willing to give him the command and make Eisenhower chief of staff—provided Marshall requested such a change.[34]

This Marshall would not do. He desperately wanted the Overlord command, but his sense of honor and duty precluded any expressions of personal preference. The president, he insisted, would have to decide what was best for the country, not for George Marshall.

At the second Cairo Conference immediately after Tehran, Roosevelt decided to retain Marshall in Washington and make Eisenhower the Overlord commander. "I feel I could not sleep at night," he explained, "with you out of the country."[35] It was an extraordinary admission. Marshall could not be given one of the greatest military commands in history, a command everyone agreed he was entitled to receive, because he had become indispensable in Washington to his commander in chief and his country. For a soldier with Marshall's values, the compliment had to counterbalance, if not outweigh, the disappointment.

President Franklin D. Roosevelt and Prime Minister Winston S. Churchill on *H. M. S. Prince of Wales* during their first summit conference at Argentia Bay, Newfoundland, 10 August 1941. Behind them are (*left to right*) Marshall, Admiral Ernest J. King, and Admiral Harold R. Stark; General Sir John Dill is on the far right.   *U.S. Army Signal Corps photograph*

Marshall as Army Chief of Staff conferring with Secretary of War Henry L. Stimson in the War Department, Washington, D. C., January 1942.
Associated Press photograph from U.S. Army Signal Corps

Chief of Staff Marshall with General Dwight D. Eisenhower during an informal press conference at Allied Headquarters in Algiers, 3 June 1943. *U.S. Army Signal Corps photograph*

Chief of Staff Marshall with General Douglas MacArthur at Southwest Pacific Area Field Headquarters, December 1943. General Walter Krueger is on the left.
U.S. Army Signal Corps photograph

Special presidential representative Marshall in Yenan, during his ill-fated mission to China, with Communist Party Chairman Mao Tse-tung (*left*) and General Chu Teh (*right*), March 1946.   *National Archives*

Secretary of State Marshall with President Harry S. Truman and two Republicans who played key roles in America's postwar bipartisan foreign policy: Senate Foreign Relations Committee Chairman Arthur Vandenberg of Michigan and U.N. Ambassador (former Senator) Warren R. Austin of Vermont, August 1947.   *National Archives*

Secretary of Defense Marshall in Korea with Far Eastern Commander in Chief General
Matthew B. Ridgway (*left*) and 8th Army Commander Lieutenant General James A. Van Fleet
(*right*), 8 June 1951.
U.S. Army photograph

Katherine and George Marshall in their garden at Leesburg, Virginia, during General
Marshall's retirement, circa 1952.
George C. Marshall Research Library

Cartoonist Bill Mauldin's tribute to Marshall at the time of his death, 16 October 1959. *Reprinted with special permission of Bill Mauldin and Wil-Jo Associates.*

Marshall's flag-draped coffin at the National Cathedral, Bethlehem Chapel, in Washington, D.C., 19–20 October, 1959.
U.S. Army Signal Corps photograph

7

THE FACES OF POWER,
1943–45

Global strategy and diplomacy were by no means Marshall's only concerns from 1941 to 1945. Throughout the war years he remained deeply involved with many of the issues that had dominated his time before Pearl Harbor, most notably the expansion and training of the army, the selection of its general officers, and the establishment of good relations with the Congress and the president. As Allied forces began to achieve major victories against the Axis, he also became increasingly involved in supporting his commanding officers in the field, achieving greater interservice unity, and planning for the postwar world. Simultaneously he remained deeply immersed in ongoing disputes over strategy and diplomacy. In all of these activities he became "the indispensable man" and one of the most respected and powerful individuals in the world at the same time the United States was becoming its most powerful nation. "Wherever this man goes he inspires reverence," Roosevelt's White House secretary wrote in mid-1944; "may God spare him."[1]

Time magazine aptly summarized both this reverence and Marshall's numerous achievements in naming him its Man of the Year in early 1944. The tide of war had turned because the United States had actualized its potential strength, the magazine claimed, and George Marshall was primarily responsible for this accomplishment. He had created, equipped, and trained the largest army in U.S. history, refused to use this force too early or improperly, recognized the importance of air power, established unity of command, and won adoption of a unified strategy. He had also established an "unparalleled" position with Churchill, Roosevelt, and his CCS colleagues, as well as an extraordinary relationship with the public and Congress. Not since Washington had Americans so trusted a soldier, and "never in U.S. history has a man enjoyed such respect on Capitol Hill." Only Marshall, one congressman maintained, "could at any time get a unanimous vote of confidence." Devoid of political ambition, he was *"civis Americanus,"* a "trustee for the nation," and "the closest thing to 'the indispensable man.'"[2]

As in 1940–41, Marshall's image was a true reflection of the individual and his accomplishments yet at the same time a conscious and cultivated creation. Aware of the extraordinary position he occupied and the serious consequences that could flow from any emotionalism, for example, he made the public mask that already covered his feelings even more impenetrable as the war progressed. "I cannot afford the luxury of sentiment," he told his wife; it was incompatible with the "cold logic" his job required. Nor could he afford anger, an emotion that would be "fatal" because it was "too exhausting. My brain must be kept clear." He could not even "afford to appear tired," for he remembered that when Pershing had once done so, dangerous rumors had spread that the war was going badly. "It was as though he lived outside of himself," his wife later stated, "and George Marshall was someone he was constantly appraising, advising and training to meet a situation."[3]

Yet the public image was an accurate reflection of the individual. Marshall had always been a private person, and in a sense he merely extended and accentuated long-held characteristics and beliefs at this time. Even the conscious effort at emotional control was neither new nor out of character.

Highly illustrative of this combination of true personality and controlled image was Marshall's consistent reaction to queries regarding his political beliefs and plans. Still refusing to vote, he humorously dismissed inquiries into his "political faith" by saying that "my father was a democrat, my mother a republican, and I am an Episcopalian." He was much more serious when it came to growing suggestions that he run for president, suggestions he tried to squelch immediately as antithetical and dangerous to his work, his image, and his beliefs. "Putting such an idea into a man's head is the first step toward destroying his usefulness," he warned a supporter in 1941. Moreover, "the public suggestion of such an idea, even by mere rumor or gossip, would be almost fatal to my interests." As long as public officials devoted all their time and thought to "the straight business of the job," he concluded, "all will go well with America, but just as soon as an ulterior purpose or motive creeps in, then the trouble starts and will gather momentum like a snowball."[4]

He felt similarly about proposed biographies, which he did his best to suppress, and about decorations, awards, and honorary degrees. Once he threatened an aide with removal should such honors be bestowed upon him. He relented on a few foreign decorations when rejection would have created a diplomatic incident, and in 1944 Roosevelt overrode his objections and obtained for him a fifth star from Congress, along with the title general of the army. Overall, however, his modesty, integrity, and lack of ambition for political office precluded the recognition that the public wanted to give him. This only reinforced the respect and awe in which he was held, as well as his effectiveness. "You are one of the most selfless public officials that I have ever known," Stimson told him in 1942.[5]

That respect and awe was further enhanced by his carefully cultivated congressional and press relations. Particularly notable in this regard was his uncanny ability at press conferences to take all the reporters' questions and then give a long, detailed reply that answered each question individually and in order. Equally notable was his ability to give mesmerizing, extemporaneous expositions on the war to political leaders. So impressed were forty-four state governors after one such exposition that they rose to give him a silent tribute before breaking into applause.[6]

Marshall's public image also benefited from his insistence on seclusion—at either Fort Myer or Leesburg where Mrs. Marshall was restoring Dodona Manor and where Molly and her two children were temporarily living. Here he could spend his all-too-rare free time with his beloved garden and grandchildren, a method of relaxation that matched the ancient Roman image Americans still cherished of the virtuous and simple citizen-soldier. "Had he wished to cultivate the legend of Cincinnatus," his biographer has noted, "he could not have succeeded better than by his life at Dodona Manor."[7]

Marshall needed all the rest and relaxation he could get at Fort Myer and Dodona Manor, for his burdens remained enormous. Throughout the war he handled those burdens with the same basic schedule he had established in 1939–41. His office workday continued to run from 7:30 A.M. to 4 or 5 P.M., preceded by a horseback ride, broken at noon by lunch and a short nap at Fort Myer, and followed by a quiet evening

111

whenever possible and bed by 9 P.M. He also continued to terrify his staff with his insistence on high quality, independence, and brevity. "By God, I finally wrote one he didn't change!" Eisenhower exclaimed after Marshall had returned a draft memorandum without editorial comment. "Did you give the old man what he wanted?" a staff officer once asked another. "No, I never have," came the reply. "Neither did I," came the rejoinder with a smile. "You never will. Nobody ever will."[8]

Full-scale U.S. belligerency did bring some changes to Marshall's daily routine, such as a late 1942 office shift from the old Munitions Building to the new Pentagon, a special global briefing every morning, and weekly lunch meetings with the Joint Chiefs and with Field Marshal Dill. With the continued exception of regular visits to Pershing, it also increased his avoidance of social calls and events. When forced to attend such events, he usually arranged for an "emergency" to be telephoned in so that he could leave early. This semi-isolation clearly fitted his personality, but it was also the result of his need for total escape and rest at the end of each day and the fact that social events, far from providing this, often increased his worries and workload. One White House dinner, for example, resulted in eight personal requests for favors that necessitated thirty-two separate letters and several telegrams.[9]

Throughout the first half of 1944, strategic issues continued to be Marshall's primary concern. While those issues had supposedly been settled at Tehran, Overlord remained a potential rather than an actual operation and one that would require enormous skill to bring to fruition. Debate also continued to swirl over ancillary operations in the Mediterranean, as well as over how to conduct the war against Japan.

Bringing Overlord to fruition was now Eisenhower's responsibility, and Marshall clearly believed his protégé could fulfill it as successfully as he had previous assignments. The chief of staff also had a general policy of delegating as much authority as possible and of not interfering with or questioning the decisions of subordinates unless they failed. "Army officers are intelligent," he would say. "Give them the bare tree, let them supply the leaves."[10] In the past, however, Eisenhower had on occasion needed support and guidance from his mentor. Marshall had clearly promised and provided it, and he continued to do so now.

Two of the most important topics they discussed during the first half of 1944 were the size of the invasion bridgehead and the generals who should be given high-level command. On the advice of British General (later Field Marshal) Sir Bernard Montgomery, the ground commander for Overlord, Eisenhower suggested an expansion of the bridgehead from three to five divisions. Marshall agreed. He also agreed, with pleasure, to the appointment of General Omar N. Bradley to command the U.S. Army group that would be created after Allied forces were established in France. One of "Marshall's men" since Fort Benning days, Bradley had been promoted rapidly and marked by his chief early in the war for high command, and throughout the Mediterranean campaigns of 1942–43 he had exhibited an exceptional capacity for leadership and team play. Below him would be the modest but highly competent General Courtney Hodges, an old friend of Marshall from his days in the Philippines; and the brilliant but eccentric George S. Patton, an individual who would cause Marshall and Eisenhower endless public grief yet provide them with some of the most extraordinary battlefield leadership of the entire war.

As global commander of all U.S. Army forces, Marshall insisted on maintaining some outstanding generals in other theaters, and he and Eisenhower were not always in complete agreement as to the merits of specific officers. Overall, however, their assessments were remarkably similar. In the few cases where there were differences, Marshall limited himself to advice and carefully avoided the temptation to order. He clearly wanted to avoid any repetition of the World War I Pershing-March conflict and any needless burdening of his field commanders, telling Eisenhower in early 1943 to "concentrate on this battle with the feeling that it is our business to support you and not to harass you and that I'll use all my influence to see that you are supported." Now he similarly told him to "list your final desires and so far as I can see now they will be approved." The concern was personal as well as professional. "General Marshall's whole attitude toward Ike was that of a father to a son," the latter's naval aide noted in 1943.[11]

Eisenhower's need for support and advice was not limited to military matters. Theater strategy was as inextricably linked to political issues as global strategy, and since his North African command he had been involved in a host of political issues that had required Marshall's help. First had been the Darlan affair, in which his willingness to place the collaborationist former premier of Vichy France in administrative charge of North Africa in return for a cease-fire order to French forces had aroused a storm of controversy and required a public defense by Marshall. This had been followed in 1943 by controversies over the surrender terms for Italy and between the different commanders in Eisenhower's multinational force. In 1944 Ike faced this latter problem again and had to exhibit exceptional diplomatic skill. With his headquarters in England, he also had to bear the full brunt of Churchill's strong personality and interference, especially during the mid-1944 revival of the Anglo-American debate over European strategy.

While Churchill had been forced at Tehran to accept Overlord, neither he nor his advisers were reconciled to a static Italian front or to Operation Anvil, the supporting invasion of southern France from Italy. Instead they wished to proceed vigorously up the Italian leg and then swing eastward, through the Ljubljana gap in the Balkans and on to Vienna. Under Churchill's constant prodding, Allied forces during January tried to break the military stalemate in Italy by an amphibious assault just south of Rome at Anzio. The beachhead barely survived violent German counterattacks and then remained isolated for five months.

To Marshall, this was the old Mediterranean "suction pump" at work again; the effort required to save Anzio temporarily made it the fourth largest port in the world.[12] Churchill's attempt to substitute the Ljubljana gap for Anvil also appeared to be another example of British willingness to subordinate the defeat of German armies to political objectives in Eastern Europe. With Eisenhower claiming that the invasion of southern France was vital to support Normandy operations and his own staff vehemently opposed to any movement into the Balkans as both politically inspired and militarily dangerous, the army chief adamantly refused to agree to the British shift.

Roosevelt completely supported Marshall. Gone were the days when the president would ignore his advice and prefer the conclusions Churchill offered. Indeed it was Marshall who drafted Roosevelt's negative reply to Churchill, something he was doing with increasing frequency. Making use of their growing power within the alliance, the Americans virtually bludgeoned the British into Operation Dragoon, the new name for Anvil and one that aptly summarized Churchill's feelings as to how he had been forced to agree.[13]

All of Marshall's efforts came to fruition during the spring and summer of 1944. On 4 June Allied forces in the Mediterranean captured Rome. Two days later Anglo-American troops successfully established themselves on the beaches of Normandy. A few weeks after the landings, the promised Soviet offensive in the East began. In July the Overlord forces successfully broke out of their Normandy bridgehead and raced across France in a breathtaking campaign of speed and maneuver. Leading that breakout was the U.S. Army Marshall had created and the generals he and Eisenhower had selected for the task. In the midst of the campaign, Dragoon was successfully launched and soon linked up with the main Allied forces. By summer's end, France had been liberated and Germany was under simultaneous attack from the east, west, south, and, with the combined bomber offensive, the sky.

Marshall watched with growing satisfaction as his generals and troops fulfilled all their promise in these brilliant operations, and in June and October he visited the front to observe firsthand. During the second visit he became involved in another strategic debate regarding how to proceed in Europe. On paper, the issue was whether further offensives should emphasize a movement from the north (Montgomery), farther south (Bradley and Patton), or across the entire front. The real issues were that each army commander thought he was capable of breaking through if provided with the lion's share of available supplies, the egos of those commanders clashed, and there was Anglo-American national rivalry for war materiel and glory in the invasion of Germany.

The truth of the matter was that by mid-September, the Allied armies had outrun their supplies. In all likelihood, neither Patton nor Montgomery could have broken through the German defenses even if one had been given all available materiel, something that became abundantly clear when Montgomery's Arnhem offensive was checked short of its objectives. Eisenhower therefore decided on a slower advance to the Rhine along the entire front, with an emphasis on Montgomery over Bradley in the crossing of that river. Both protested. So did Churchill, but Marshall supported Ike completely. "Sometimes when I get tired of trying to arrange the blankets smoothly over several prima donnas in the same bed I think that no one person in the world can have so many illogical problems," a grateful Eisenhower wrote a few months later. "I read about your struggles . . . , and went right back to work with a grin."[14]

While the debate over European strategy had raged throughout 1943 and 1944, another strategic debate with quite different issues and personalities had been taking place regarding the Pacific war. This was essentially a U.S. theater, and the conflicts that erupted were thus national rather than international in nature. On the surface those conflicts concerned proper strategy, but the real issues were interservice and interpersonal rivalries.

Army-navy rivalry was nothing new. It had existed throughout U.S. history, often with negative consequences, and while other nations had similar rivalries, the depth of animosity in the United States was exceptional. It went far beyond the competitiveness and emotions of the annual army-navy football game, and on numerous occasions it had not been clear whether the two services viewed a foreign power or each other as the primary adversary. The controversy over strategic air power and a separate air service added another layer to this interservice conflict, with air arguments that naval as well as ground forces were obsolete infuriating the admirals.

Marshall clearly recognized the revolutionary impact of air power on warfare. He made his air chief, General Arnold, a member of the JCS and strongly supported a large air force, the strategic bombing campaign against Germany, and air autonomy within the army. He opposed for the present an independent air force, however, and consistently emphasized the fact that air power was not a panacea or a substitute for balanced forces. This proved to be an effective compromise that minimized conflict within the War Department during World War II.

Minimizing army-navy conflict was more difficult, though before Pearl Harbor a series of factors had enabled Marshall to reduce interservice rivalry substantially. Preoccupied with building the army, he had left the initiative for strategic planning to the navy. Equally important, Germany's 1940 victories had led naval planners to forgo their previous preoccupation with the Pacific and agree instead to the hemispheric and Atlantic-first approach that the army already favored. Finally, naval chief Admiral Stark was personable and easy to work with, and he and Marshall quickly became friends. "Stark and I are on the most intimate personal basis," Marshall noted in early 1941, "and that relationship has enabled us to avoid many serious difficulties."[15]

All of that changed in early 1942. With the United States a full participant in the war, army planners took the initiative in developing strategic plans, most notably the cross-channel concept, while naval planners once again became preoccupied with the Pacific. The war against Japan was primarily a naval conflict, and Pearl Harbor dramatically altered naval perspectives and assessments. Some navy planners even questioned continued adherence to the Germany-first approach, while others more diplomatically argued that greater effort would now be required simply to conduct a successful holding action against Japan. Foremost in making these arguments was Stark's replacement as naval chief, Admiral Ernest J. King, who consistently pressed for greater forces in the Pacific and just as consistently met opposition from Marshall's planners.

King was very different from the personable Stark. A brilliant strategist, by some accounts even more talented than Marshall, he was also opinionated, short-tempered, highly irascible, and rude. "When the going gets rough they call on the sons of bitches" was his supposed motto, and navy legend had him shaving with a blowtorch. This was not an individual Marshall could befriend. King was, however, open to diplomacy and reason, at least on occasion. Marshall effectively used both to create a viable working relationship. On one day in 1942, for example, the admiral angrily stormed out of Marshall's waiting room because of an unavoidable delay in a scheduled meeting ("He is the most even-tempered man in the world," one of his daughters wryly noted. "He is always in a rage"). Upon discovering what had happened, Marshall immediately went to King's office to explain, apologize, and warn of the disastrous repercussions of a blow-up between the two of them. "We can't afford to fight. So we ought to find a way to get along together." After a pause to absorb the words and calm down, King recognized the graciousness of the gesture and wisdom of the comment. "We will see if we can get along," he answered, "and I think we can." Aside from "one or two pretty mean fights," they did.[16]

The result was a constructive collaboration, if not a friendship, between two men who "probably did not like one another very much."[17] At its base lay King's continued adherence to a Europe-first strategy and cross-channel operations in return for Marshall's agreement to support more resources for the Pacific. In effect, King supported Marshall's lead in Europe, and Marshall did likewise for King's proposals for the war against Japan, even to the extent of threatening the British on numerous occasions with a Pacific-first strategy. This quid pro quo was not totally equal, however. Whereas King gave Marshall a virtual free hand in regard to European strategy and command, the presence of General Douglas MacArthur in the Pacific made it impossible for Marshall to give King similar support in regard to that theater.

MacArthur was one of the most controversial soldiers the United States has ever produced. Graduating first in his class at West Point, he had been quickly recognized for brilliance and had risen rapidly to high command. Matching that brilliance was an enormous ego and ambition, along with a dose of paranoia. He referred to himself in the third person, was determined to fulfill what he considered a personal destiny, and often saw dark forces determined to thwart him. By 1931 he was already army chief of staff, and it was apparent to many that his ambition could easily spill over into the political realm. Roosevelt considered him one of the two most dangerous men in the country (Louisiana Senator Huey Long was the other) and was relieved when MacArthur retired and departed for Manila in 1935 to train the army of the soon-to-be-independent Philippines.

In 1941 Marshall convinced Roosevelt that the Far Eastern situation in general and the recent specific decision to reinforce and hold the Philippines required a commander of MacArthur's proved military capabilities. He was therefore recalled to active duty and put in charge of all U.S. as well as Filipino forces on the islands. That did not prevent the Japanese from destroying his air forces, successfully invading the main Philippine island of Luzon, and forcing him into a doomed defense on the Bataan peninsula in late 1941 and early 1942. At that point Marshall convinced Roosevelt that MacArthur would be more valuable as a rallying point and active commander than a martyr or prisoner of war. On the army chief's initiative, he therefore received a presidential order to leave Bataan for Australia, where he would be given command of Allied forces in the Southwest Pacific and awarded the Congressional Medal of Honor. Here he became not only a rallying point but also a major problem in terms of strategy and interservice relations.

Strategically, MacArthur suffered from a severe case of "localitis." Convinced that his theater was the most important in the war, he even called for a reversal of the Europe-first approach and a shift to the Pacific. When such calls remained unheeded, he and members of his staff concluded that Marshall, despite all his previous support, was part of the dark forces conspiring against him. So was the navy, which refused to think highly of him or even consider letting him control its ships. Subordination of MacArthur to the navy was equally unthinkable, for he far outranked the new Pacific naval commander, Admiral Chester W. Nimitz.

MacArthur was also a political problem. Roosevelt's critics in early 1942 spoke of recalling the general to Washington where he would become the supreme U.S. commander, a clear usurpation of the powers properly belonging to the Joint Chiefs and the commander in chief. By 1943–44, some Republicans were talking about him as a presidential nominee. With the majority of Americans agreeing with MacArthur that Japan rather than Germany was the primary enemy, the Pacific commander was clearly a potential threat to the president.[18]

In his strategic views, interservice relations, political ambitions, and personality, MacArthur was Marshall's antithesis. Here was the vain, egotistical, and political general par excellence. Here was also a proven and brilliant battlefield commander, however, and with his charisma MacArthur provided a strong psychological boost to the Allied cause. Marshall therefore continued to support him strongly. He even wrote MacArthur's Medal of Honor citation in 1942 and undertook a world-circling trip after the Cairo-Tehran conferences of late 1943 in order to visit him. "I was fighting his battles from the start to the finish," Marshall later and accurately maintained, and talk of personal hostility dating back to World War I conflicts between MacArthur and Pershing's staff was "damn nonsense. I did everything in the world I could for him."[19]

That included violating his strong unity of command principle to ensure MacArthur autonomy. With the navy unwilling to place its aircraft carriers under the general and Marshall unwilling to subordinate him to the navy, the Joint Chiefs divided the Pacific into two theaters, one primarily naval and the other primarily army and air. Admiral Nimitz was given command of the vast Pacific Ocean areas and MacArthur the Southwest Pacific area. In 1942 the navy would control the first stage of operations around Guadalcanal, while MacArthur would take control in later stages against New Guinea and the major Japanese base at Rabaul (Operation Cartwheel). Naval and amphibious forces would be made available to support his operations but would not be under his direct command.

Additional command problems arose when Guadalcanal developed into a major campaign and forced a shift of the fleet into the South Pacific. The navy would not tolerate MacArthur's controlling that fleet under any circumstances. A compromise was worked out in early 1943 and Rabaul effectively isolated, but soon another conflict erupted over the proper direction and command of future U.S. offensive operations against Japan. Admiral Nimitz wished to emphasize a naval movement due westward across the Central Pacific to Formosa through the Gilberts, Marshalls, Carolines, and Marianas islands. This would bypass the main Philippine island of Luzon and relegate MacArthur to a backwater. Unwilling to tolerate this, the general proposed top priority for a series of movements from Australia and New Guinea designed to culminate in the invasion and liberation of Luzon. His rationale was openly psychological and political as well as military; he had sworn to return to the Philippines, and such a return was necessary to eradicate the memory of the stinging defeats of 1942 and rebuild U.S. prestige in the area. Not for the first or the last time, MacArthur was equating his own interests with those of the United States.

From 1942 through 1944, the Joint Chiefs and their planners consistently argued over these strategies and command relationships in the Pacific. Marshall found himself in the unenviable position of being both a mediator between the navy and MacArthur and an advocate for his Pacific commander, a position that strained his relations with Admiral King. Yet on the issue of Luzon versus Formosa, the army chief initially agreed with King. Rather than reach a definite decision, however, the JCS from mid-1943 to mid-1944 essentially compromised and postponed by endorsing both sets of offensive plans, something that proved possible because of the increased forces sent to the Pacific and the rapid success of those forces despite fierce Japanese resistance.

While militarily questionable, this dual approach solved a series of interservice and political problems in the Pacific. It also appears to have thoroughly confused the Japanese and kept them off balance, providing the United States with military as well as political gains. In late 1943 Nimitz took Tarawa and Makin in the Gilberts. The Marshalls fell in February 1944. Simultaneously MacArthur completed the isolation of Rabaul and leapfrogged along the northern coast of New Guinea onto the island approaches to the Philippines. During the summer, Nimitz conquered Saipan, Tinian, and Guam in the Marianas and virtually annihilated the Japanese naval air arm at the Battle of the Philippine Sea. At the same time logistical problems and the virtual collapse of Chinese resistance made the Formosa operation impractical and devoid of strategic importance. In early October the JCS finally agreed with MacArthur by sanctioning the invasion of Luzon, to be followed by a shift northward rather than westward for Nimitz to Iwo Jima and Okinawa. Later that month the Americans successfully landed at Leyte Gulf in the Philippines, while the navy inflicted heavy casualties on what remained of the Japanese fleet. As in the European theater, 1944 appeared to be the year of unbroken victories.[20]

One month earlier, Marshall had traveled to Quebec for another Anglo-American strategic summit conference (Octagon). There Churchill had summarized the results of the past few months by stating that since the last conference, Allied affairs "had taken a revolutionary turn for the good. Everything we had touched had turned to gold." Under the impact of an almost unbroken string of victories, the CCS quickly reached accord on final plans for the total defeat of Germany and Japan. Indeed on the horizon loomed the possibility of ending the European war in 1944.[21]

That possibility soon disappeared as Eisenhower's offensive met with increasing logistical problems and German resistance. By October the

Allied advance had been stopped west of the Rhine; in December the Germans launched a major counteroffensive in the Ardennes, the so-called Battle of the Bulge. Also in October the Japanese increased the length of battles and number of U.S. casualties in the Pacific by using suicidal ground defenses within an interlocking system of caves and bunkers and by introducing the suicidal kamikaze air attacks that would take so many U.S. ships and lives in the following year.

The growing casualty figures were a solemn reminder of the true costs of the war, as well as a warning that the fighting was far from over. Marshall had always made sure those casualty figures were placed before the president, and he maintained a constant awareness of the enormous cost of the conflict as well as an intense concern for the welfare of his men. No matter how busy his schedule, he found time every day to read a summary of their complaints and to reply to at least six of their letters. At the beginning of the war, he sent a personal letter to the family of each American soldier who fell, but the growing number of deaths made the continuation of such a personal touch impossible.[22] Compared to other major powers engaged in the conflict, especially the Soviet Union, U.S. casualties remained extraordinarily light. In terms of U.S. history, however, the final figure of more than 400,000 dead was surpassed only by the Civil War.

Marshall was not spared the personal loss of loved ones. In May 1944 his stepson Allen, with whom he had been quite close, was killed on the Italian front. In July two of his friends from World War I days died in France. Theodore Roosevelt, Jr., who had come ashore with his troops on D-Day, fell to a heart attack, while General Lesley McNair, the individual most responsible for training the army and one of Marshall's closest subordinates, was hit by misdirected Allied bombs. In November Field Marshal Sir John Dill, head of the British Joint Staff Mission and a man who had become one of Marshall's closest friends, died in Washington of aplastic anemia.

Dill and Marshall had first met as military counterparts during the 1941 Atlantic conference. Soon they were corresponding "personally and very frankly" on a first-name basis. Marshall was thus quite pleased when Dill was appointed to head the Washington mission, and over the next three years their friendship blossomed under almost-daily contact and the "implicit trust" they developed in one another. It was a friendship based on the many similarities in their careers, ideas, personalities, and values, with each having become, as one scholar has noted, "the conscious paradigm of the staff officer. When they met, the recognition was mutual."

Marshall considered Dill "the finest soldier and the greatest gentleman I have ever known" and admitted to his widow having "personally lost a dear friend, unique in my lifetime, and never to be out of my mind." At the funeral, according to one observer, "Marshall's face was truly stricken."[23]

Dill's death was a political as well as a personal tragedy. No other person had been more responsible for smoothing out Anglo-American differences and allowing the CCS to function so well. For three years he had played a pivotal role in Washington, albeit largely behind the scenes and unappreciated by a prime minister who in 1941 had forced him to resign as army chief. Earlier in 1944 Marshall had had to launch a major effort simply to prevent his relief and replacement. "To be very frank and personal," he now informed Churchill, "I doubt if you or your Cabinet associates fully realize the loss you have suffered." To make Dill's contribution clear and preserve his memory, Marshall not only buried him in Arlington national cemetery but also had an equestrian statue erected to him there and obtained passage of a special congressional resolution in his honor.[24]

These deaths brought the war home to Marshall and only increased his desire to end it as soon as possible. But that was not his only concern by late 1944. With victory on the horizon, political issues, never truly dormant, began to occupy more of his time and effort.

Primary responsibility for many of these political issues rested with Stimson and his civilian subordinates in the War Department, especially Assistant Secretary John J. McCloy. Marshall thus played a peripheral role in such controversial decisions as the forced relocation of Japanese-Americans and the refusal to bomb the Auschwitz death camp. On numerous occasions, however, he chose to become deeply involved in political issues because of their close relationship to the makeup and use of the armed forces.

A few of these issues were domestic in nature and concerned army recruitment policies. He successfully lobbied Congress for the establishment of the Women's Army Auxiliary Corps (WAAC) in 1941 and for a regular nonauxiliary corps (WAC) in 1943, and throughout the war he firmly defended this pioneering effort against its numerous detractors. That defense was based on issues of military and managerial efficiency, however, not women's rights. Using females in clerical positions they already occupied in civilian life made common sense and freed more men for combat duty. At no time did the conservative Marshall seek to use the military to advance social causes. On the contrary, he continued the army's traditional racial segregation policies on the grounds that one should not conduct "experiments" in wartime "which would inevitably have a highly destructive effect on morale—meaning military efficiency." In the case of WACs, however, this obsession with morale and efficiency resulted in an important advance for women's rights. Some claim this was not mere coincidence and that beneath the managerial mask Marshall strongly believed that qualified females who wanted to serve should have the right to do so. In 1950 he would create a political furor by insisting that a liberal Jewish woman, Anna M. Rosenberg, be made assistant secretary of defense for manpower.[25]

Concern with morale and efficiency during the war also led Marshall into political quicksand on occasion. In late 1943, for example, he dropped his traditional anonymity in labor disputes and risked his nonpartisan status by publicly attacking railway workers who were threatening to strike. He risked that status again in 1944 when he secretly contacted Republican presidential nominee Thomas Dewey in an effort to prevent him from revealing that Allied intelligence had broken the highest Axis codes.[26] So successful were this and other efforts that the full story of Magic, Purple, Ultra, and Enigma would not be revealed for another thirty years.

Despite his involvement in these domestic incidents, most of the political issues that concerned Marshall at this time involved war aims and postwar policies. While he firmly believed that soldiers should play little if any role in such matters, he also clearly recognized that war was an instrument of policy and could not be divorced from them. The strategic debates of 1942–43 had reinforced this point. Now he began to deal intensely with an even broader range of international political issues.

At the Casablanca Conference in early 1943, Roosevelt had enunciated the key Allied war aim as unconditional surrender of the Axis powers. Actually this had long been the unstated goal of the Grand Alliance and lowest common denominator between its members. Roosevelt's verbalization of it at this time was primarily a political move to reassure the public as well as the Russians and Chinese in the light of the Darlan affair and the present paucity of Anglo-American military assistance. Marshall and his JCS colleagues supported this presidential statement of policy, but they had some doubts as to its specific application and psychological effect on the enemy. Consequently they requested a presidential clarification and modification prior to Overlord that would differentiate between the German government and the people. Roosevelt refused. Nevertheless, unconditional surrender was modified in practice for the Italians and the Japanese.[27]

Marshall also took an interest in military occupation policies. In early 1943 he established a Civil Affairs Division within the general staff. Later that year military planners prepared their first occupation plans for Germany (Rankin), and in October a European Advisory Commission was established to plan Allied policy. Anglo-American conflict over occupation zones hampered the commission's work. Despite the fact that Eisenhower's forces would be entering Germany with the British in the north and the Americans in the south, Roosevelt demanded a northern zone of occupation for the United States until September 1944, when his advisers finally convinced him of the impracticability of such a shift. At that point, however, conflict erupted over the nature of the Allied occupation. Led by Treasury Secretary Morgenthau, one group pressed for a policy to keep Germany permanently pacified by means of a long and harsh occupation that would include a virtual ban on industrialization. The State and War departments opposed such a policy as counterproductive, vindictive, and unenforceable. Marshall also feared long-term occupation could destroy the "sacred trust" of the American people in their armed forces.[28]

The question of occupation policy was related to broader questions of postwar policy in general, questions in which political and military factors could not be neatly separated. Senior army and navy representatives were therefore brought into the State Department's Advisory Committee on Postwar Foreign Policy and special postwar committees were established during 1943-44 within the JCS, as well as the individual services. In late 1944, a high-level State-War-Navy Coordinating Committee was established to deal with the increasing number of politico-military issues that were arising.

Civilian and military planners agreed that the United States should under no circumstances retreat into isolation as it had at the end of World War I. That policy, they insisted, had constituted an unwise withdrawal from global responsibilities that had only encouraged aggression and resulted in the present world war. Instead of repeating its error, the country should take advantage of this second chance to maintain close postwar relations with its allies, enforce the peace that would be created once the Axis were defeated, and play a major role in a new collective security organization that should have substantial power to prevent any repeat of the 1930s. During 1944, Allied representatives meeting at

Dumbarton Oaks in Washington established the basis for this organization, the United Nations, while other representatives meeting in Bretton Woods, New Hampshire, established the basis for a postwar international financial system. This time the United States clearly intended to participate and assert fully its enormous power in the postwar world.

Such an assertion would necessitate a revolution in U.S. military as well as foreign and economic policy. An extensive peacetime military establishment would be needed for occupation and long-term international peacekeeping duties. It would also be needed for national defense. The events of the past six years had reinforced for Marshall and his colleagues the importance of interservice coordination and military preparedness in this regard and the fact that in any future war, the United States would not have time to create a large, prepared force. Consequently Marshall established a special division within his staff for postwar planning and recalled his old friend John McAuley Palmer to help, while the Joint Chiefs and the Congress began to examine possibilities for a large, coordinated postwar military establishment.[29]

Postwar political questions also began to dominate alliance negotiations. The agenda for the early 1945 Big Three summit conference at Yalta in the Crimea was as political as it was military in nature, with major topics including occupation policies, postwar governments, and the United Nations organization as well as plans for the defeat of Hitler and Japan. The three powers agreed to coordinated military offensives against Germany, specific zones of occupation, and basic occupation policies. In the Far East the Soviet Union promised to enter the war against Japan within three months of Germany's defeat in return for territorial concessions in Manchuria and the North Pacific. In Poland the West agreed to recognize a Soviet-supported government if its base was broadened to include non-Communist elements from the London-based Polish government-in-exile and if free elections were held. Along with this went a tripartite declaration promising free elections throughout Europe. Big Three differences over the powers and membership of different segments of the postwar United Nations were compromised, and a meeting was set for San Francisco in April to write the organization's charter.[30]

Yalta has become notorious as the conference during which a dying Roosevelt, advised by the politically naive JCS, supposedly gave away half of the postwar world to Stalin for meaningless Soviet promises. Similarly critics have attacked Marshall, his JCS colleagues, and Roosevelt for naiveté on the whole range of politico-military issues that arose throughout World War II. Rather than gear their strategy, war aims, and postwar policies to checking Soviet influence, as Churchill supposedly desired to do, they insisted on a simplistic and dualistic approach to war and peace whereby total military victory became the only objective. This had disastrous postwar consequences, most notably a massive extension of Soviet power. Once again the United States had won a war but lost the peace because of the blindness of its leaders to harsh and complex political realities.[31]

Such assessments are largely incorrect. Recent scholarship has shown that Churchill was by no means as astute or anti-Soviet in motivation as he later claimed, for example, and that Roosevelt was far from politically naive regarding the Soviet Union in the postwar world.[32] As for Marshall and his JCS colleagues, at Yalta they did not even participate in political discussions. On a broader level, they were well aware of political factors and constantly took them into account in planning strategy.

Marshall later stated that the JCS "probably devoted more time" in their "intimate discussions" to political factors than to any other subject. What they refused to do was attempt to make political decisions, or even to give political advice, on the grounds that this would be a usurpation of presidential prerogatives. "Political factors may exercise a determining influence on military operations, therefore they must be given careful consideration," Marshall had noted in late 1942. "Yet soldiers must not assume to lead or to dictate in such matters." Far from fitting the "image of political illiteracy he cultivated," one scholar has concluded, Marshall appears to have been "supremely political" in following the advice of a British colleague to "understand the ways of politics without becoming involved in them."[33]

The critics also fail to recognize the serious constraints under which Roosevelt and his military advisers had to work. The most important of these was the crucial importance of the Soviet Union to the war effort. Throughout the years 1941–45 the eastern front remained the largest and most important front in the war against Germany. The Soviets lost twenty million people here and, in the process, decimated the German Army. Allied victory was impossible without this effort, even in 1945. Marshall had based his earlier gamble to create only ninety divisions on the continuation of this effort. Forced to commit the last of these during the Battle of the Bulge, he and Eisenhower now needed a Soviet offensive to prevent stalemate, or worse, on the western front. The Joint Chiefs also considered early Soviet entry into the war against Japan to be of "incalculable importance." As in Europe, this situation would result in an inevitable extension of Soviet power. With Axis defeat, the JCS warned, the Soviet Union would be in a position of "assured military dominance" in Northeast Asia, as well as Central and Eastern Europe and the Middle East.[34]

Compounding these constraints were those imposed by the nature of the U.S. government and its people. Those people demanded quick and decisive victory in Europe, minimal casualties, and a redeployment to the Pacific as soon as possible. From their previous behavior one could also assume, as did Roosevelt and Marshall, that they would not tolerate a long occupation period.

The politico-military situation at the time imposed additional restraints. The European Advisory Commission had already worked out the German zones of occupation. Within Germany the Red Army was already approaching Berlin, while Eisenhower had not yet crossed the Rhine. In the Far East, the Soviets appeared capable of entering the war only at the last minute and then grabbing as much territory as they wanted. That they would agree to coordinated offensives in Germany, to limit their zone and divide Berlin, to enter the Far Eastern war so quickly and for so few territorial concessions—all of these could be considered U.S. victories rather than giveaways.

The real victory, however, was the ability of the Allies at Yalta to compromise their differences and proceed with a unified plan for German and Japanese defeat. Coalitions were notorious for their inability to do this, an inability Hitler clearly believed would reappear to save him. That it did not reappear at Yalta Marshall considered a critical defeat for the Germans. "They have always planned on a split of the Allies," he told the press soon after the conference. "They never for one moment calculated that the Allies could continue to conduct combined operations with complete understanding and good faith."[35]

During the next two months the military and political situations changed dramatically. In March Eisenhower's forces successfully crossed the Rhine with unexpected ease, captured nearly 350,000 German forces in the Ruhr, and broke the back of German resistance in the West. By late April they were advancing at unprecedented speed across central Germany, and Eisenhower had shifted the focus of his offensive from a planned move by Montgomery on Berlin to a move by Bradley into central and southern Germany. Simultaneously the diplomatic situation deteriorated dramatically. Amid complaints that he was breaking his promises in regard to Poland, Stalin accused the West of using secret surrender negotiations in northern Italy as a pretext for a separate peace. Marshall and his staff drafted the sharp reply that Roosevelt sent, with its "bitter resentment . . . for such vile misrepresentations," as well as its fear that such accusations could imperil final victory.[36] But the army chief refused to overrule Eisenhower and sanction the drives on Berlin and Prague that the British now requested.

To the contrary, Marshall agreed totally with Ike that these drives were militarily unjustified and dangerous. Personally he was also "loath to hazard American lives for purely political purposes." That did not mean either general would oppose a Berlin or Prague assault if the president considered the political gains worth the military risks. Neither would attempt to make such a political decision, however, or recommend such action on military grounds. As Marshall's biographer has noted in this regard, "it was not the failure by the military leaders to think of political consequences but their refusal to make political decisions that their critics apparently deplore. On that point the position of Marshall and Eisenhower was in the soundest political tradition of the Republic." Moreover, even the supposed political gains were questionable. The Soviets threatened to respond to a Prague assault with a move into Denmark, and Berlin probably would have been "returned" to the Soviet Union in the same way other Soviet zone territory overrun by Eisenhower's armies was "returned" after German surrender.[37]

In the midst of this debate President Roosevelt died of a massive stroke on 12 April. Marshall was placed in charge of the funeral arrangements by Eleanor Roosevelt and for the burial made his first visit to Hyde Park. For six years he had served directly under this extraordinary man. During the last two of those years, their relationship had become exceptionally close as each developed a deep respect for and trust in the other's abilities. Partially as a result of this respect and partially as a result of Hopkins's serious illness, Marshall by 1945 had clearly become the president's foremost adviser. Yet his reserve and fear of being manipulated had led him to maintain a formal distance from his commander in chief and to refuse invitations to the president's home. Now, however, it was time to pay final respects.

Marshall quickly returned to Washington to brief the new president, Harry S. Truman, to settle the continuing Berlin debate, and to deal with the final stages of the war. The end came quickly. During the last week of April, Soviet and U.S. forces achieved a juncture on the Elbe River. Hitler committed suicide a few days later in his Berlin bunker. On 8 May his successors surrendered unconditionally. Finally it was over.

The war against Japan continued, but its outcome was beyond doubt now that Germany had been totally beaten.

Perhaps more than any other individual, Marshall was responsible for this victory. It was he who had planned and directed the actualization of U.S. potential military strength and in the process created the largest and most effective military-industrial machine in history. From the Pentagon he now controlled a force of 8⅓ million men deployed in nine theaters around the globe and supported by an economic base and logistical system of unprecedented magnitude. The managerial skill required had been enormous. Indeed Marshall had now brought the managerial revolution in warfare, of which he had always been a part, to its apogee. For good reason Churchill labeled him the "organizer of victory."[38]

Yet he had done much more than create and manage a war machine. He had carefully selected and supported its commanders, devised the core global strategy for its use, and successfully fought for Allied acceptance of that strategy. He had also been primarily responsible for the unprecedented interservice and civil-military coordination in the United States and for the extraordinary Anglo-American coordination—from the CCS structure in Washington down to unity of command in each theater. "Our greatest triumph," he told Churchill in this regard, "lies in the fact that we achieved the impossible, Allied military unity of action."[39] In achieving all of this he had shown exceptional abilities as a diplomat and statesman, as well as a soldier and manager, and had raised the power and stature of the United States in the world arena to unprecedented levels.

Finally and perhaps most important, Marshall had not fallen victim to either militarism or personal ambition. Throughout the war he had maintained an understanding of and respect for civilian values, as well as an ability to subordinate his personal desires to the service of his country. As *Time* magazine had noted in choosing him as its Man of the Year, "American democracy is the stuff Marshall is made of." Churchill's physician later commented that "his goodness seemed to put ambition out of countenance."[40]

Most of those with whom Marshall had worked during the war agreed, and their praise and thanks now began to pour in. Eisenhower rated his confidence and support "the strongest weapon that I have always had in my hand. . . . Our army and our people have never been so deeply indebted to any other soldier." Admiral Stark concurred: "I simply thank God for you from the bottom of my heart. I don't know how we could have gotten along without you."[41]

The most moving tribute came from Stimson. Before a select audience of high-ranking War Department officials, the seventy-seven-year-old secretary acknowledged on 8 May "my great personal debt to you," as well as his deep respect for Marshall's abilities and selflessness. "You have never thought of yourself," he said. "I have never seen a task of such magnitude performed by man." Beyond that, Stimson emotionally continued, it was "rare in late life to make new friends; at my age it is a slow process but there is no one for whom I have such deep respect and I think greater affection. . . . I have seen a great many soldiers in my lifetime," he concluded, "and you, sir, are the finest soldier I have ever known." At least one general in the audience openly wept. As for the totally self-disciplined Marshall, he was "strangely silent" when he returned home that evening.[42]

If Stimson delivered the most moving tribute, Churchill may have inadvertently delivered the most meaningful one. "That is the noblest Roman of them all," he told his physician. The compliment clearly referred to Marshall's character, but it possessed additional meaning in the light of the enormous wartime growth of U.S. power and the consequent comparison by many, including future Prime Minister Harold Macmillan, of the emerging "American Empire" to the old Roman one.[43] Marshall had been the key military architect of this new empire. In terms of his own values, he was also a fascinating link to the ancient one with which his nation was now being compared.

8

THE LIMITS OF POWER,
1944–47

At the time of Germany's surrender in May 1945, the United States was by far the most powerful nation in the world. Three months later it illustrated the depth of that power when it destroyed Hiroshima and Nagasaki with atomic bombs and forced Japan to surrender. World War II was officially over, and the armed forces Marshall had done so much to create, forces that now numbered over 12 million men, stood triumphant on every continent and ocean. Behind them stood an equally massive industrial base. Tremendously expanded as a result of World War II, fully recovered from the Great Depression, and protected from wartime destruction by its distance from active theaters, the U.S. economy was producing more than 50 percent of the world's total goods.

The United States by 1945 had fully realized the potential it had first shown a half-century earlier. "What Rome was to the ancient world," Walter Lippmann had prophesized in 1938–39, "what Great Britain has been to the modern world, America is to the world of tomorrow." By 1945 "tomorrow" had arrived. With good reason Americans felt that the twentieth century had become, in newspaper publisher Henry Luce's words, the "American Century." Possessing enormous power and believing it neither could nor should retreat again into isolation, the United States would now fulfill Woodrow Wilson's earlier vision by accepting

131

"wholeheartedly our duty and our opportunity as the most powerful and vital nation in the world" to act decisively in the international arena and to create a new world order of peace, prosperity, and democracy.[1]

Such rosy images of the postwar era were quickly dashed as Americans learned that their virtually unlimited military and economic power could not always be translated into diplomatic success. In both Europe and Asia, long-term problems that had been exacerbated by World War II defied American solutions and revealed the limits of what had at first appeared to be Washington's unlimited power in the postwar world. During 1945 and 1946, as both army chief of staff and special presidential emissary to China, Marshall would discover these limits.

Throughout World War II, the forgotten China theater had provided Marshall with an early example of the limits of American power. While Allied forces were achieving stunning victories on every other front by 1943–44, in China they continued to be ineffective against the Japanese despite a large influx of American aid. "Everything seems to go wrong," Roosevelt had complained to the army chief in October 1943.[2] A year later, continued failure in this theater had forced a major change in U.S. strategy and made a political casualty of one of Marshall's favorite subordinates.

The Sino-Japanese conflict was the oldest of the numerous regional wars that had fused in December 1941 to create World War II. Beginning in 1931 with the Japanese conquest of Manchuria and escalating in 1937 to full-scale if undeclared war, it pitted the powerful Japanese Army against a coalition of Chinese forces under the nominal leadership of Kuomintang Generalissimo Chiang Kai-shek. U.S. support of Chiang in this struggle had been one of the major causes of the Japanese-American conflict that had culminated in Pearl Harbor, and Americans tended to view him as a loyal, valiant, and democratic ally in the struggle against the Axis. Although the Europe-first strategy after Pearl Harbor precluded any immediate large-scale activity in aid of Chiang, Washington did promise increased Lend-Lease supplies. It also sent Lieutenant General Joseph W. Stilwell, one of Marshall's most valued subordinates, to head the U.S. military mission in China and serve as Chiang's chief of staff. His primary function would be to provide supplies, training, and leadership to Chiang's forces and to mesh the Chinese war effort into the total Allied effort.

As Stilwell discovered, the reality of the China theater was quite removed from the American image. While officially the president of the

Chinese Republic and an ally of the United States, Chiang was in reality an authoritarian warlord who exercised limited control from his temporary capital of Chungking and who had no intention of allowing Stilwell to control and use his forces against Japan. Before the outbreak of full-scale hostilities with Japan, he had been engaged in a campaign to unify China by force and obliterate his Communist rivals under the leadership of Mao Tse-tung. The Japanese invasion forced a suspension of that effort and the creation of a united front with Mao, but Chiang viewed this as limited and temporary. After Pearl Harbor he expected the United States to take primary responsibility for defeating the Japanese while he built up his forces with Lend-Lease aid so that they could destroy Mao after Japan had been defeated.

Americans remained unaware of these facts. Ever since the enunciation of the Open Door Notes in 1899–1900, if not earlier, they had tended to view China as a special ward to be protected against the rapacious Europeans and guided toward American-style democracy. With his nationalist orientation, his conversion to Christianity, and his beautiful, American-educated wife, Chiang seemed to many Americans the Chinese George Washington who would help to fulfill this vision. Henry Luce's publishing empire strongly reinforced this image, naming the generalissimo and Madame Chiang its Man and Wife of the Year in early 1938. U.S. government propaganda after Pearl Harbor also built up Chiang as a means of mobilizing public opinion and because Roosevelt wished to make China a great power after the war.[3]

Marshall was aware that the China command would be extremely difficult and had chosen Stilwell because of his unique qualifications for this assignment. He had served in China on three separate occasions as language instructor (1920–23), battalion commander (1926–29), and military attaché (1935–39) and was probably more knowledgeable about the country than any other high-ranking American officer. He was also an outstanding general and fighter. Marshall was familiar with these strengths, having served with Stilwell in China during the 1920s, where they had become friends, and having then made him a valued instructor at Fort Benning. After Pearl Harbor he appeared to be the best officer to serve as head of the U.S. military mission and Chiang's chief of staff. Stimson at first favored Lieutenant General Hugh Drum, who had been Marshall's primary competitor for the chief of staff position in 1939, but when Drum once again revealed his ego and arrogance by treating this difficult assignment as beneath him, the secretary agreed to give it to Stilwell.[4]

In retrospect the assignment was more than difficult; it was impossible. Chiang's Kuomintang government was both unable and unwilling to play the role Washington had assigned it in the war, and Washington was unwilling to play the role Chiang wished to assign it in his separate wars against the Japanese and the Communists. The United States wanted to equip and train Chinese units to fight the Japanese army; Chiang demanded that the United States send troops and planes for this purpose while supplying the army he was saving for later use against Mao. From the American point of view, Stilwell concluded in mid-1942, Chiang's government was "playing the USA for a sucker" by "looking for an Allied victory without making any further effort on its part to secure it" while expecting "to have piled up at the end of the war a supply of munitions that will allow it to perpetuate itself indefinitely."[5]

Angry and disgusted by these realities, Stilwell quickly developed contempt for the corrupt and incompetent Kuomintang and for Chiang personally. The former he labeled "a gang of fascists" similar to the Germans save for their inefficiency, and he nicknamed Chiang "Peanut" in the privacy of his diary. His feelings were far from well hidden, and they outraged the Chinese leader. So did his efforts to contact and work with the Communist forces in Yenan against the Japanese, and the blunt, undiplomatic style that had earned him the nickname "Vinegar Joe."[6]

Stilwell's difficulties were compounded by complex command relationships and related personality conflicts. As head of the U.S. military mission to China, he controlled Lend-Lease supplies, but as chief of staff to Chiang, he was subordinate to a government leader who wanted to control those supplies himself. He was also subordinate to the Joint Chiefs and Roosevelt as head of the U.S. China-Burma-India (CBI) theater, while as commander of Chinese forces in Burma, he was responsible to Chiang and to the British command in India. In 1943 he was also appointed deputy to the newly created Southeast Asia Command (SEAC) under British Admiral Lord Louis Mountbatten. "The only one, it seems, that the general was not responsible to," a wartime reporter quipped, "was God." With good reason CBI became known in some circles as "Confused Beyond Imagination."[7]

To make matters worse, "Vinegar Joe" disliked the British as much as he did Chiang, calling them by such epithets as "monocled ass," "pisspot," and "pig-fucker."[8] There was also conflict with some of his American colleagues, most notably Major General Claire L. Chennault. A retired air corps pilot who had served before 1941 as adviser to Chiang's air force and supervisor for a group of U.S. volunteer fighter pilots known as the Flying Tigers, Chennault was a fervent believer in air power. Recalled to active duty and promoted in 1942, he challenged Stilwell's emphasis on building up Chinese ground forces and pressed instead for the creation of a large strategic air force and air bases in China from which to bomb the Japanese.

Stilwell disagreed and pointed out that the enemy would overrun the air bases unless a strong Chinese army was available to defend them, but Chiang strongly supported Chennault's plan since it would not involve use of the army he was saving for his postwar battles. Chennault was further aided in this dispute by the fact that he possessed an independent Lend-lease supply line and an assistant, Joseph Alsop, who was a relative of the Roosevelts and consistently undercut Stilwell. With good reason an early scholar of U.S. policy in this area during the war titled his study the "China Tangle."[9]

As a result of all these factors, as well as his own continued belief in air power as a cheap way out of complex politico-military problems, Roosevelt backed Chennault and seriously considered recalling Stilwell. Marshall warned his subordinate to be more diplomatic but strongly supported him against his detractors and was able to save him on two separate occasions. He and his JCS colleagues also pressed for greater emphasis on the China theater and a Burma campaign at the expense of the Mediterranean. This position outraged the British, who thought much less of Chinese abilities and importance than did the Americans, and it led to some of the most explosive CCS sessions of the entire war. Stilwell confided in his diary that one such session at the November 1943 Cairo Conference almost ended in a brawl when "Brooke got nasty and King got good and sore. King almost climbed over the table at Brooke. God, he was mad. I wish he had socked him."[10]

In 1944 the disaster Stilwell had predicted took place as the Japanese launched a successful offensive that quickly overran half of the principal Chinese air bases and threatened to knock China out of the war completely. Simultaneously Chiang threatened to withdraw his forces from Burma, thereby endangering the future of that campaign. Fully backing his subordinate and friend, Marshall pressed upon Roosevelt the seriousness of the situation and obtained presidential approval of a blunt telegram warning Chiang that either he now place Stilwell in complete charge of Chinese forces or face a total cut-off of American supplies. Stilwell personally delivered the telegram to Chiang and gleefully recorded that "the harpoon hit the little bugger right in the solar plexus and went right through him."[11]

The victory was short-lived. After procrastinating, Chiang made clear to Roosevelt his belief that Stilwell was the real problem and, supported by special presidential envoy Patrick J. Hurley, stated he no longer had any faith in the American commander. Rather than follow through on his earlier threat, Roosevelt now ordered Marshall to recall Stilwell and replace him with a more diplomatic officer. Marshall protested but was forced to agree. Major General Albert C. Wedemeyer, formerly one of Marshall's chief strategic planners and currently Mountbatten's deputy chief of staff, took over and quickly established better relations with Chiang.[12]

The combination of Chinese military failure and the Stilwell fiasco convinced Marshall and his JCS colleagues that China could not be relied upon as a major force in the war against Japan. This played a major role in their decision to invade Luzon instead of Formosa and to push northward against Iwo Jima and Okinawa in order to obtain alternative bases and jumping-off points for the bombing and invasion of the Japanese home islands. To tie down the large Japanese Army in China, they began to look more and more to the Soviet Union. This in turn played a major role in Roosevelt's decision at Yalta to agree to territorial concessions at China's as well as Japan's expense in return for a Soviet promise to enter the war against Japan within three months of Germany's surrender. The U.S. effort to use China as a major force in the war had ended in total failure.

China was not the only issue to defy easy solution. Soviet-American relations by mid-1945 had deteriorated sharply, threatening American plans for the war against Japan and the postwar world. And in the Pacific the Japanese continued to fight tenaciously despite their hopeless position and inflicted high casualties on the Americans.

By April 1945, Churchill and Roosevelt were complaining to Stalin about violations of the Yalta accords in regard to Poland while the Soviet leader was accusing the West of duplicitously negotiating a separate peace under the guise of surrender negotiations in northern Italy. The Yalta spirit of cooperation was collapsing almost as rapidly as the German armies in the west, and many of Roosevelt's advisers began to call for a much tougher policy toward the Soviets. Stalin, they claimed, respected only force, and with the end of the war his need for American aid would give the United States an effective position for some tough bargaining.

Roosevelt died in the midst of this reassessment, and it is impossible to know what he would have done had he lived. His successor, however, clearly believed that a change in policy with some very blunt talk was in order. On 23 April, less than two weeks after taking office, President Truman called his top military and political advisers together to tell them that the "one-way street" of Soviet-American relations could not and would not continue. In regard to the specific issue of disagreements regarding the drafting of a U.N. charter in San Francisco, he intended to go ahead with American plans "and if the Russians did not wish to join us they could go to hell." Later that day he lectured visiting Soviet Foreign Minister Molotov on fulfilling the Yalta accords regarding free elections in Poland and warned him that future friendship could not be on the basis of a one-way street. "I have never been talked to like that in my life," Molotov replied. "Carry out your agreements," Truman retorted, "and you won't get talked to like that."[13]

Many of Marshall's advisers had been calling for such a change in policy for months. "I have sat at innumerable Russian banquets and become gradually nauseated by Russian food, vodka, and protestations of friendship," Major General John R. Deane of the U.S. military mission in Moscow had written in December 1944. "It is amazing how these toasts go down past the tongues in the cheeks," to be followed by additional Soviet demands and American acquiescence. Future collaboration, Deane insisted, would be worthless unless based on "mutual respect and made to work both ways."[14]

Marshall had agreed with Deane "in toto" and forwarded the letter to Stimson, who in turn sent it to Roosevelt. A few months later the army chief drafted the president's blunt rejoinder to Stalin over the surrender negotiations in northern Italy. Both Marshall and Stimson had qualms about the new president's assertiveness on 23 April, however. Stimson warned that the United States "might be heading into very dangerous water," and Marshall noted the serious military consequences of any break with Stalin at this time. Whereas the military situation in Europe was "secure," the Far East remained more dubious. Here the army chief hoped not merely for Soviet participation, which he knew would eventually come because it was in Moscow's interests to enter the war, but for such participation "at a time when it would be useful to us." The Russians, he warned, "had it within their power to delay their entry into the Far Eastern war until we had done all the dirty work."[15]

Marshall was deeply troubled by this possibility because of what had been taking place in the Pacific. Japan's fleet, air forces, and merchant marine had been virtually destroyed, long-range American bombing attacks were reducing Japanese cities to rubble, and Tokyo's military position was clearly hopeless. Nevertheless, the Japanese continued to put up savage resistance, using kamikazes and other suicidal tactics that prolonged the battles and increased American casualties enormously. The February 1945 invasion of the island of Iwo Jima resulted in a four-month battle and 26,000 American casualties. Of the more than 20,000 Japanese defending the island, only 218 were taken prisoner. The invasion of Okinawa on 1 April was even worse. Before the battle ended in June, U.S. forces would suffer 75,000 casualties. Seventy-four hundred Japanese surrendered, but 110,000 were killed.

Although naval and air force leaders believed that bombardment and blockade of Japan might force a surrender, Iwo Jima and Okinawa convinced Marshall and his advisers that an invasion of the home islands would be both necessary and costly. Early Soviet entry could take some of the pressure off his forces, but such entry was not likely if the United States pressed for a diplomatic showdown over Poland. Moreover, with major forces scheduled to be transferred to the Pacific as soon as Germany surrendered, the U.S. bargaining position on European issues would not be very strong.

Nor would that bargaining position get any better in the foreseeable future, for as the JCS and their planners clearly realized, the United States was not the only nation to emerge from World War II with vastly increased power. Equally noteworthy was the "phenomenal development" of Soviet military and economic strength, a development they had in 1944 labeled "epochal in its bearing on future politico-military international relationships." When combined with total Axis defeat and postwar British exhaustion and weakness, the result would be an inevitable extension of Soviet influence and power that not even the strength of the United States could hope to overcome. To the contrary, the Joint Chiefs warned, Axis defeat would leave the Soviet Union "in a position of assured military dominance" in Eastern Europe, the Middle East, and Northeast Asia even if it did not enter the war against Japan, while Soviet and U.S. strengths and geographic positions were such "as to preclude the military defeat of one of these powers by the other" in the postwar world.[16]

As chairman of an important Senate committee investigating the national defense program during World War II, Truman had developed an enormous respect for Marshall and stood in virtual awe of him. The army chief's 1945 reservations and warnings therefore carried enormous weight with the new president. Equally important, Truman's assertiveness in no way led the Soviets to be more conciliatory. In June the president therefore backed away from further confrontation. Instead he called a dying Harry Hopkins out of his sickbed to meet Stalin in Moscow, and the two soon succeeded in negotiating a compromise settlement on the Polish issue. Once again U.S. power had its limits.

Ironically, at the very moment the limits of U.S. diplomatic power were being illustrated, American scientific and military power were on the verge of achieving one of their greatest triumphs: the atomic bomb. For years Marshall and Stimson had poured funds into the top-secret Manhattan Project to develop a nuclear weapon before Germany did. First they had used general army allocations; then they had successfully pleaded with the congressional leadership for appropriations without explanation. Now their efforts were reaching fruition; the United States had clearly won its race with Germany, and at the end of 1944 Marshall was informed that a bomb would be ready for use by 1 August. Germany surrendered before that date arrived. Japan was another matter, however, and Stimson began to think about using this potentially devastating weapon against Tokyo in the hope that it might force a surrender and make invasion of the home islands unnecessary.

Earlier in the war, Stimson had successfully pleaded with then-Senator Truman not to investigate the top-secret project. "I can't tell you what it is," he had said to Truman at that time, "but it is the greatest project in the history of the world." After the cabinet meeting on the day of Roosevelt's death, Stimson privately informed the new president of the great secret he had previously refused to explain to him. A special high-level Interim Committee was quickly established to examine the question of using an atomic bomb against Japan.[17]

Throughout the war, the assumption among the few who knew about the Manhattan Project had been that any bomb successfully developed would be used against the enemy. Now doubts began to be raised, especially by some scientists involved in the project, who feared that such use would make postwar international control of nuclear energy impossible. To avoid such a situation, these individuals suggested informing the Soviet Union of the bomb's existence, explicitly warning Japan, and providing a public demonstration of the weapon on a deserted island. For the most part the Interim Committee rejected these suggestions as technically impossible and/or politically counterproductive, recommending instead that the bomb be dropped on Japan without warning as a way of shocking the Japanese into surrender. The committee did agree, however, that a nonspecific warning be issued to Tokyo and that the Soviets be informed of the new weapon.[18]

Because of the deterioration in Soviet-American relations, some administration officials began to see the bomb as an alternative to Soviet entry into the war and as a means of impressing the Russians with American power and making them more manageable on other issues. Some scholars have argued that this anti-Soviet motivation, not the belief that the bomb could save lives by forcing a Japanese surrender without invasion, was the primary factor in the decision to use the weapon.[19] Most recent studies disagree, pointing out that those policymakers who did possess anti-Soviet motivations for dropping the bomb saw this aspect of the decision as a diplomatic "bonus." Forcing a Japanese surrender short of invasion remained the key issue.[20]

Marshall clearly believed that from a military point of view, the bomb should be dropped on Japan, but he was by no means convinced that by itself it would force a Japanese surrender. Consequently he and his colleagues on the JCS continued to recommend bringing the Soviets into the war and preparing to invade the home islands as well as dropping the bomb. He was also well aware that use of the bomb was by no means solely a military issue. "Don't ask *me* to make the decision," he told Assistant Secretary of War McCloy. While he clearly favored use of the weapon on military grounds, he also realized that other, "primordial considerations" were involved. Manufacturing centers, he argued, should be targeted only after a "purely military" target had been hit and after the enemy had been warned to advise civilians to leave, for the United States "must offset by such warning methods the opprobrium which might follow from an ill-considered employment of such force."[21]

One month later, the related issues of the bomb, Japanese surrender, and Soviet-American relations were joined at the Big Three summit conference in the Berlin suburb of Potsdam. The contrasts between this meeting and its predecessor at Yalta only five months earlier were striking. Truman had replaced Roosevelt, and midway through the conference the British electorate, looking to the postwar world, replaced Churchill with Clement Attlee of the Labour party. Of the original Big Three, only Stalin remained by the end of the conference. The tone and topics of the sessions were as different as the participants. Postwar issues now dominated. So did harsh disagreement rather than cooperation and compromise, with most difficult issues left for the foreign ministers to resolve later.

In the middle of the conference, Truman received detailed information regarding the successful test of the atomic bomb at Alamogordo, New Mexico. His assertiveness at the ensuing plenary session showed the change this weapon made in his attitude. Soon after he told Stimson he was "very anxious to know whether Marshall still felt that we needed the Russians in the war or whether we could get along without them." Marshall did not answer directly. He noted that the Soviets were already pinning down Japanese forces in Manchuria by amassing troops along the border and that the atomic bomb had decreased the value of their assistance, but he warned Stimson that even if Japan did surrender without their participation, the Soviets would be able to march into Manchuria anyway and "get virtually what they wanted in the surrender terms." Stimson inferred from this comment and others that "Marshall felt as I felt sure he would that now with our new weapon we would not need the assistance of the Russians to conquer Japan" and so informed the president.[22]

Simultaneously Truman approved the Potsdam Declaration, which did not mention the bomb but warned Japan to surrender or face "utter and complete destruction." He also fulfilled the letter if not the spirit of the Interim Committee's advice regarding informing the Soviets by "casually" telling Stalin at the end of the 24 July plenary session that "we had a new weapon of unusual destructive force." The Soviet leader knew exactly what Truman was talking about as a result of his own atomic research and the work of spies, but he feigned ignorance as well as lack of interest. Stating that he was pleased, he simply expressed the hope that Truman would make "good use of it against the Japanese." That evening, however, he told his advisers that the Soviet atomic bomb project would have to be accelerated. The World War II alliance was fast dissolving into mutual suspicion and deception.[23]

On 6 August 1945 a single atomic bomb obliterated more than 80 percent of the city of Hiroshima and killed approximately 130,000 people. Two days later, which also happened to be the exact date on which they had promised to do so, the Soviets declared war on Japan. These events precipitated a major debate within the Japanese cabinet, where moderates had been attempting to begin negotiations for a compromise peace with the Americans through Soviet mediation. Extremists were opposed. So was a United States intent on unconditional surrender. Now facing apparent annihilation and diplomatically isolated by the Soviet declaration of war, the moderates, with the emperor's support, took control and offered to surrender on 10 August with the sole proviso that he be retained. That was too late to prevent a second atomic bomb from destroying Nagasaki on 9 August, but it did lead to peace soon after. The United States agreed to the Japanese offer so long as the emperor remained subject to the authority of the Supreme Commander of Allied

Forces in the Pacific, a position Marshall obtained for MacArthur. On 14 August Japan accepted these terms, and on 2 September the official instrument of surrender was signed aboard the U.S. battleship *Missouri* in Tokyo Bay.[24]

The greatest war in history was officially over, apparently as a result of an extraordinary display of American scientific and military power. Unfortunately the cold war between the United States and the Soviet Union had simultaneously begun, and in that conflict the bomb would frighten the Soviets not into accommodation or surrender but into greater insistence on security through control of Eastern Europe and greater diplomatic rigidity. At their first meeting in London during September, the Allied foreign ministers proved unable to agree on anything, not even a public communiqué announcing their disagreements. Six months later, Churchill was warning that an "iron curtain" now divided Europe. Once again Americans were facing limits to what had appeared to be their unlimited power.

Marshall did not overly concern himself with such issues during the fall of 1945. His primary task had been successfully completed with the Japanese surrender, and he now looked forward to his retirement with Katherine in both Leesburg and Pinehurst, North Carolina, where they had recently bought a winter home. Congratulations and tributes poured in from all directions. The most notable once again came from Secretary Stimson, who devoted more than half of his final press conference on 19 September to praise of the army chief's character as well as his accomplishments. "I have had considerable experience with men in Government," he reminded the reporters. "General Marshall has given me a new gauge of what such service should be." President Truman concurred, labeling him "the greatest military man this country has ever produced." A few months later the president reluctantly accepted Marshall's resignation and on 26 November personally awarded the army chief his only wartime decoration, a second Oak Leaf Cluster to his World War I Distinguished Service Medal. "In a war unparalleled in magnitude and horror," Truman read from the official citation, "millions of Americans gave their country outstanding service. General of the Army George C. Marshall gave it victory."[25]

The major discordant note during the interim between Japanese surrender and Marshall's retirement consisted of congressional and public demands for immediate demobilization. The army chief had long been aware that he would face such demands, for he had experienced them at the end of World War I and knew from his study of history that they had followed the completion of all previous U.S. wars. Hoping to break this pattern, he had attempted during the war to plan for a gradual and partial demobilization that would leave the United States with a postwar military establishment sufficient to enforce its political objectives in the world and had asked his old friend John McAuley Palmer to help with this task, as well as long-term postwar military planning.

Palmer and his associates had once again recommended universal military training as the best way to meet the country's military needs, and as early as 1943 a bill to establish UMT in the postwar era had been introduced in Congress.[26] Marshall strongly endorsed this proposal in a series of public statements, most importantly his published and highly acclaimed Biennial Report to the Secretary of War on 1 September 1945. In the process, he boldly illustrated the revolution World War II had wrought in U.S. security conceptions.

As had been true after World War I, the arguments for UMT once again focused on the belief that military preparedness would avoid rather than cause war by deterring would-be aggressors. This time, however, Marshall and his colleagues also argued that technological and geopolitical changes necessitated a much larger perspective on deterrence than Americans had previously considered. Dismissing hemispheric security as insufficient in the modern world, the army chief bluntly stated that the United States "must be prepared to defend its interest against any nation or combination of nations" willing to use force. "We are now concerned with the peace of the entire world," he insisted, and "the peace can only be maintained by the strong."[27]

In the form of a large standing army, Marshall readily admitted, such strength could be "subject to the behest of a group of schemers" and thereby constitute a menace to American liberties. The citizen-soldier concept embodied in UMT, however, was "the guarantee against such an abuse of power." It would establish not a large, expensive, and dangerous standing army, but rather an enormous pool of trained men who would only be called up when needed. It was thus "the only sensible, business-like, democratic, and financially possible way" for the United States to prevent war and maintain its global interests while preserving its domestic system.[28]

Throughout 1945 Marshall consistently emphasized these themes in pressing for UMT and opposing demands for the immediate return and demobilization of all troops. He was largely unsuccessful. Although Truman formally called for and Congress paid lip service to UMT, support for the measure remained "soft" and it never passed.

Part of the problem was the traditional American refusal at the end of a war to plan for the future. In 1945 this refusal was reinforced by a general belief that atomic weapons made large armies superfluous. Equally important, growing intra- and interservice conflicts over appropriate postwar coordination and force levels weakened support and arguments for UMT. Marshall found that even his army staff did not share his strong belief in the citizen-soldier concept and that it favored a postwar force larger than he thought necessary or politically obtainable. Meanwhile, public demands for immediate demobilization proved too powerful to be overcome. By the end of November, four million men had already been demobilized. Marshall warned on 29 October that such rapidity without the adoption of a permanent peacetime military program translated into "disintegration, not only of the armed forces but apparently of all conception of world responsibility and what it demands of us," but his pleas were ignored. Despite his enormous prestige, the chief of staff had to face some personal limits of power in late 1945.[29]

Marshall was not solely concerned with the military aspects of America's new role in international relations. The "world of suffering people," he stated in his farewell speech on 26 November, now looked to the United States to avoid another global catastrophe, but their thoughts

> are not concentrated alone on this problem. They have more immediate and terribly pressing concerns—where the mouthful of food will come from, where they will find shelter tonight and where they will find warmth from the cold of winter. Along with the great problem of maintaining the peace we must solve the problem of the pittance of food, of clothing and coal and homes. Neither of these problems can be solved alone. They are directly related, one to the other.[30]

In this statement Marshall neatly summarized what one historian has aptly labeled the "peace and prosperity" theme that would dominate postwar American thinking.[31] As enunciated at the time and later by numerous policymakers, that theme consisted of the belief that the rise of Hitler and other totalitarian leaders had been the result not merely of European appeasement and American isolationism, but more basically of the Great Depression. Desperate economic conditions, proponents of this theory maintained, led people to an equally desperate support of dictators who promised relief in return for power. Because such dictators were in American eyes the primary causes of war, ensuring American and worldwide prosperity would ensure world peace as well as democracy.

This was to be one of the primary goals of postwar American foreign policy, a policy Marshall probably thought he would view only from afar while in retirement. Little could he have realized that he would make his words a reality less than two years later with the economic recovery program that bore his name.

The awareness that he would play some role in the postwar world actually came to Marshall much more quickly than this. On 27 November, the day after his farewell speech, he and Katherine arrived at Leesburg. Immediately the telephone rang. It was President Truman asking him to undertake a special postwar mission to China. Not one to refuse a request from his commander-in-chief, Marshall curtly accepted but said nothing to Katherine, who had gone upstairs for a nap. She woke up to hear the news of the mission being announced on the radio. "I could not bear to tell you until you had had your rest," he said to his bitterly disappointed wife. "My retirement," he informed General MacArthur in an interesting piece of understatement, "was of rather short duration."[32] It had lasted one day.

The decision to send Marshall to China in late 1945 was the result of continued long-term problems in that country, as well as an immediate crisis caused by the sudden resignation of the U.S. ambassador. No one had truly expected Stilwell's recall in late 1944 to "solve" China's problems, and it had not done so. His successor, General Wedemeyer, had been much friendlier and more diplomatic with Chiang. So had the new ambassador, former Major General, Secretary of War, and special presidential envoy Patrick J. Hurley. Sino-American relations clearly improved during 1945 as a result of these personnel changes and as a result of the highly limited expectations the JCS now held regarding the Chinese war effort. But the economic and political situation within China did not improve. To the contrary, Kuomintang corruption, economic chaos, and conflict with the Communists continued unabated. By the time Japan surrendered, China appeared to be on the verge of civil war and anarchy.

American policymakers were troubled by this situation for numerous reasons. Their longstanding special interest in China and wish to transform it into a Western-style democracy and great power sprang from more than simple altruism. With Japan totally defeated, a massive power vacuum existed in the Far East. If China did not fill it, an increasingly hostile Soviet Union would. Soviet forces had already occupied Manchuria and were in the process of stripping away the area's wealth.

The Soviet Union was also aiding Mao's Communist forces, which had grown tremendously in size, influence, combat effectiveness, and political appeal as a result of their guerrilla war against the Japanese and Kuomintang ineffectiveness and corruption. If civil war broke out, American observers warned, Chiang would be incapable of winning unless the United States intervened massively on his side. Such intervention would lead to increased Soviet intervention on the Communist side, however. It also ran counter to U.S. foreign and military policy regarding the Far East and was impossible in the light of the demobilization then taking place. Without massive American intervention, the result of civil war would be a stalemate that would leave China divided and weak or a Communist victory. The Soviets would extend their influence and power in either event.

Some foreign service officers in China concluded that the future lay with Mao rather than Chiang and that his communism was by no means an insuperable barrier to a cooperative relationship with the United States. For both nationalistic and ideological reasons, there was little understanding or love between the Marxist-Leninist Soviets and the peasant-oriented Chinese Communists, and in 1944–45 Mao was anxious to befriend the United States. But because of the growing conflict with the Soviet Union, the general belief in the United States that all Communists were subordinate to Moscow, and the wartime buildup of Chiang Kai-shek, Washington never seriously considered a pro-Mao policy.[33]

Given this fact, as well as Chiang's weakness and the inability and unwillingness of the United States to intervene militarily, Washington formulated a two-pronged policy in 1945. It would continue to provide Chiang with limited assistance in return for reform measures that, it was hoped, would improve the economic and political situation and thereby blunt the Communists' appeal. Simultaneously the United States would try to mediate a Kuomintang-Communist settlement that could avoid civil war and create a new coalition government under Chiang's leadership. If successful, this policy would result in a strong, peaceful, and democratic China. As one scholar has recently noted, it would also neutralize and transform the Communists, minimize Soviet influence in China, and remove that country as an area of Soviet-American conflict.[34]

Ambassador Hurley had been pursuing such a policy when on 27 November he suddenly announced his resignation and attacked both the State Department and the administration for foiling his efforts. To head off domestic criticism, as well as add to the chances of success by supplying a highly prestigious and able negotiator, Truman decided to replace Hurley with a special mission headed by Marshall, who was designated the president's special representative with the personal rank of ambassador and given the power virtually to write his own instructions. Although this would be the general's first full-fledged diplomatic assignment, he had actually been negotiating with heads of state as well as officers for the last six years and had clearly illustrated his abilities in this field. As General Walter Bedell-Smith later stated, "his whole service had been a preparatory course for high-level negotiations."[35]

Looking forward to retirement and private time with her husband after the hectic pace of the last six years, Mrs. Marshall was extremely upset over what she labeled this "bitter blow." President Truman, she angrily wrote to one of Marshall's wartime aides, "should never have asked this of him and in such a way that he could not refuse."[36] Many of the general's subordinates and friends agreed, though primarily on the grounds that no matter how gifted and prestigious a negotiator Marshall might be, his mission was doomed to failure. Stilwell had already tried to trade U.S. aid for reform of the Kuomintang and failed, and the ideological differences, past history, and depth of animosity between the Kuomintang and the Communists made coalition government impossible.

To make matters worse, Marshall would be wearing two contradictory hats in China. On the one hand he was supposed to be the impartial mediator. On the other he was supposed to support and build up Chiang Kai-shek while minimizing Soviet and Chinese Communist influence. The second mission made his impartiality suspect for successful completion of the first, while American unwillingness and inability to intervene militarily meant he did not possess the power to fulfill the second if the first failed.

Marshall was not totally powerless, however. In addition to his negotiating skills and enormous prestige, he could threaten to provide or withhold U.S. aid in moving Kuomintang forces into Manchuria and supporting them while evacuating the Japanese. Possession and use of this power, he and administration officials believed, would give him leverage to force both sides into important concessions; the threat to move Kuomintang troops would pressure the Communists, while the threat not to would pressure Chiang. As his biographer has noted, Marshall was going to China "not merely as an honest broker but as a tough persuader who could promise the carrot or the stick to the negotiating parties."[37]

Whether this carrot and stick were substantial enough to force major concessions, and whether they were believable, remained open questions. Would the United States refuse to aid Chiang, for example, if he rejected concessions? The secret answer was no; if negotiations broke down, Marshall was informed by Truman, Secretary of State James Byrnes, and Under Secretary Dean Acheson in response to his specific queries, he was to aid Chiang even though the United States would, in his words, "have to swallow its pride and much of its policy in doing so."[38] If Chiang suspected this, as he did, there was no reason for him to negotiate in good faith. If the Communists suspected it, as they did, there was no reason to trust Marshall's mediation.

Despite these overwhelming problems, Marshall's prestige, diplomatic abilities, and efforts at evenhandedness were so great that his first few months in China were successful. By late February his mediation had resulted in a cease-fire and the cessation of troop movements, to be overseen by a special executive headquarters made up of Kuomintang, Communist, and U.S. representatives; a series of resolutions that provided a blueprint for a new coalition government leading to a constitutional democracy; and agreement in principle to integrate the armed forces of the two sides. Most of these successes came as a result of efforts in the so-called Committee of Three, a negotiating body in which Marshall, Communist leader Chou En-lai, and Kuomintang leader Chang Chih-chung were able to work together. Nicknamed the "professor" by his two colleagues, Marshall proved to be a highly effective negotiator and mediator. "I doubt seriously whether any other person in the world could have done as much in so short a time," General Wedemeyer reported. The agreements constituted a "stupendous accomplishment."[39]

When Marshall temporarily returned to the United States in March to obtain additional financial aid for China, however, the agreements quickly collapsed. The cease-fire had never been fully extended to Manchuria, and extremists on both sides who had always opposed negotiations now took advantage of this fact, Marshall's absence, and the simultaneous withdrawal of Soviet occupation forces to violate the accords in an effort to gain control of the province. These violations had an enormous impact because of the continued lack of any real trust between the two parties. So great was this lack of trust that Chou and

Chang had found it "safer" to use and retranslate into Chinese Marshall's English translation of their sessions than to rely on either one's record of what had been said. Such intense suspicion meant that the long-term success of the accords depended almost totally on Marshall's personal guarantee, and when he left, so did that guarantee. Although Marshall's "international prestige and the very stature of the man have dominated the field and brought about conciliatory action," Wedemeyer noted and warned in this regard, the "permanence of his accomplishments" was clearly "contingent upon his physical presence."[40]

Even if Marshall had remained, it is highly questionable whether the accords could have worked. Each side essentially viewed the other as a mortal enemy and coalition as a threat rather than an opportunity. Both had agreed to negotiations primarily for tactical reasons, and their leaders were increasingly attracted to advisers who believed all pretense to compromise could be abandoned because total military victory was obtainable.

Marshall's efforts were further undermined by the fact that the contradictory nature of his assignment regarding impartial mediation combined with support of Chiang was becoming apparent to both sides. This clearly lessened his effectiveness when he returned to China with Mrs. Marshall in April. Chiang correctly suspected that U.S. policy would be to help him even if he refused to make concessions and therefore treated Marshall's veiled threats of nonsupport as bluff. Indeed he totally ignored the American's military as well as political advice by launching a major military campaign in Manchuria against the Communists who had recently taken over key areas from the withdrawing Soviets. The Communists in turn began to believe that the United States was following, in Chou's words, a hypocritical "double policy" in China. A short-term truce was arranged on 6 June, but it quickly collapsed, and by 17 June a gloomy, overworked, and increasingly short-tempered Marshall was warning Truman that negotiations had "reached an impasse." Kuomintang officials, he noted, incorrectly believed that they could quickly defeat the Communists in battle and that the United States would support them militarily.[41]

By summer the extremists were clearly in charge of both camps. In Nanking two prominent Chinese liberals were assassinated. Soon after Communist guerrillas in the Anping incident ambushed a U.S. marine convoy in North China, killing three Americans and wounding twelve. By August the Communists were publicly attacking Marshall, and

Chiang, ignoring his warnings, was preparing a major offensive against them. "My battle out here is never ending," he wrote Eisenhower a few months later, "with both ends playing against the middle—which is me." A cutoff of U.S. ammunition forced the generalissimo to take Marshall's "stick" seriously and temporarily back down, but by the fall his forces were on the move once again in northern China and Manchuria. Marshall's warning that "the Communists have lost cities and towns but they have not lost their armies" fell on deaf ears. In November a new National Assembly met without any Communist representation, Chou returned to Yenan, and Chiang proceeded in his efforts to obtain a military solution. After more than 300 meetings and a year of work, the Marshall mission had clearly failed.[42]

President Truman had offered to issue a recall order whenever Marshall requested it, and the general now did so. On 7 January it was officially announced. In a public statement on that date, Marshall labeled "the complete, almost overwhelming" mutual suspicion between the two parties as "the greatest obstacle to peace." He also blamed the actions of militarists and extremists on both sides for the failure of mediation and looked to moderates, specifically "liberals in the Government and in the minority parties" who would act under Chiang's leadership, as China's only possible salvation.[43]

The problem lay not with Marshall but with the contradictory nature of his assignment. In a broader context, the real problems were the virtual impossibility of obtaining a peaceful settlement in China and the limits on U.S. power in the area. Americans had a difficult time believing this, for they had grown accustomed to viewing China through an American prism and tended to see their own power to transform that society as limitless. Nationalists and Communists, they argued, should be able to compromise as easily as Democrats and Republicans at home and to unify around Chiang as their George Washington. In the aftermath of total victory over the Axis, they saw their power and prestige as more than sufficient to obtain and enforce such an agreement and, in time, to turn China into a thriving Western-style democracy. As one American senator allegedly stated, "With God's help we will lift Shanghai up and up, ever up, until it is just like Kansas City."[44]

Marshall was much more of a realist. His entire career had been an education in the uses, misuses, and limits of power, and the Stilwell fiasco had clearly illustrated those limits in this situation before he even departed for China. Nevertheless, he shared with most other Americans a belief in the universality and exportability of certain American concepts. Particularly noteworthy in this regard were his professorial lectures on creating an American-style, nonpolitical army subject to civil control and the need to appoint "umpires" between the two armies analogous to those used in baseball games. Equally noteworthy were the American beliefs he projected onto the Chinese: that the key issue was misplaced as opposed to well-founded mistrust; that the Communists could be co-opted by minority representation in the government; and that Kuomin-tang reform was both possible and the only way to blunt their appeal.

Like Stilwell and many other Americans, Marshall had thought China could be remade in the American image. And like Stilwell, he had discovered that it could not and would not be and that American power in the area had severe limits. "I know Marshall now believes he made a mistake in ever thinking coalition was desirable or useful or pos-sible," a member of the U.S. embassy staff noted in late November. As Stilwell's biographer has concluded, "China was a problem for which there was no American solution."[45]

Marshall's education regarding the limits and aspects of power did not end with the failure of his mission. On the contrary, China was simply the beginning of a virtually new career for him with power, albeit one that would be diplomatic rather than military in nature. As the of-ficial announcement of his recall made clear to a surprised world, Mar-shall was being brought back to Washington to become secretary of state.

9

CREATING A NEW
FOREIGN POLICY,
1947–49

Although Marshall was secretary of state for only two years, from January 1947 to January 1949, his tenure witnessed some of the most important and revolutionary developments in the history of U.S. foreign relations. Under the impact of its growing conflict with the Soviet Union, the United States during these years articulated an activist, global foreign policy highlighted by the Truman Doctrine, the Marshall Plan, the containment policy, and moves that would culminate in the creation of West Germany and the North Atlantic Treaty Organization (NATO).

While by no means primarily responsible for all of these initiatives, Marshall played an important role in the formulation of many of them. Of at least equal importance was his pivotal role in winning bipartisan congressional and public support for them during a time of intense domestic partisanship and in reasserting State Department control over the foreign policymaking process. It is far from accidental in this regard that Marshall's tenure as secretary of state coincided with the reemergence of the State Department as the key formulator and conductor of U.S. policy, as well as with the creation of this new global approach to foreign affairs.

The initiation and declaration of the cold war had actually preceded Marshall's appointment by at least a year. Emerging from World War II as the only remaining powers, separated by radically different ideologies and histories, and no longer bound together by fear of the common enemy, the United States and the Soviet Union had begun to eye each other warily even before the war officially ended. Once it did end, the suspicions and disagreements increased dramatically. Within a month of Japanese surrender, the first meeting of Allied foreign ministers in London had ended in complete deadlock. Some progress was made on peace treaties for Germany's satellites during the December meeting in Moscow, but soon a series of public statements announced that a major conflict was in progress.

The first three months of 1946 witnessed the dispute over withdrawal of Soviet troops from northern Iran, Stalin's speech resurrecting ideological conflict between capitalist and Communist worlds, and Winston Churchill's warning in Fulton, Missouri, that an "iron curtain" had descended across central Europe. By summer the foreign ministers meeting in Paris had deadlocked again over the future of Germany, the United States had halted reparations payments from its occupation zone, and Moscow had rejected both the American Baruch Plan for international control of atomic energy and the political strings regarding Eastern Europe that Washington was attaching to a Soviet postwar loan request. The Soviets also tightened their grip on Eastern Europe and resumed their demands on Turkey for a new treaty regarding control of the Dardanelles. The United States responded by sending a naval task force into the eastern Mediterranean and uniting the British and U.S. occupation zones in Germany.

A major Soviet-American confrontation was thus already taking place as 1947 began. The American people still lacked an overall explanation of the nature and extent of this confrontation, however, and policymakers similarly lacked a coherent analytical framework to interpret Soviet actions and a global policy to counter them. The State Department under Marshall's direction would soon provide all of these.

The decision to appoint Marshall stemmed from personal and policy conflicts between President Truman and Secretary of State Byrnes. Byrnes had tended to conduct foreign policy independently, as if he were the chief executive—or at least still Truman's senior in the Senate. The president found this increasingly intolerable, especially when Byrnes exhibited a willingness to compromise with the Soviets in Moscow during late 1945 that was out of step with the increasingly tough, anti-Soviet stance of the administration. "I'm tired of babying the Soviets," Truman told him in January. Byrnes quickly swung back to a hard line, but it was too late. Health problems compounded his difficulties while providing a convenient excuse for submission of his resignation in April 1946, to become effective once the satellite peace treaties had been negotiated and an appropriate successor found.[1]

Truman quickly decided that Marshall would be the best choice. He had venerated the general for many years and highly valued his political and diplomatic as well as his military abilities. Indeed it was Truman who had previously sent Marshall to China, and the eventual failure of that impossible mission in no way lessened his high opinion of the general. As a former senator, Truman also knew how effective Marshall could be with Congress and how capable he was of removing issues from the arena of partisan debates. These abilities had played a major role in the president's decision to send Marshall to China. They played an equally important role in the decision to appoint him secretary of state. "This gives me a wonderful ace in the hole," he replied when informed of Marshall's acceptance of his offer in the spring of 1946.[2]

Continuing Chinese negotiations precluded Marshall from taking over the State Department at that time, but by year's end the lack of success in those negotiations had led the general to request his own recall. Truman decided to combine that recall with the announcement of Marshall's new position, thereby submerging the failure of the mission under the euphoria of making one of the country's most respected individuals secretary of state. The tired Marshall agreed. "My answer is in the affirmative if that continues to be his desire," he wired from China. "My personal reaction is something else."[3]

Marshall's nonpartisan image was even more important to Truman in early 1947 than it had been a year before, for in the interim the Republicans had won control of Congress. Any foreign policy initiative by the administration would thus require bipartisan support, and Republican pleasure over the Marshall nomination clearly illustrated the general's ability to obtain that support. Chairman Arthur Vandenberg put the nomination through his Senate Foreign Relations Committee without hearing or opposition and obtained full Senate approval on the same day. Upon arrival in Washington on 21 January 1947, Marshall moved to reinforce his bipartisan and apolitical image, as well as squelch some recent rumors, by being "explicit and emphatic" in announcing to the assembled press that he was not a candidate for any political office and could under no circumstances be drafted to run. He then went to the White House for his swearing-in ceremony.[4]

Although Marshall was the first high-ranking soldier to serve as secretary of state, he had little problem adapting to his new civilian environment. "I found the problems from the viewpoint of geopolitical location and of pressure to be almost identical in many respects with those of the war years," he later commented. "There was the same problem between East and West; the same limitations as to our capability; the same pressures at home and abroad, in regard to various areas, and there was the same necessity for a very steady and determined stand in regard to these various problems."[5] There was also the same need for strong leadership and organizational reform. The State Department that Marshall inherited had for many years been plagued by serious problems in these areas, as well as by poor morale and lack of influence, and under President Roosevelt it had been relegated to a secondary role in the policymaking process. Marshall's appointment clearly gave the department some badly needed prestige, but the new secretary recognized that more than this was necessary. Still the great organizer, he began by reforming the department's chaotic administrative structure.

Marshall had been "horrified" to discover that each department subdivision tended to act on its own as "a separate industry" and report individually to the secretary. Equally appalling to his orderly administrative mind, no agency had specific responsibility for long-term planning.[6] The result was an almost total lack of coordination and vision, with the secretary assuming enormous burdens and buried in a mass of details. Using the army in general and the War Department reorganization of 1942 in particular as his models, Marshall the efficient manager created a Policy Planning Staff, a Central Secretariat, and a clear chain of command that ran up to the under secretary of state, who served as his chief of staff, and then directly to him.

Marshall did on occasion carry his penchant for administrative efficiency too far, particularly in his emphasis on reaching a single conclusion as quickly as possible and his consequent insistence that the under secretary present him with only one recommendation, to be approved or disapproved. "Gentleman," he once told a group of arguing section chiefs, "don't fight the problem, decide it." At least one of his subordinates worried that such an approach isolated him from the decision-making process and ignored the fact that diplomatic problems were often "not susceptible to an answer" but only to "an action which is less disagreeable than some other action and probably no action is altogether good." Overall, however, his reorganization was highly successful. According to a later self-study, it freed the department for an extraordinarily creative period and established in the Policy Planning Staff a badly needed "focus of creative thinking." As one official noted, "George Catlett Marshall brought order to the conduct of foreign relations. . . . The change was felt from top to bottom and called forth a great surge of ideas and constructive effort."[7]

At least as important as reorganizing the department was the need to obtain and retain the services of exceptional subordinates. Here Marshall was also very successful. Dean Acheson, Byrnes's under secretary, agreed to remain in office for a limited period of time and serve as Marshall's chief of staff. Former Assistant Secretary of War Robert Lovett would then replace him, and for now he was brought in as assistant to Under Secretary for Economic Affairs Will Clayton, who also remained in his post. Soviet specialist Charles Bohlen was retained first as Marshall's special assistant and then as the department's counselor, while the new secretary tapped another Soviet specialist, George F. Kennan, to head the Policy Planning Staff.

Seldom if ever had such an array of talent been assembled within the department and given such latitude. Acting in the same way George Washington had in selecting cabinet members, Marshall had recognized his own limitations in this new environment and surrounded himself with the best and brightest young men available, men who could initiate bold proposals, implement them in his name, and take over once he retired. Acheson and Lovett would be outstanding as Marshall's second in command, and each would eventually succeed him in a cabinet post, Acheson as secretary of state and Lovett as secretary of defense. Bohlen proved to be a highly effective adviser to Marshall in his negotiations with the Soviets and went on to complete an extremely distinguished diplomatic career. So did Kennan, who quickly became Marshall's key idea man. He played a pivotal role in the formulation of key U.S. cold war policies, most notably the Marshall Plan, authored the famous containment policy, and then achieved additional fame as an ambassador, adviser, and diplomatic historian. With good reason two journalists have dubbed these individuals four of the six "Wise Men" who virtually created postwar U.S. policy. With equally good reason Acheson entitled his memoirs of his years in the State Department *Present at the Creation*.[8]

Although Marshall may not have been the intellectual equal of these men, he was clearly their leader and one of the most respected and extraordinary individuals in each of their lives. Their memoirs and recollections, by no means notable for humility or compliments about others, are unanimous in their praise of him and their awed descriptions of his personality, abilities, and impact. "I have never gone in for hero worship," Bohlen stated, "but of all the men I have been associated with, including presidents, George Catlett Marshall is at the top of the list of those I admired. He had the ability to evoke the loyalty, respect, and affection of those who had the privilege of working with him. He was a man of absolute integrity. You felt the firmness, as if it were written in large letters all over him." Acheson agreed. "The moment General Marshall entered a room," he recounted, "everyone in it felt his presence. It was a striking and communicated force. His figure conveyed intensity, which his voice, low, staccato, and incisive, reinforced. It compelled respect. It spread a sense of authority and of calm."

This was not a matter of mere image. Acheson described in some detail Marshall's extraordinary decision-making process, particularly the ability of this lifelong soldier to focus on nonmilitary factors, think in nonmilitary terms, view all elements of a problem, and hold them "in solution in his mind until it was ready to precipitate a decision." Acheson labeled this ability "the essence and the method—or rather the art—of judgment in its highest form . . . which requires both mastery of precise information and apprehension of imponderables," and he considered it "an act of God" that this "Man for All Seasons" had become secretary of state at such a critical time in world history. "His personality infected the entire State Department," Bohlen wrote. "It gave it a sense of direction and purpose. . . . We realized we were working for a great man."[9]

The lifelong self-control and emotional distance remained. "I shall expect of you," he informed Acheson, "the most complete frankness, particularly about myself. I have no feelings except those I reserve for Mrs. Marshall." Yet these memoirs and recollections clearly illustrate that for all his austerity and aloofness, Marshall established personal relationships with each of these men that were almost familial in their closeness. Lovett remarked years later that he and Marshall "worked together almost as brothers." Acheson treasured memories of the general dining at his home on occasion and reminiscing at length about his past while Mrs. Marshall was hospitalized. One scholar has noted that Bohlen was "touched by the human side of the secretary" and that "the relationship between the two became so close that one colleague likened it to that of a father and son." Kennan, on the other hand, stated that "I was not close to him personally" and that "I puzzled him. He was not used to people like me." Yet he added that "like everyone else, I admired him, and in a sense loved him, for the qualities I saw in him."[10]

Some of those qualities were quite personal, touching, and humorous. "Kennan," he once said when that individual was pouring drinks, "they tell me you are a good head of a planning staff, and for all I know you are, but . . . who the hell ever taught you to put the ice in before the whiskey?" Upon arrival in Paris on one occasion, he presented Bohlen and his wife with a photograph he had just ordered taken in Washington of their two-year-old son. Kennan recalled one episode "that endeared him to me beyond all others" when a policy initiative backfired and led to severe press criticism, and he asked Marshall what he had done incorrectly. "The only trouble with you," the secretary replied, "is that you don't have the wisdom and perspicacity of a columnist. Now get out of here!"[11]

Marshall and his advisers were in fundamental accord regarding U.S. foreign policy. They agreed that political isolationism was a dated and discredited policy, that world peace, democracy, and economic prosperity were inseparable, and that the United States, in its own as well as humanitarian interests, should assume primary responsibility for all three. Marshall had previously asserted these themes in his 1945 biennial report and "farewell" address, and he reasserted them at Princeton University on 22 February during his first speech as secretary of state. "If the world is to get on its feet," he warned, "if the productive facilities of the world are to be restored, if democratic processes in many countries are to resume their functioning, a strong lead and definite assistance from the United States will be necessary." The new generation of Americans, Marshall maintained, needed to develop "a sense of responsibility for world order and security."[12]

By the time Marshall delivered that address, most of his subordinates and cabinet colleagues had also concluded that the Soviet Union was the major threat to world peace, democracy, and prosperity and that cooperation with Moscow was impossible. Kennan had explained why as early as February 1946 in his famous Long Telegram sent from the Moscow embassy. Like their Czarist predecessors, the Soviets were extremely insecure, believed the outside world was perpetually hostile, and saw expansion as their only viable defense against that hostility. No U.S. concessions could alter this distrust and expansion, and a permanent settlement with the Soviet Union was thus not possible. To the contrary, the Soviet definition of "security" equaled U.S. insecurity, for Moscow could not feel safe as long as any independent power center existed.[13]

In mid-1947, after Marshall had become secretary of state, Kennan amplified and publicized these ideas beyond the confines of the State

Department by publishing under an ill-concealed pseudonym an article entitled "The Sources of Soviet Conduct" in the journal *Foreign Affairs*. Here he placed greater emphasis on ideology and Stalin's dictatorship as determinants of Soviet behavior but reached the same basic conclusions: due to internal factors, the Soviets were hostile, expansionist, and threatening to U.S. security. No concessions or goodwill by the United States could change that hostility or stop that expansionism. Soviet policy simply "moves inexorably along the prescribed path, like a persistent toy automobile wound up and headed in a given direction, stopping only when it meets with some unanswerable force." The United States, Kennan argued, should provide that "unanswerable force" through adoption of a policy of "firm containment" that would "confront the Russians with unalterable counterforce at every point where they show signs of encroaching upon the interests of a peaceful and stable world." If successful, such a policy would not only check Soviet expansion but in the process would maintain sufficient pressure to force a change in Soviet attitudes as well as actions.[14]

Most administration officials agreed with such reasoning. Marshall was one of them, albeit with a few reservations. He had clashed with the Soviets before, had long believed that they respected only tough talk, and by no means thought of them as altruistic or friendly. Moreover, he had read the Long Telegram before appointing Kennan to head the Policy Planning Staff and had to agree with such basic components of administration foreign policy in order to be a member of the cabinet; Secretary of Commerce Henry Wallace, who in his diary had labeled Marshall "very strongly anti-Russian" in November 1945, had already been dropped from that body because of his lack of agreement. Nevertheless, as an individual slow to make up his mind before all the facts were available, Marshall was not yet ready to dismiss totally the idea of postwar cooperation—even if everyone else in the administration was.[15]

The Moscow Foreign Ministers Conference of March–April 1947 would be the key turning point in this regard for Marshall. Even before that conference, however, his general views regarding both the Soviet Union and America's role in the world led him to support the anti-Soviet stance others were urging. During his 22 February speech at Princeton, he had stated that the new generation of Americans needed to develop "a sense of responsibility for world order and security." Simultaneously the British in effect asked the United States to assume this responsibility with specific regard to the eastern Mediterranean by informing the State Department that they were no longer capable of supporting the Greek government against Communist guerrillas or Turkey against Soviet demands for revision of the Dardanelles treaty. State Department personnel "realized at once," according to one official, "that Great Britain had within the hour handed the job of world leadership, with all its burdens and all its glory, to the United States."[16] They and members of the administration were virtually unanimous in the belief that London's offer should, indeed must, be taken.

Marshall agreed. "A crisis of the utmost importance and urgency has arisen" with "a direct and immediate relation to the security of the United States," he informed congressional leaders at a 26 February White House meeting called to obtain their support for this dramatic departure in U.S. foreign policy. Communist success in Greece would make the Turkish situation more critical and open the door to Soviet domination "over the entire Middle East to the borders of India." Such extension of Soviet power would have a major impact on Hungary, Austria, Italy, and France. The situation thus constituted "the first crisis of a series which might extend Soviet domination to Europe, the Middle East and Asia." Only U.S. power could prevent this. "We are at the point of decision," he warned.[17]

Marshall's logic was an early example of what would later be called domino theory, a theory at least partially discredited during the 1960s and 1970s by the Vietnam War and now considered overly simplistic and alarmist. During this crisis, however, the secretary's approach was considered too low key by some of his subordinates. Under Secretary Acheson, feeling his chief had "flubbed" his statement by not being sufficiently dramatic, chose to rouse the congressional leaders with some extraordinary imagery. "Like apples in a barrel infected by the rotten one," he warned, the Greek "corruption" would carry the Communist "infection" to Asia Minor, Africa, the Far East, and Europe, thereby giving the Soviets world domination at minimal cost. Only the United States could prevent this and save Western civilization. "Not since Rome and Carthage had there been such a polarization of power on this earth."[18]

Truman's rhetoric was even more sweeping. Convinced by his aides as well as Senator Vandenberg that he needed to "scare the hell out of the country" if he wished to obtain support for $400 million in aid to Greece and Turkey, the president on 12 March enunciated a universalistic U.S. foreign policy to "support free peoples who are resisting attempted subjugation by armed minorities or by outside pressures." This Truman Doctrine was a call to arms for a global, ideological crusade.[19]

The Greek and Turkish governments were hardly democratic, and some of Marshall's advisers such as Kennan and Bohlen opposed the president's anti-Communist and universalist rhetoric. So did the secretary himself. Due to its postwar demobilization as well as the realities of power, the United States did not have the force to back up such sweeping rhetoric, and without sufficient force, Marshall often warned, it was unwise to hit a man across the face and call him names. At that moment the new secretary was also on his way to Moscow to see the men Truman had just attacked; such a statement was not the best way to begin negotiations. And while Marshall was being urged by many "to give the Russians hell" in those negotiations, "my facilities for giving them hell . . . was 1⅓ divisions over the entire United States. This is quite a proposition when you deal with somebody with over 260 and you have 1⅓." Moreover, unlike many of his advisers, Marshall still believed negotiations might succeed.[20]

The Moscow Foreign Ministers Conference disabused him of this notion. During forty-three separate sessions from 10 March through 24 April, Marshall watched Soviet Foreign Minister Molotov live up to his nickname of "stone ass" and his reputation for intractability and obstructionism. On 15 April the frustrated American went directly to Stalin in a fruitless effort to break the deadlock. It had been almost two years since their last meeting, and Stalin was aware of the fact that he had aged considerably in the interim. "You look just the same as when I saw you last time," he told Marshall, "but I am just an old man." Some of his comments could have been interpreted as a mellowing with age. "These were only the first skirmishes," he said in reply to Marshall's complaints. The need for compromise was usually recognized "after people had exhausted themselves in dispute," and although success might not be achieved at this conference, "compromises were possible" in the future. For now it was "necessary to have patience and not become depressed."[21]

Marshall did not interpret Stalin's comments as reassuring. During their three previous meetings, the Soviet leader had exhibited a strong desire and ability to obtain concrete results in a short period of time. Partially on his insistence, the Tehran Conference had lasted less than a week, Yalta only slightly more, and Potsdam two. Now, however, he appeared unconcerned by the fact that five full weeks had been wasted in meaningless name calling or by the dire conditions within Germany and the rest of Europe as a result of wartime devastation and the lack of a clear and unified policy for Germany.

With his last hope for progress thus dashed and with an awareness of what had happened to his predecessor Byrnes when that individual had successfully compromised with Stalin in Moscow, Marshall now accepted the belief of his subordinates and the rest of the U.S. delegation that the Soviets had no interest in reaching agreement on policies in Germany. To the contrary, they seemed to be stalling deliberately in the hope that Germany's and Europe's desperate economic situation would get even worse, thereby opening the door to greater Communist influence and eventual Soviet domination.

Whether such conclusions were correct remains unclear; conceivably the Soviets had no such master plan and simply wanted reparations before agreeing to any united policy on Germany. What is clear is that Marshall had now joined wholeheartedly with his advisers and colleagues in the belief that cooperation was, in Kennan's later words, "a pipe dream" and that Soviet policy constituted a menace. In late April the Moscow conference ended with the promise to meet once again in London during November. For Marshall such a meeting held no hope of progress. He was not ready to call for a total, public break with the Soviets, but he was quite ready, indeed anxious, to initiate unilaterally a new European recovery policy. It was vital to find "some initiative to prevent the complete breakdown of Western Europe," he told Bohlen, and the day after his return he ordered Kennan to set up the Policy Planning Staff ahead of schedule and immediately address this issue. "The patient is sinking while the doctors deliberate," he warned the American people; "action can not await compromise through exhaustion."[22]

Kennan and his staff concluded that the basic problem was not the Soviet Union or communism. Rather it was the economic, political, and social chaos, and the spiritual crisis of confidence, caused by the war's devastation. In despair, West Europeans were voting for local Communist parties in unprecedented numbers and might very well elect them to power or accede to their takeover in France and Italy. And these parties, administration officials insisted, were Soviet "fifth columns," similar to the ones Hitler had used in the 1930s, that would give Moscow control of Europe. Yet, as Kennan emphasized, the Soviets were merely taking advantage of an existing crisis, not creating one. What was needed was a U.S. initiative directed at the real problem, an initiative to restore the economic health of Western Europe and with it the Europeans' faith in themselves and their values. Much as Lend-Lease had been given to those willing to fight Germany during World War II, so economic aid should now be given to those willing to work together for the economic rehabilitation of their society.[23]

These conclusions were not new. For months Washington officials had been discussing such a program to solve a host of politico-economic problems ranging from those Kennan enunciated to the expansion of U.S. export markets. And ever since World War I, U.S. policymakers had been emphasizing the need for the United States to take responsibility for the economic well-being of Europe as a means of ensuring prosperity, democracy, and peace. Such goals could not be obtained, however, without economic integration as well as rehabilitation, and that integration had to include Germany. So far efforts to achieve this had been blocked at least as much by France as by the Soviet Union. American economic aid for a multilateral European recovery program could overcome French objections. It could also remake Europe's political economy in the American image, thereby aiding U.S. as well as European economic growth and guaranteeing a future of peace and prosperity.[24]

Kennan was not the only individual to recommend such a program during the spring of 1947. Journalist Walter Lippmann enunciated a similar proposal in March and April. So did the State-War-Navy Coordinating Committee in an April report, Acheson in a major public address before the Delta Council in Cleveland, Mississippi, during May, and Clayton in an internal State Department memorandum that same month. Like Marshall, all of them emphasized the need for quick action.[25] Their advice also fit in with the "peace and prosperity" and "world leadership" themes Marshall had enunciated in 1945 and February 1947, and appealed as a strategy that was peaceful, humanitarian, and made use of America's greatest strength: its economic power.

By late May Bohlen was drafting from the Kennan and Clayton recommendations a major address for Marshall to deliver suggesting American economic aid to Western Europe. In and of itself such aid would be neither new nor very reassuring, for the United States had already granted or loaned billions of dollars to individual European countries without any positive results. Rather than continue this way, Marshall's advisers wanted future funds tied to a comprehensive, multilateral plan, authored by the Europeans themselves, for European (including German) economic rehabilitation and integration rather than merely relief. Not wanting to take responsibility for the further division of Europe, they and Marshall agreed that the Soviet bloc should be invited to join; clearly, however, they hoped for and planned on Communist rejection.[26]

To publicize and promote such a bold initiative, Marshall needed a public forum with extensive press coverage in the immediate future. Harvard University's commencement on 5 June was chosen because it met these requirements and because Marshall had already been offered an honorary degree there on three separate occasions (Wisconsin and Amherst were also considered). Belatedly the secretary now agreed to join eleven others in receiving honorary degrees and after the formal ceremonies to make a brief address to the alumni and graduates. That address would quickly (if somewhat incorrectly) become known as the Marshall Plan speech.

The honorary degree recipients on 5 June were an eclectic group that included a four-star general (Omar Bradley), a world-reknowned poet (T. S. Eliot), a key civilian figure in the Manhattan Project (J. Robert Oppenheimer), and a former U.S. senator (James W. Wadsworth). Attired in a civilian suit rather than a uniform or academic robes, Marshall nevertheless remained the most notable figure in the group, "a soldier and statesman whose ability and character brook only one comparison in the history of the nation" his citation read, and he led the precession of honorary degree recipients. In the afternoon, after the commencement ceremonies and lunch, he followed the alumni president, the governor of Massachusetts, and General Bradley in offering a brief public address. It was only 1,500 words in length, and the low-key delivery lasted a mere ten minutes.[27] What Marshall suggested, however, mostly in two critical paragraphs, was of enormous significance.

The countries of Europe needed help, he said, and the United States was willing to provide it. "Our policy is directed not against any country or doctrine," he insisted, "but against hunger, poverty, desperation and chaos. Its purpose should be the revival of a working economy in the world so as to permit the emergence of political and social conditions in which free institutions can exist." Those nations willing to participate in this task of recovery, Marshall suggested, should take the initiative by coming up with a collective plan themselves. The role of the United States would be to provide "friendly aid" in both the drafting and later support of such a program.[28]

This was not the Marshall Plan per se, for at that moment there was no such plan. Rather it was a suggestion that the United States would react favorably if the Europeans took the initiative by creating and presenting such a plan to Washington. Led by British Foreign Minister Ernest Bevin, who had been forewarned of the Marshall proposal, they quickly did so. With U.S. assistance they developed and forwarded in

September a proposal for $17 billion in aid over a four-year period to revive the economies of sixteen countries and the western zones of Germany. The Soviet Union and Eastern bloc countries had been invited to participate, and Molotov had even flown to Paris in June for the opening sessions. He objected vehemently to listing his nation's resources and needs as well as the multilateral nature of the plan, however, and as Marshall's advisers had hoped and predicted, he soon denounced it, withdrew, and forced the East Europeans to do similarly. Soon after the Soviets responded with their own "Molotov plan" for Eastern Europe and with a Communist Information Bureau (Cominform) to replace the Communist international organization (Comintern) abolished during World War II.

While European and U.S. negotiators worked out the details of the Marshall Plan, Truman called Congress into special session and requested nearly $600 million in short-term aid to see Western Europe through the coming winter. Marshall's testimony was once again effective, and Congress agreed in mid-December. A few days later, the president sent the $17 billion European Recovery Program (ERP) to Capitol Hill. Returning from the final, fruitless foreign ministers' meeting in London, Marshall now plunged into a major public relations campaign to sell the program. Working closely with Senator Vandenberg and other Republican leaders ("We could not have gotten much closer unless I sat in Vandenberg's lap or he sat in mine," he later stated), Marshall testified before congressional committees and warned that quick and decisive action was necessary to restore Europe's economy and to preserve Western values and world peace. Beyond that, he traveled extensively throughout the country in a successful effort to mobilize public support for the program. "I worked on that as hard as though I was running for the Senate or the presidency," he later recalled. "That's the thing I take pride in, putting the damned thing over. Anybody, well, you take a campaign or anything like that, there's nothing so profound in the logic of the thing. But the execution of it, that's another matter."[29]

As he had been doing since 1945, Marshall in his statements noted the dramatic changes that had taken place in the world, attacked isolationism as a dated and dangerous policy, emphasized the inseparability of peace, prosperity, and democracy, and insisted that the United States had a responsibility in its own interests, as well as those of others, to ensure all three. Now, however, he no longer showed the caution and fear of rhetorical excess that had marked his first months in office. To the contrary, he warned that the Soviets threatened nothing less than the future of Western civilization and world peace, that they would "oppose and sabotage" the restoration of Western Europe "at every turn," and that on the future of the ERP, the "greatest decision in our history," hinged nothing less than "the survival of the kind of world in which democracy, individual liberty, economic stability, and peace can be maintained."[30]

This shift in Marshall's rhetoric can be traced to his dismal experiences with Molotov throughout 1947, the rapidly deteriorating situation in Western Europe, and his agreement by this time with Truman that Congress would act quickly only under fear of communism; "there is a notion, held by some in Washington," Walter Lippmann disapprovingly commented in this regard, "that the only way to win the support of Congress for the Marshall Plan is to frighten it."[31] Equally important in motivating Marshall was his fervent belief in America's new global mission and the fact that, unlike the Greek-Turkish crisis of 1947, this was not a potential military confrontation for which the United States was unprepared. Rather it was an economic and psychological crisis for which he possessed overwhelming power in the form of America's enormous economic and financial strength. For once, the United States had ready the means needed to obtain its goals in the international arena—provided he could convince Congress to let him use those means.

By the time Congress voted on the ERP in March–April 1948, it was being commonly referred to as the Marshall Plan. Truman supported and furthered this association in his own statements, thereby ensuring the secretary of state a form of historical immortality. Partially that had been the president's aim. Marshall had been denied such immortality when Eisenhower had been appointed to command Overlord; here was a fitting substitute for the man Truman respected above all others. Of equal if not greater importance, only through association with the general could the plan get through a Republican Congress in 1947–48. "Can you imagine its chances of passage in an election year in a Republican congress," he asked one of his aides, "if it is named for Truman and not Marshall?"[32]

As in most such situations, the naming of a plan for one person involved some distortion. Marshall was important in the ERP's initiation and passage but by no means the sole or even the primary figure. The concept was more than twenty-five years old and had long been a component of U.S. foreign policy. Kennan and Clayton were primarily responsible for the specific proposals enunciated by Marshall in 1947, and

Bohlen drafted the Harvard speech from their memoranda. Lippmann and Acheson publicly stated the key ideas beforehand, and the Europeans with U.S. assistance actually worked out the program as requested. Vandenberg was so critical to securing its passage that Marshall later said he "was just the whole show when we got to the actual movement of the thing."[33]

At every stage, however, Marshall had been the key initiator, organizer, and mover. It was he who had pressed for quick action, mobilized subordinates, revised and delivered the pivotal public address, provided the critical testimony to Congress, conceived and implemented with Vandenberg the bipartisan approach, and served as the plan's most effective public spokesman. The European Recovery Program was by no means totally altruistic. Rooted in self-interest, it was an extremely appropriate and effective strategy for the United States to pursue in defense of those interests. It also had some negative consequences; it accelerated the division of Europe into two hostile camps and increased West European dependency on the United States. Yet the self-interest on which it was based was enlightened in the sense that the program helped others in the process of helping the United States, attempted to preserve the most cherished of Western political values, and tapped the deepest humanitarian instincts and abilities of the American people. It also succeeded in achieving European recovery and integration and in reviving European hope.

For all of this Marshall clearly deserved his second Man of the Year selection from *Time* magazine in January 1948 and the Nobel Prize he would receive in 1953. As *Time* noted in explaining its selection, Marshall was "the man who offered hope to those who desperately needed it," as well as the symbol of the U.S. decision to assume world leadership.[34]

A month after the Harvard commencement address, *Foreign Affairs* published Kennan's "The Sources of Soviet Conduct." Although he used the pseudonym "X," readers quickly identified the author and realized that containment was to be the official U.S. policy toward the Soviets. Exactly what containment meant remained an open question, however. While the Marshall Plan was the heart of that policy, it was by no means its entirety. Economic reconstruction of Western Europe required the economic reconstruction of the western occupation zones of Germany, and that in turn required political reconstruction in those zones. Many West Europeans believed that some form of politico-military organization with the United States was also necessary. Consequently preliminary talks began in late 1947 and early 1948 regarding the formation of a West German government and the creation of a military alliance.

Kennan had never conceived of the Soviet threat as primarily military, but he recognized that Europeans needed to feel secure if recovery was to take place and therefore grudgingly supported an alliance. He also realized that the Soviets, in reaction to the Marshall Plan, would tighten their control in Eastern Europe and perhaps precipitate a crisis.[35] This is exactly what happened during the first six months of 1948. Soviet reaction in turn led to Western reaction, which led to further Soviet reaction. A vicious cycle was thereby created that completed the division of Germany and Europe while bringing the two superpowers to the brink of military confrontation.

The first step in this escalation was the February 1948 Communist coup in Czechoslovakia. While predicted by Kennan as a nonthreatening by-product of Soviet fear and weakness in the light of the Marshall Plan initiative, it touched a raw Western nerve: memory of the 1938 Munich appeasement that had paved the way for the outbreak of World War II. General Lucius Clay, commander of the U.S. occupation zone in Germany, feared that war might now be imminent. His fears were reinforced when in March the Soviets, reacting to early moves to form a West German government, walked out of the Allied Control Council. In Washington Truman responded by pressing for passage of the ERP and linking it to restoration of selective service and approval of universal military training. The ERP passed the Senate (69–17) in late March and the House (329–74) in early April, and it played a role in Communist losses during the Italian elections a few weeks later. Congress also reinstituted the draft (but again rejected UMT). In May the Western European nations signed the Brussels Pact, a military alliance, and invited U.S. participation.

Congress had already approved collective defense treaties with the 1947–1948 Rio Pact and Organization of American States (OAS), agreements Marshall had helped to negotiate with Latin America during conferences in Brazil and Bogotá, Colombia. These could be rationalized as within the U.S. tradition under the general rubric of the Monroe Doctrine; an alliance with Europe was another matter entirely. In June, however, Congress sanctioned such participation, too, with the Vandenberg Resolution. At the same time U.S. and West European representatives meeting in London recommended the formation of a German republic out of the western occupation zones. Hoping to stop this as well as reassert his authority in Eastern Europe that was being eroded by the rebellion of Yugoslav leader Tito, Stalin responded with a blockade of the western zones of Berlin.

As with previous responses that were perceived by the other side as dangerous initiatives, this one led to exactly what Stalin had wished to prevent in establishing the blockade. While Marshall and Truman rejected suggestions to break it with an armed convoy, they did institute a successful airlift of supplies into West Berlin and a highly effective counterblockade of the entire Soviet zone in Germany, send long-range bombers to England, and accelerate negotiations for the creation of a West German government and a North Atlantic Alliance. In September 1948 a West German constituent assembly met, and in May the following year a republic was proclaimed. NATO was created in April 1949, with Senate approval given in July. Tito's break with Stalin succeeded in the interim while the Berlin airlift continued to circumvent the blockade. By May 1949 Stalin had given it up as a total, counterproductive failure.

Long before that date, the success of U.S. policies had become evident. As early as November 1947, Kennan had concluded that the expansion of Soviet domination "has now been brought substantially to a standstill." A year later the situation appeared even brighter. "In every field," Marshall informed his European colleagues in September 1948, "the Russians are retreating. From now on Berlin is the only foothold which they have against us. Everywhere else, and particularly in Germany, they are losing ground." Clearly, "we can really say that we are on the road to victory."[36]

That success created its own problems, however. Kennan had always looked upon containment as a temporary, politico-economic strategy designed to restore Europe, and with it additional power centers, so that the United States and the Soviet Union would not be in head-on collision. With his policies working, he therefore suggested in August 1948 a move to disengage Soviet and U.S. forces from Germany and reunify that country as a neutral player in the cold war. Few agreed with him. The Soviets, his colleagues reminded him, could not be trusted to keep such an agreement, while West Germany was essential to West European recovery and defense efforts. Those defense efforts were critical, they insisted, because, unlike Kennan, they saw the Soviet Union as a military threat. Henceforth containment would become increasingly militarized, globalized, rigid, and an end in and of itself rather than a means.[37]

U.S. success was also limited to Europe. In China Chiang's economic and military position deteriorated sharply in early 1947, as Marshall had feared and predicted it would. The secretary agreed to rescind the arms embargo and sent General Wedemeyer back to China on a fact-finding and morale-boosting mission, but Wedemeyer reported that the corrupt and "spiritually insolvent" Kuomintang lacked the popular support necessary to win and expressed doubts about Chiang's desire and ability to reform. Yet he recommended a long-term aid program without prior reform, a program that included economic assistance, material support, and U.S. financial and military advisers, on the grounds that a Communist victory could not be tolerated. To prevent such a victory in Manchuria, he further recommended an international trusteeship over the area.[38]

Wedemeyer's call for expanded aid to Chiang without preconditions echoed the cries of the so-called China lobby in Congress and the recommendations of the War and Navy departments and the JCS, who were developing with their contingency war plans a concept of national security requirements much more global and military in nature than Kennan's. The Soviet Union, they argued, constituted a worldwide military menace to the United States. A local Communist victory anywhere extended Soviet power and, according to the logic of containment, had to be prevented at all costs. Consequently Chiang had to be supported no matter what his weaknesses.[39]

Marshall and his advisers disagreed. A Communist victory in China would not necessarily lead to Soviet domination and would in no way threaten U.S. security the way Communist success in Western Europe would. Of more immediate importance, aid would be wasted on the corrupt and incompetent Kuomintang unless preceded by reforms, while Chiang's military and economic needs were so enormous that even the United States could not meet them without a major economic and military commitment that was both unwise and impossible. Economic aid would have to come at the expense of the ERP, while U.S. postwar demobilization meant the armed forces necessary to ensure Chiang victory were not even available. And the Soviet Union could easily match the U.S. level of aid at little cost.

Even with its enormous power, U.S. resources were thus limited and should not be dissipated in a fruitless and dangerous military crusade, especially in an area of secondary importance to the United States and at the expense of commitments to the much more critical European continent. Clearly recognizing these constraints on U.S. power, Kennan favored a limited form of "asymmetrical" containment whereby the United States would rely primarily on its economic strength to help revive industrial "strong points" and thereby recreate a multipolar, balance-of-power world in which the full burden of containing the Soviets would not fall on an overextended United States. "Steps should be taken," he recommended to Marshall in May 1947, to dispel the idea that the Truman Doctrine "is a blank check to give economic and military aid to any area in the world where the communists show signs of being successful." To implement this strategy in the Far East, Kennan wanted to "liquidate" the U.S. commitment in China and instead build up Japan and the Philippines.[40]

Marshall agreed. Strategy, after all, involved the establishment of priorities and the application of limited resources appropriately so as to achieve certain ends, something he had clearly learned as a soldier. Europe remained the primary area of U.S. interest and the area in which limited U.S. intervention could be decisive. In China the reverse was true. And in general strategic terms, he warned a congressional committee, trying to apply counterforce "wherever the Communist influence is brought to bear . . . would be a most unwise procedure" in that it would be equivalent to "handing over the initiative to the Communists," thereby enabling them to "spread our influence out so thin that it could be of no particular effectiveness at any one point." In specific regard to China, intervention to defeat the Communists would be limitless, indecisive, and constitute both an economic burden and a military responsibility "which I cannot recommend as a course of action for this Government."[41]

Simply to sit back and allow Chiang to fall was impossible, however, because the China lobby and its supporters could respond by blocking passage of the critical ERP. Already in late 1947 they had successfully tacked funds for China onto the administration's short-term aid bill for Western Europe. Marshall and his advisers consequently decided on a policy of limited aid to Chiang that would be sufficient, in Kennan's words, "to satisfy American public opinion and, if possible, to prevent any sudden and total collapse of the Chinese government." The result was the $400 million China Aid Act of 1948 and a decision to keep Wedemeyer's report classified.[42] As in World War II, the United States would pursue a Europe-first policy while trying to hold in the Far East and mollify public opinion. Unlike World War II, the effort would be unsuccessful.

Public opinion and politics also foiled Marshall's preferred policy in

Palestine, a League of Nations mandate where Britain found itself by 1947 caught between conflicting World War I promises to Jewish nationalists seeking to recreate their ancient homeland (Zionists) and Arab nationalists who sought self-determination and viewed Jewish immigration as a European colonial invasion. Adopting a pro-Arab policy during the 1930s, Britain had severely restricted Jewish immigration at the same time the United States and other nations were restricting all immigration and the violently anti-Semitic Nazis were taking over Germany and Europe. No haven for Europe's persecuted Jews was thus available at the moment one was most needed. By 1941 Nazi persecution had turned to genocide as the Germans implemented their "final solution" to exterminate European Jewry. Close to six million were murdered in the Holocaust that followed. The Allies did nothing to stop it. Indeed the War Department rejected pleas to destroy the Auschwitz extermination camp gas chambers even though the air force was dropping bombs less than five miles away, while Assistant Secretary of the State Breckinridge Long continued his successful efforts to allow as few refugees into the United States as possible.[43]

Revelation of Nazi atrocities after the war led to massive public support in the United States for an end to Britain's immigration restrictions in Palestine and the establishment of a Jewish national home for Holocaust survivors—Arab and British protests notwithstanding. In 1947 Britain handed the problem over to the United Nations, and a special commission recommended the partition of Palestine into Jewish and Arab states. The General Assembly agreed, with both the United States and the Soviet Union voting in the affirmative. Britain then announced it would withdraw completely from the area in May 1948. Violence increased, and full-scale war between Arabs and Jews was clearly imminent. With the same well-meaning naiveté and historical ignorance that a senator had exhibited in his desire to raise Shanghai to the level of Kansas City, America's U.N. ambassador now urged Arabs and Jews to come together and "settle this problem in a true Christian spirit."[44]

The State Department's Near East Division opposed partition on the grounds that unavailable U.S. troops would be needed to enforce it and that U.S. support would alienate the Arabs, thereby providing the Soviet Union with an opportunity to extend its influence into the oil-rich and strategically vital Middle East. Marshall agreed. So did the newly created Defense Department and the U.S. intelligence community, and during the spring of 1948, they attempted to reverse the partition decision. White House advisers David Niles and Clark Clifford, as well as Zionist leaders, countered that reversal would cripple the prestige and effectiveness of the fledgling United Nations and be profoundly immoral in the light of the Holocaust and Allied inaction during the war, inaction that had prominently featured the War and State departments. It would also alienate American voters who supported partition, non-Jewish as well as Jewish, just before a presidential election in which Truman was clearly the underdog. Consequently Niles and Clifford pressed not only for continued U.S. support of partition but also for immediate recognition of the state of Israel upon its establishment.

In a repetition of his reaction during the 1942 strategic debate, Marshall became incensed that domestic political factors were interfering with expert advice and carefully conceived policy, and he incorrectly tended to see this as the only issue. He made his feelings clear at a 12 May White House meeting, stating in what Clifford labeled "a righteous God-damned Baptist tone" that the presidential adviser's recommendations were a "transparent dodge to win a few votes" and that his very presence in the room was the result of domestic politics, which should not be determining U.S. policy. If the president took Clifford's advice, and if Marshall broke his lifetime refusal to vote, "I would vote against the President." Nevertheless Truman agreed to recognition. Whether he did so primarily to gain votes, because of Zionist pressure, to support the U.N., out of guilt, or because he thought it was morally correct remains a matter of historical dispute. So is the question of how important his stand proved to be in his stunning upset victory over Republican Thomas Dewey six months later.[45]

Several of Marshall's friends urged him to resign over this disagreement, but he correctly answered that the final decision constitutionally belonged to the president, not the secretary. He would resign, however, after the 1948 election. If the Republicans won, he would not be wanted. If the Democrats won, he would not be so desperately needed for a bipartisan policy and could finally begin in good conscience the retirement he so deeply craved. It was also a retirement he desperately needed, for the 67-year-old Marshall was exhausted from the strenuous pace and enormous burdens of the last ten years. A full one-third of his days as secretary of state had been spent at international conferences, the rest juggling multiple crises. By his own count, he had had only nineteen days off since 1939. Acheson compared him in late 1947 to "a four-engine bomber going only on one engine." Then in mid-1948 doctors concluded that one of his kidneys needed to be removed. Marshall continued his hectic pace until Truman's reelection in November, but a month later he entered the hospital and successfully underwent the surgery. Acheson was named his successor in January.[46]

"To say what makes greatness in a man is very difficult," Acheson wrote Marshall at that time. "But when one is close to it, one knows. Twice in my life that has happened to me—once with Justice Holmes and once with you."[47] As he and numerous others realized, Marshall's achievements as secretary of state had been extraordinary, and no one doubted that he richly deserved a belated retirement. Truman, however, still needed him. In September 1949 he gave Marshall light responsibilities by appointing him chairman of the American Red Cross. By 1950, however, another crisis had erupted that he believed required the general's forceful leadership.

10

DENOUEMENT IN KOREA
AND AT HOME,
1949–59

In June 1950, the cold war became hot when the United States committed military forces to combat in Korea. In the midst of this crisis, President Truman asked Marshall once again to oversee a U.S. military effort, albeit in a civilian role—this time as secretary of defense. Marshall was confirmed and sworn in on 21 September 1950. He would hold this position for only one year. Within that brief time, however, he would be forced to deal with three critical and interrelated issues: the creation of an armed force to fight in Korea, the determination of proper strategy and objectives in the conflict, and the firing of General Douglas MacArthur for his refusal to accept that strategy and those objectives. Although the three issues were specific and unique to this situation, they were also illustrative of the broad themes in America's rise to world power that Marshall had dealt with throughout his entire career: military preparedness, global strategy and policy, civilian control over the military in a democratic society, and the inseparability of military from political issues.

All of these came to a climax in Korea, and Marshall's views emerged victorious on each of them. In the process, however, this most apolitical of soldiers became himself politicized and for the first time a target of serious partisan attack. To refuse to run for political office or even to vote, Marshall was forced to realize, did not mean that a soldier could avoid politicization. To the contrary, if war and politics were inseparable, so were soldiers, statesmen, and politicians.

The position Marshall assumed in September 1950 was a relatively new one and, ironically, one that he had played a major role in creating. At the end of World War II, he had supported a postwar military policy that included not simply universal military training but also unification of the armed forces and greater civil-military coordination. After extensive bureaucratic and political battles, Congress moved on these ideas two years later by passing the National Security Act of 1947. It institutionalized the JCS as a permanent body, separated the air force from the army, placed all three services in a single Department of Defense, set up the Central Intelligence Agency, and established the National Security Council to ensure civil-military coordination. In effect, it created the defense establishment we still live with today.

The act was better on paper than in reality. Many civilians had opposed the concentration of military power inherent in unification. So had a navy fearful of being overwhelmed by the army and the air force. The result was not true unification but rather a federated system whereby each service retained autonomy and the secretary of defense had limited powers. To make matters worse, severe postwar budget cuts quickly pitted the services against each other. The resulting turmoil may have played a role in the subsequent nervous breakdown and suicide of James Forrestal, the former secretary of the navy who had become the first defense secretary.[1]

The situation did not improve under his successor, former Assistant Secretary of War Louis Johnson. On the contrary, Johnson's decision to support the air force's B-36 bomber program over the navy's supercarrier plans led to the so-called Revolt of the Admirals—a bitter dispute that rocked the Defense Department in 1949.[2] Congress sought to solve the bureaucratic problems this and other episodes had revealed by increasing the powers of the defense secretary, but by this time the department was highly demoralized and polarized. Moreover, no congressional legislation could restore the civil-military coordination that had broken down as a result of friction between the abrasive Johnson and Secretary of State Dean Acheson. Clearly a new defense secretary was needed.

That new secretary would have to do more than simply restore interservice and interdepartmental harmony. He would also have to expand the armed forces as a whole, for the postwar demobilization and large budget cuts that had precipitated the Revolt of the Admirals had also left those forces unprepared for any conflict except a nuclear one. This military policy had been justified on numerous grounds, including the need for a balanced budget and the relative cheapness of nuclear over ground forces ("more bang for the buck"), the fact that the cold war was primarily political and economic rather than military in nature, and the belief that the U.S. nuclear monopoly and a buildup of West European forces could best deter any hostile moves by Soviet armed forces. Even Marshall, although he supported in late 1948 "some attempt to recoup our lost military stature," joined his advisers in rejecting a buildup of ground forces for Europe.[3]

During 1949 and 1950, however, all of these assumptions were called into question. While the cold war became increasingly globalized and militarized, a sense of frustration and failure grew within the United States over the results of containment. Although many of those results, such as continued recovery in Western Europe, were quite positive, they appeared inconclusive to a public used to more decisive military victories. And by late 1949 these successes had been overshadowed in the public mind by apparent failures elsewhere. This was particularly true in China, where Communist forces defeated the Nationalists on the battlefield and by year's end forced Chiang Kai-shek to withdraw from the mainland to the island of Formosa.

Marshall had anticipated this scenario as early as 1946 if the Nationalists continued to ignore his advice. So had his State Department subordinates, and in the aftermath of the Communist victory Secretary Acheson released the department's "White Paper," a collection of documents and statements emphasizing the same points Marshall had been making since the failure of his 1945-46 China mission. Most notable in this regard was the assertion that the Kuomintang had been responsible for its own demise and that the United States could not have saved Chiang without a massive commitment that was impossible in the light of other, more important commitments in Europe, as well as the lack of sufficient U.S. military forces. The White Paper further implied that Mao's victory was not necessarily disastrous, for Asia was of secondary importance in U.S. global strategy and Chinese nationalism could preclude Soviet control of the area.[4]

Implicit in such arguments was a future U.S. policy of withdrawal in Asia and the Western Pacific on both strategic and political grounds. Strategically, the JCS as well as the State Department maintained, the Europe-first approach and paucity of U.S. military forces still precluded any major effort to save Chiang or become involved in an Asian ground war. Politically withdrawal could accelerate the Sino-Soviet clash that the experts expected and thus turn Mao into another Tito. Even recognition of Mao's government was possible in such a situation. In January 1950 Acheson articulated this policy and sketched a U.S. "defense perimeter" in the Western Pacific that included neither Formosa nor Korea.[5]

Although essentially correct, such assessments ignored the antagonism the Communists had developed against the United States for aiding Chiang during the Chinese civil war, as well as the American public's continued emotional commitment to China. Communist antagonism led to attacks against American property and representatives in that country and by February 1950 to a Sino-Soviet alliance that made talk of a split between the two nations seem absurd. The old and emotional public commitment to "saving" China led to a belief that this critical area had now been permanently "lost" to the Soviets and that such a loss constituted a devastating defeat for the United States.

Equally if not more devastating to the American public was the almost simultaneous announcement that the Soviet Union had exploded an atomic device. Although scientists had warned that the U.S. nuclear monopoly could not last, Soviet success only four years after Hiroshima was a frightening shock. Four years after their total victory in World War II, Americans found themselves less secure, and more vulnerable and threatened, than they had ever been previously.

Rather than question their basic assumptions, Americans blamed the Truman administration for these alleged policy "failures." Their wrath and hysteria were fueled by the discovery of Soviet nuclear spies, and by a belligerent Republican right wing that gained power after the party's shocking defeat in the 1948 presidential campaign and rejected the bipartisan foreign policy Marshall and Vandenberg had created a few years earlier. Strategically, many of the former isolationists in this wing argued, Asia was more rather than less important than Europe. Politically, they maintained, their party's previous refusal to challenge Truman's foreign policy had resulted in electoral defeat. As a result of such reasoning, Republicans began to attack the administration savagely for "losing" both China and the nation's nuclear monopoly. For some extremists, the losses were the result of treason rather than blundering, especially after State Department official Alger Hiss was accused of espionage. In February 1950, Senator Joseph McCarthy of Wisconsin made the first of his notorious charges regarding Communists in the State Department.[6]

Such public and partisan attacks reinforced a growing tendency within the administration by 1949 to view the cold war in hard-line military and global terms. Despite Kennan's emphasis on containment as a temporary strategy of limited, primarily nonmilitary means and selective application, a growing chorus in Washington began to view it in exactly the opposite terms. The Sino-Soviet Treaty was interpreted as a sign of total Chinese subservience to the Soviet Union requiring the application of containment to Asia not merely by the rebuilding of Japan but also by politico-military support for the European powers against Communist-led anticolonial movements in Southeast Asia. In Europe, the Berlin crisis and the formation of NATO simultaneously reflected and reinforced a growing reliance on military containment and a tendency to think in terms of a permanently divided, bipolar world.

The reasons for this shift were numerous. Partially it resulted from conceptions of national security within the Defense Department that were different from and much more expansive than Kennan's. There was also a natural tendency to think in terms of Soviet capabilities rather than intentions, capabilities that took on frightening proportions after the Soviet atomic bomb. Confusion existed in Washington over the relationship between Soviet foreign policy and local Communist movements, as well as whether containment was a means or an end, a flexible strategy or a rigid doctrine. Some of Kennan's rather loose and easy-to-misinterpret language exacerbated this confusion and fueled what he considered a gross distortion and misrepresentation of his ideas. So did the administration's rhetorical excesses in its efforts to sell the anti-Soviet foreign policy to Congress, the fact that many officials had never agreed with the limited containment Kennan had espoused, and the inability of his formulations to deal adequately with irrational fears.[7]

Throughout 1948 and 1949 Kennan found himself fighting an increasing futile rear guard action against the global, military version of containment. By 1950 he had quit the State Department in disgust, and in time he would disavow the policy he had authored. Nevertheless, as the author of the "X" article, he would be forever known as the father of containment. In an ironic historical version of musical chairs, his reputation would rest on a policy he opposed, while Marshall, denied immortality as commander of the cross-channel operation he had championed, would receive it for the economic policy Kennan truly desired.

While this public and administration shift toward global, military containment gradually gathered momentum, Soviet detonation of an atomic device in late 1949 served as the immediate catalyst for its verbalization as official policy. Prior to that detonation, U.S. strategy for Europe and NATO had rested on Washington's ability to deter any Soviet military attack with the threat of nuclear retaliation. This threat was believable, however, only so long as the United States possessed a nuclear monopoly and would not face Soviet retaliation, a situation that ceased to exist when the Soviets exploded their first atomic bomb. With its military strategy obsolete, the Truman administration now decided to develop a much more powerful "superbomb" (the hydrogen bomb) and a new, expansive military and national security policy. In April 1950 that new policy was enunciated within a framework of global, military containment in National Security Council Paper 68 (NSC-68), an extraordinary document of seventy typed, single-spaced, legal-sized pages.

Primarily the work of Paul Nitze, Kennan's successor as head of the Policy Planning Staff, NSC-68 argued that the Soviet threat was military, ideological, global, and total, and that it required a massive program to rearm the United States and its allies before the Soviets initiated a war in the belief that they could win. Cost was now considered immaterial not simply because of the danger Moscow posed but also because the administration had rejected the sanctity of the balanced budget in favor of the Keynesian deficit spending concepts that had been used during the New Deal and World War II. If necessary, NSC-68 argued, the United States could afford to spend up to 20 percent of its gross national product on rearmament, rearmament that had to include conventional as well as nuclear forces so as to be able to wage whatever limited conflicts the Soviets or their proxies might instigate.[8]

NSC-68 constituted, in the words of two scholars, "the most elaborate effort made by United States officials during the early Cold War years to integrate political, economic, and military considerations into a comprehensive statement of national security policy." It was also a military call to arms with profound and disturbing repercussions for the future, most notably in its equation of Soviet expansionism with local Communist movements, its emphasis on global military containment, and its implicit rejection of Kennan's multipolar world in favor of a zero-sum game whereby any gain for the Soviets was a loss for the United States, and vice-versa.[9]

Whether the government would have ever agreed under normal circumstances to the defense expenditures recommended in NSC-68 must remain a matter of conjecture. The document did receive presidential approval and become a reality via congressional legislation in late 1950–51 but primarily because of new circumstances that were anything but normal: an undeclared war in Korea.

Formerly part of the Japanese empire, Korea had been promised its independence during World War II and at war's end had been occupied by U.S. and Soviet forces. As the cold war developed in Europe, the temporary dividing line between the two occupation forces at the thirty-eighth parallel north latitude became a permanent political division. The Soviets rejected U.S.-sponsored resolutions in the U.N. calling for elections to unify the peninsula, and by 1949 each side had established a Korean government friendly to itself. As the two powers subsequently removed their occupation troops from the peninsula, each Korean government threatened to unify the country by force. On 25 June North Korean forces struck first, invading South Korea.

The Truman administration immediately interpreted this not in local terms but as a Soviet-directed move and major escalation in the cold war, analogous to Hitler's occupation of the Rhineland in 1936, that required an immediate military as well as a diplomatic response. While the U.N. Security Council branded North Korea the aggressor and agreed to collective military action, something it was able to do because the Soviet Union was boycotting the council over its refusal to recognize the People's Republic of China, Japanese occupation commander General MacArthur was placed in charge of all U.S., South Korean, and U.N. forces and ordered to halt the North Korean attack. It soon became apparent that large-scale U.S. ground forces would be needed to do this, forces that did not exist. In such a situation Truman decided to call upon Marshall to create these forces, much as he had during World War II, by proposing him as Johnson's successor to head the Defense Department.

The president had more in mind than merely building up the army for this immediate crisis, however, when he nominated Marshall. In the background stood the more general need to fight another coalition war, this time with U.N. allies, to create a new defense policy in line with NSC-68, to restore interservice and interdepartmental cooperation after the recent battles under Johnson, and, he hoped, to recreate some semblance of a bipartisan policy as the cold war became hot. Marshall's reputation was based in part on his past successes in all of these areas, and he was thus one of the best possible candidates to be secretary of defense at this time.

In August 1950, however, Marshall was also approaching seventy and, while clearly recovered from his kidney surgery, no longer capable of the demanding schedule he had maintained between 1939 and 1949. Yet he agreed to serve, on condition that his term be limited to six months and that Lovett be appointed under secretary so as to be able to succeed him. Partially his agreement stemmed from his sense of duty. Partially it stemmed from his recognition that, as Lovett noted, what was needed in the Defense Department was not a workhorse but someone with sufficiently high stature to restore cooperation with the State Department and the Congress, as well as between the services; bring the armed forces up to wartime standards; and clarify the relationships among MacArthur, Washington, and the U.N.[10] This Marshall could provide no matter what his age and condition.

Unlike his experience in 1947, Marshall did not receive Senate confirmation without hearings and opposition. Part of the problem was the need to amend the 1947 National Security Act, for in line with the American tradition of civil control over the military, that act had explicitly stated that no officer active within the last ten years could be appointed defense secretary. Behind this legal issue, however, was the fact that the bitter partisanship surrounding foreign policy had already eroded Marshall's apolitical status. With the failure of his China mission in 1945–46 and his suppression of the Wedemeyer report in 1947–48 as "ammunition," right-wing Republicans had begun to blame him for the U.S. failure in China.

These individuals did not have enough votes or support to stop his confirmation, but they were able to use the amendment issue to force hearings, to interrogate him, to prevent the unanimous recommendation that had greeted his nomination as secretary of state in 1947, and even to question his loyalty. "General Marshall is not only willing, he is eager to play the role of a front man for traitors," said Senator William Jenner of Indiana on the Senate floor in a vicious diatribe against Truman and Acheson, as well as the general. "The truth is this is no new role for him," for rather than being "the greatest living American" as Truman had claimed he was, "General George C. Marshall is a living lie."[11]

Such a verbal barrage did not stop overwhelmingly favorable votes in both houses to amend the National Security Act and appoint Marshall. Nor did they cow him personally. During the hearings he answered Jenner's often outrageous questions with a combination of dignity, honesty, and contempt, a combination best summarized by his reply when asked why he had joined in the suppression of the Wedemeyer report. "I did not join in the suppression of the report," he responded; "I personally suppressed it."[12]

Jenner's inquisition and barrage did give Marshall a foretaste of later attacks, however, as well as reveal the level of hysteria and distortion of the facts already prevalent in the country. Only such an environment can account for Marshall's being seriously asked whom he was "protecting" by refusing to write his memoirs ("A great many people," he sardonically replied); why he had permitted "the signing of the master Lend-Lease agreement that gave the Russians priority at the expense of the American fighting forces" (it did not); why he had recommended one of Alger Hiss's World War II appointments (he had not); why he had accepted in 1945 the job "to force Generalissimo Chiang Kai-shek to take Communist China and its armies into the Nationalist Government [sic]"; why he had not protested the World War II policies that supposedly "handed half the world on a silver platter to Stalin"; whether he favored "surrendering American sovereignty into the hands of an international superstate" and transforming the armed forces "into a permanent foreign legion"; and whether he would agree "unequivocally" if confirmed not to be "dominated by or carry out the policies of" the supposedly treasonous Secretary of State.[13] With such "logic" and ideas spreading, Marshall received Senate confirmation by a 57–11 vote and on 21 September became the third secretary of defense.

One of Marshall's primary tasks during his first months in office was to build up U.S. military forces. This he was able to do in a very short time as a result of his managerial talents and previous experiences. Building an army was nothing new for him. Indeed this was the third time he had undertaken such a task. As he later commented, "I was getting rather hardened to coming in when everything had gone to pot and there was nothing you could get your hands on, and darned if I didn't find the same thing when I came into the Korean War. There wasn't anything." Actually there was a draft law already in place this time, something that made his task a good deal easier. By April 1951 he had succeeded in doubling army strength, with more men obtained in the preceding ten months than in the entire eighteen-month period from August 1940 to February 1942.[14]

Once again, however, Congress refused to act on the measure he considered vital to prevent another round of unpreparedness in the future: universal military training. For Marshall, UMT had long been the obvious solution to the problem of reconciling global military commitments with a democratic form of government. To its numerous critics, however, UMT was expensive, unpopular, and an unnecessary form of government coercion. For all his successes and prestige, Marshall never was able to overcome this opposition and obtain UMT legislation.

Another key task for Marshall was the restoration of harmony within the defense establishment and with the State Department. Here his prior relationships with key individuals proved invaluable. Three of the four members of the JCS—Generals Bradley, Collins, and Vandenberg—had been his subordinates and protégés during World War II, while Secretary of State Acheson had been his under secretary in 1947 and remained one of his warmest admirers. Of equal importance was Marshall's fervent belief in civilian control over the military and civil control over policy formulation. Emphasizing these principles while making use of the high esteem in which he was held, he was able to restore harmony within the Defense Department and achieve a new level of civil-military coordination with State. Although a five-star general, he made clear his status as a civilian official and his belief in civil primacy. At the regular interdepartmental meetings that he arranged, he deferred to and sat with Acheson on the civilian side of the table, thereby signaling, in the words of his biographer, "that defense and foreign policy were parts of a whole once more."[15]

Marshall played virtually no role in the formulation of early U.S. strategy and policy in Korea because they had already been determined by the time he became secretary of defense. Indeed, a week before he took over, General MacArthur had implemented Washington's directives by launching an amphibious assault behind the North Korean lines at the port of Inchon and simultaneously breaking out of the Pusan bridgehead on the southern tip of the Korean peninsula. It was a daring gamble that MacArthur had himself conceived and pressed upon a doubting JCS, and it succeeded brilliantly. Within a few weeks, the North Korean Army was routed, and its remnants fled back across the thirty-eighth parallel.

Now, however, a crucial strategic decision had to be made with enormous political ramifications: whether MacArthur should cross the thirty-eighth parallel with his forces. The original U.S. and U.N. objective in Korea had been to "halt aggression" by defeating the North Korean invasion. This had been done by the end of September, but the speed and totality of the victory led many officials to return to the broader, 1948 objective of unifying the peninsula. With the North Korean Army virtually destroyed, there appeared to be nothing in the way of this objective, and Marshall thus joined with the rest of the administration in sanctioning a movement by MacArthur into the North. By 19 October his forces had taken the North Korean capitol of Pyongyang and were heading toward the Yalu River boundary with China and the Soviet Union.

That geographical fact raised the specter of possible Chinese or Soviet intervention, especially after some of MacArthur's aircraft crossed the boundary and strafed a Soviet airfield, and it led President Truman to meet with MacArthur at Wake Island and the Joint Chiefs to place some limits on his movements so as not to offer a provocation. Korean rather than U.S. troops were to approach the Yalu, for example, and under no circumstances were either to cross that river. Far from reassured, the Chinese secretly began to move their own troops across the Yalu and in late October offered a sharp warning by attacking Mac-Arthur's forces and then withdrawing. Refusing to believe that the Chinese would seriously consider a war with the United States and the United Nations, MacArthur ignored this warning and in late November launched his two-pronged "home by Christmas" offensive to the Yalu. The Chinese counterattacked in force, wrecking the offensive and throwing U.S. and U.N. forces into headlong retreat. On 28 November MacArthur warned that he now faced "an entirely new war" for which neither his strength nor his directives were adequate.[16]

For a while total defeat loomed on the horizon. One of MacArthur's two wings had to be evacuated by sea, and the other was forced to retreat below the thirty-eighth parallel with no clear answer as to whether it would be able to hold a defensive line on the peninsula. By early 1951 MacArthur had been able to establish such a line and begin a counteroffensive. This time, however, his superiors decided that operations and objectives should remain limited in Korea. Sensing a Soviet trap to weaken NATO and keep U.S. forces tied down and bled white in Asia, military and civilian leaders in Washington returned to their original goal of "resisting aggression" south of the thirty-eighth parallel, and barred any military actions that could expand this objective.[17]

MacArthur found such limits intolerable. As a theater commander he believed they would maximize only his casualties. As an old "Asia-firster" he disagreed with the European orientation of U.S. national policy and the fact that this orientation was so limiting of his possibilities. As an individual with an enormous reputation and ego, he had little respect for his military and civilian superiors in Washington and wished to erase his recent and humiliating defeat with a massive counterattack.

And as a politically oriented and ambitious general, he knew that his ideas would receive strong support from the Republican party and the American people. Consequently he attacked in public the limitations under which he had been placed and proposed a dramatically different approach: a major escalation of ends and means in Korea no matter what the consequences elsewhere. Since the Chinese Communists had attacked U.S. forces, MacArthur reasoned, the United States was now justified in making war on China by naval blockade, bombing Manchurian "sanctuaries," and "unleashing" Chiang Kai-shek against the mainland. The Soviet Union, he insisted, would not intervene to save China, and European concerns and qualms should not be allowed to dictate policy in this more important region.

MacArthur was entitled to propose alternative courses of action. As a field commander, however, he was bound to obey the directives of his military and civilian superiors if they remained unconvinced of the wisdom of his approach. This he refused to do. Equally if not more damaging, he publicly attacked those directives and his superiors while trying to conduct his own alternative foreign policy in the Far East. In early December he informed the press that the limits placed on his operations were "without precedent" in military history. In March he issued a public ultimatum to Peking at the very moment Washington was trying to arrange peace talks, thereby wrecking an early opportunity for a negotiated settlement. Then, on 5 April House Minority leader Joseph Martin publicly read a letter in which MacArthur criticized the Europe-first strategy, called for the unleashing of Chiang Kai-shek, and attacked the entire limited war concept.[18]

Truman and Marshall had previously attempted to control their increasingly uncontrollable Far Eastern commander by insisting in December that he issue no public statements without prior clearance. The public ultimatum and the Martin letter were direct violations of this order; their contents revealed a continued refusal to accept the strategy and policy agreed upon by his superiors, a contempt for them, and a willingness to embarrass them politically. Put bluntly, MacArthur was guilty of gross military insubordination as well as "localitis," arrogance, political maneuvering, and attempted usurpation of civil prerogatives. President Truman now faced one of the greatest challenges to civilian control of the military, as well as one of the greatest crises of his crisis-filled presidency.

For the president, insubordination was the critical issue and one that required MacArthur's dismissal. "I fired him because he wouldn't respect the authority of the President," the feisty Truman stated more than twenty years later. "I didn't fire him because he was a dumb son of a bitch, although he was, but that's not against the law for generals. If it was, half to three-quarters of them would be in jail. That's why when a good one comes along like General Marshall . . . why, you've got to hang onto them, and I did."[19] Despite this later bravado, the decision was by no means easy. Given MacArthur's popularity and ability, relieving him with a war in progress might lead to political as well as military disaster. While personally ready, the president therefore turned to Marshall and his other advisers for their opinions before acting.

Marshall and MacArthur had long been considered polar opposites within the army in terms of ideas and personalities, and on no other issue were their differences so apparent. Nevertheless, contrary to Truman's later recollections, Marshall did not encourage the president to act or tell him that MacArthur should have been fired two years earlier.[20] The theater commander was a living legend with enormous popular support, and his relief could have dire political consequences. Furthermore, Marshall had always believed that field commanders should be allowed great leeway in selecting their methods. Consequently he had supported MacArthur in the past and urged caution regarding any response to the general's excesses. By April, however, MacArthur's behavior had clearly become intolerable. Yet Marshall continued to urge caution and warn of the consequences in Congress of MacArthur's relief. With the Joint Chiefs he also searched desperately for some alternative course of action. Neither he nor they could find any in the light of what MacArthur had already and repeatedly done. On Sunday, 8 April, Marshall and the JCS met and unanimously recommended that MacArthur be relieved. He and General Bradley informed the president on the following day and, with Acheson already in full accord, Truman acted. On 10 April the president summarily relieved MacArthur as U.N. commander; U.S. commander in chief, Far East; supreme allied commander in Japan; and commanding general, U.S. Army Forces in the Far East. Eighth Army commander General Matthew Ridgway replaced him in Korea.[21]

The howls of indignation that followed the announcement of MacArthur's dismissal made previous right-wing attacks on the administration seem mild in comparison. The president, according to Senator McCarthy, was a "sonofabitch" who must have been drunk on "bourbon and benedictine" when he dismissed the general. Labeling that dismissal equivalent to appeasement of world communism, newly elected Senator Richard M. Nixon called for restoring MacArthur to command and Senate censure of the president. Others called for Truman's impeachment. The country, Senator Jenner charged, was "in the hands of a secret inner coterie which is directed by agents of the Soviet Union. We must cut this whole cancerous conspiracy out of our Government at once. Our only choice is to impeach President Truman and find out who is the secret invisible government which has so cleverly led our country down the road to destruction."[22]

Marshall was not spared this vituperation. As early as April 1950, Senator McCarthy had labeled him "completely unfit" and "completely incompetent," and in December he had demanded Marshall's resignation. The firing of MacArthur escalated this rhetoric. Nor was it any longer limited to extremists like Jenner and McCarthy. In a unanimously approved manifesto, the Republican Policy Committee indicted the "Truman-Acheson-Marshall triumvirate" for abandoning China and preparing a "super-Munich" in Asia.[23]

MacArthur returned to a tumultuous welcome and an invitation to address a joint session of Congress. In a virtuoso performance and in the ensuing congressional hearings, he reiterated and defended his approach by attacking the entire concept of limited war ("there is no substitute for victory") and by calling for the bombing and blockade of China along with the "unleashing" of Chiang Kai-shek. This, he argued, would not provoke the Soviet Union. Moreover, Korea was *the* test, and Asia was more important than Europe. Consequently the United States should proceed unilaterally if the European allies refused to agree with U.S. plans. The Joint Chiefs, MacArthur insisted, backed his strategic concepts for Korea, and politicians had no right to intervene in military affairs.[24]

MacArthur was followed at the hearings by Marshall and the JCS. Their testimony directly contradicted him on numerous critical points. Quite telling in this regard was Marshall's insistence that he and the Joint Chiefs did not support MacArthur's politico-military ideas as opposed to those of the administration. On the contrary, although there were "no disagreements" between the president, the defense secretary, and the Joint Chiefs, "basic differences of judgment" had existed and continued to exist between them and MacArthur. His overall strategy risked all-out war in the Far East with no definite gains but with the definite possibility of losing European allies, exposing Europe to successful attack by the Soviet Union, and leaving the United States in subsequent world isolation. General Bradley forcefully reiterated and expanded upon these points. MacArthur's policy, he warned in his famous summary, would involve the United States "in the wrong war, at the wrong place, at the wrong time and with the wrong enemy."[25]

The testimony of Marshall and the Joint Chiefs did much to defuse the situation and win support for Truman. Most congressmen were now forced to agree that the president had acted within his constitutional authority and that his policy was prudent and appropriate. The Mac-Arthur presidential boomlet quickly faded, and General Ridgway proceeded with administration policy in Korea. In June Marshall visited the peninsula to review the situation personally.

Although the immediate military and political crisis had passed by the summer, the vicious public attacks by the Republican right wing against members of the administration continued unabated. On 14 June Senator McCarthy launched a direct assault on Marshall from the Senate floor with a 60,000-word attack that had actually been written in essence by an Ohio journalist. Placed in the *Congressional Record* and later published as *America's Retreat from Victory: The Story of George Catlett Marshall,* it was a classic McCarthy diatribe and character assassination that turned favorable published references into attacks by ripping quotations out of context, invented other quotations, and cited as facts unsubstantiated accusations. Using such tactics as well as questionable assumptions and conclusions regarding U.S. foreign policy in general, McCarthy erected an edifice filled with so many lies and illogical statements that one hardly knew how to question it or defend Marshall. While never using the word *treason,* he clearly was accusing America's most respected soldier and statesman of just that. Marshall, he insisted, had made common cause with Stalin since 1943 and had been part of "a conspiracy so immense and an infamy so black as to dwarf any previous such venture in the history of man."[26]

"God bless democracy," Marshall had written three years earlier. "I approve of it highly but suffer from it extremely."[27] At no time in his career was this comment more accurate. He was admittedly far from the only public official to be attacked by McCarthy or the only American to be falsely accused during this anti-Communist hysteria and witch hunt of the early 1950s, and he probably suffered less personal injury and loss than most of the other accused. Indeed, in his refusal to respond in any way to the charges, he seemed to be unaffected by the slander and hysteria swirling beneath him. Nevertheless, given his intense dislike of partisan politics, McCarthy's attack may have reinforced his determination to retire as soon as possible. And ironically, an opportunity for retirement finally presented itself a few months later.

Marshall had originally agreed to be secretary of defense only for six months and then let Lovett replace him, but each month seemed to bring a new crisis that precluded resignation. This was particularly true during the winter of 1950–51 when the military situation in Korea was critical and again during the spring and summer when any resignation would have been interpreted as a MacArthur victory over Truman. By September, however, a window of sorts had opened. U.N. forces under General Ridgway had been able to stabilize the front and launch successful counteroffensives back across the thirty-eighth parallel, while the MacArthur relief and hearings were beginning to fade from popular memory. The administration admittedly remained tainted with charges of treason as well as burdened with an unpopular war and other problems, but the period of severe crisis had clearly passed. The war was under control, the armed forces mobilized, and interservice and interdepartmental coordination restored. A powerful field commander's rebellion had been effectively stopped and established strategy and policy successfully reasserted. That was an enviable record for one year of service. It was time to retire.

On 12 September Marshall casually announced his resignation effective that day to both his staff and the press. This time, it would be permanent. He was seventy years of age and desired nothing more than to be allowed, finally, to become a private citizen. Truman acquiesced, perhaps because he realized how much he had asked of Marshall and how much had been given, perhaps because Marshall's politicization at the hands of McCarthy and others negated some of the key reasons for having him as secretary of defense. And in the light of that politicization as well as a probable Republican victory in the 1952 presidential election, there was no chance Marshall would be recalled by the next administration. Ironically the McCarthy-Jenner assaults had finally guaranteed Marshall the retirement he had so desired since 1945.

Marshall's actions as secretary of defense were the final and most important assertions of the values and beliefs he had maintained in a lifetime of public service. Once again he had been asked to build a military force for overseas use after a period of unpreparedness, to plan for its appropriate employment so as to accomplish key goals of U.S. foreign policy, and to coordinate the civilian and military components of a war effort. Once again he had done so and in the process revealed his outstanding abilities as a soldier, administrator, and statesman. He had also, once again, reaffirmed the Europe-first strategy in U.S. national security policy, recognized the inseparability of military and political affairs and the real limits on U.S. power, and strongly defended the principle of civilian control over the military.

Inadvertently, however, Marshall had in the process helped to promote some of the very things he opposed. Lost amid the furor surrounding the Truman-MacArthur controversy was the fact that the Korean conflict militarized and globalized the cold war to an unprecedented degree and that it opened the door to an unlimited and disastrous overextension of U.S. power during the 1950s and 1960s. It was in the aftermath of Korea that the United States committed ground forces to NATO, recognized and decided to defend Chiang's regime on Formosa, and signed bilateral defense pacts with a host of Asian countries. It was also in the aftermath of Korea that the United States formally committed itself to the French military effort against the Vietminh in Indochina, a commitment that would lead to one of the longest and most divisive wars in U.S. history.

Linked to these problems were unresolved issues regarding the conduct of global military affairs in a democratic society. Marshall had played a pivotal role in reasserting the basic constitutional principle of civilian control over the military. In the process, however, the equally important constitutional principle of checks and balances had been violated by the waging of an undeclared executive war. A dangerous precedent for later executive usurpation of power was thereby reinforced, if not established. Moreover, the Truman-MacArthur controversy by no means found all the civilians on one side and all the soldiers on the other. To the contrary, MacArthur had been supported by numerous civilians in Congress and the Republican party while Truman had triumphed not because of any monopoly on civilian support but because the military establishment led by Marshall and the Joint Chiefs had supported him.

In effect, a global and militarized containment policy composed of a Europe-first strategy and a concept of limited executive war in the Far East, a strategy and policy supported by the civilian and military leaders of the executive branch of government and one political party, had triumphed over an Asia-first and unlimited war strategy and policy enunciated by a charismatic theater commander and the opposition party in the legislative branch. While the latter strategy and policy may have been a recipe for disaster, the former would prove quite destructive, domestically as well as internationally, in the ensuing decades. Despite

Marshall's beliefs and efforts, whether and how the United States could be a global power with military might abroad while maintaining its democratic system at home remained in 1951 unanswered questions.

They were no longer questions for Marshall to deal with, however. After fifty years of public service, he would leave them to others. His long-awaited retirement was finally at hand, and for the next seven years he would enjoy his gardening at Leesburg and his winter cottage in Pinehurst, North Carolina. The retirement was admittedly not total, for after declining Truman's offer to be reappointed head of the Red Cross he had agreed to become chairman of VMI's fund-raising organization and to accept Pershing's old position as chairman of the American Battle Monuments Commission. These were thoroughly apolitical and honorary assignments, however, and Marshall virtually disappeared from the political scene in late 1951 to, quite literally, tend his garden.

This did not mean his name dropped out of sight. To the contrary, Senator McCarthy made a point of keeping that name, as well as his own, in the limelight with his scurrilous attacks. Nor did Marshall's enormous influence come to an end. His civilian protégés Acheson and Lovett remained as secretaries of state and defense, respectively, and in 1952 his most notable military protégé won the Republican presidential nomination. If he had suggested this outcome ten years earlier, Eisenhower wrote to his former chief, Marshall would have had him locked up as dangerous.[28]

He might have also dismissed him as lacking in character had he known what Eisenhower would do, or rather retreat from doing, in the ensuing political campaign. Angered by McCarthy's outrageous attacks against his former chief, Eisenhower defended Marshall at a press conference in Denver and then decided to pay tribute to him while campaigning in McCarthy's home state of Wisconsin. He quickly changed his mind, however, when advisers and Republican politicians warned him that such a tribute was politically inexpedient. McCarthy thus sat on the stage with Eisenhower in Milwaukee while the Marshall tribute and defense was deleted from Ike's speech.[29]

Marshall never expressed any bitterness over the episode and probably understood it as one of those compromises that, while personally offensive, was inevitable in politics.[30] It was nevertheless a cowardly performance that outraged many people, including Mrs. Marshall and President Truman. It also haunted Eisenhower for the rest of his life, and in the ensuing years he did everything in his power to compensate for it. Marshall was invited to his swearing-in ceremony and to state dinners, and in 1953 he was appointed head of a distinguished commission to represent the United States at the coronation of Queen Elizabeth II of England. Eisenhower also insisted that Marshall have the presidential suite when he visited Walter Reed Hospital, and in 1964 Ike was one of the speakers at the dedication of the Marshall Library at VMI. Mrs. Marshall was appeased by these efforts and later told Marshall's biographer not to "attack President Eisenhower about the McCarthy thing; he did everything in the world to make it up to George and me."[31] He may very well have done so, but that could not and did not erase this stain on his reputation.

Probably more gratifying to Marshall than such personal touches were Eisenhower's actions as president, especially his retention of Marshall's key foreign policies. In the 1952 campaign the Republicans had attacked containment as defeatist and promised a more aggressive policy. After his victory, however, Eisenhower retained containment as the basic U.S. policy, as well as the asymmetrical version and the Europe-first approach that Marshall had championed. In this and other moves, Eisenhower effectively isolated the party extremists and returned control to the moderates with whom Marshall had helped to forge postwar U.S. foreign policy. With Eisenhower's indirect help, the Senate in 1954 censured and isolated McCarthy; three years later he was dead.[32]

Throughout the decade, honors continued to pour in on Marshall. The 1951 VMI celebration of the Battle of New Market was dedicated to him, and he joined George Washington and Stonewall Jackson in having an arch named in his honor. At Elizabeth II's 1953 coronation, the entire audience stood up as he walked to his seat, while Churchill, Alanbrooke, and Montgomery turned out of the ensuing procession to shake hands with him. In that same year, he was given one of the world's most prestigious awards—the Nobel Peace Prize—for the European Recovery Program. Typically he considered the prize "a tribute to the American people" rather than a personal award and in his acceptance speech once again emphasized the inseparability of peace, prosperity, and democracy.[33] As the memoirs of military and political leaders during the 1940s were published, the chorus of praise continued to grow.

Marshall continued to refuse to write any memoirs. He reportedly turned down a million-dollar contract for such a volume, and on the one occasion when he did agree to give an oral history interview to two officers working on the official JCS history, he insisted that his comments were not for attribution. In 1956–57 he relented slightly by agreeing to an official biographical project and to a series of interviews with biographer Forrest C. Pogue. At first he found those interviews uncomfortable. "I feel like I'm on a dissecting table having my liver removed," he complained. "If you don't give me answers to some of these questions about your youth, the Freudians will get you," Pogue warned in reply, after which Marshall laughed and began to speak freely.[34]

"It seems to me that as I grow older the birds fly faster," Marshall had confided to Bradley in 1948, and the retirement years flew by with increasing rapidity.[35] Inevitably they were punctuated by increasing health problems. Marshall had developed a bad cold and flu during the fall of 1953 and had carried this illness with him to the Nobel Prize ceremony in Norway. Upon his return, he remained bedridden until February and never fully recovered his strength. In January 1959, soon after his seventy-eighth birthday, he suffered a crippling stroke and was confined to a wheelchair in Walter Reed Hospital. Brain spasms that followed took away his sight, hearing, speech, and memory and reduced him to a shell of a human being kept alive only by machines. When Churchill paid a visit to him and the terminally ill John Foster Dulles, he left Marshall's room in tears. On the evening of 16 October 1959, the agony ended.[36]

Typically Marshall had forbade the massive type of state funeral that Pershing had had and MacArthur would have. He gave explicit orders that there was to be no ceremony in the National Cathedral, no lying in state in the Capital Rotunda, no huge invitation list, no funeral eulogy, and no long list of honorary pallbearers. Mrs. Marshall altered this slightly by having his unopened coffin rest overnight at the National Cathedral and by adding a few honorary pallbearers, but the brief funeral service itself on the following day was at the Fort Myer Chapel as he had wished. Presidents Truman and Eisenhower sat next to each other and across from the family. Following the brief service, the casket was taken to the site in Arlington National Cemetery chosen by Marshall years before, next to the graves of Lily and her mother. The traditional rifle volleys and taps followed, and the coffin was lowered into the ground.

The final farewells had thus been paid to the man who had played so prominent a role in America's rise to world power and whose selfless service inspired comparison with only one other soldier in U.S history. Like Washington, Marshall had provided a model of such service for the Republic as well as policies and advice that had been critically important to its survival and growth.[37] Indeed, under Marshall's guidance the United States by mid-twentieth century had fulfilled many of Washington's prophecies and had become the greatest power the world had ever seen.

Appropriate use of that power, however, required understanding of its nature, its limits, and its relationship to the most cherished of American values. Marshall recognized this, a fact illustrated by his linkage of economic with military factors, his emphasis on Europe over Asia, his acceptance of limited as well as unlimited war, and his support for citizen-soldiers and civilian control of the military. On occasion he had admittedly fallen victim to the oversimplifications and visions of omnipotence that often accompany power. Overall, however, most of his beliefs, actions, and legacies emphasized realistic limits—the domestic as well as international limits on the power he had done so much to create. Whether those legacies would survive and his advice be heeded now lay in the hands of his successors.

CHRONOLOGY

31 December 1880	George Catlett Marshall, Jr., born, Uniontown, Pennsylvania.
September 1897–June 1901	Cadet at Virginia Military Institute (VMI), Lexington, Virginia.
September–December 1901	Commandant, Danville Military Institute, Danville, Virginia.
2 February 1902	Commissioned second lieutenant of infantry, U.S. Army.
11 February 1902	Marries Elizabeth C. Coles.
May 1902–November 1903	Duty in Philippines.
December 1903–August 1906	Duty at Fort Reno, Oklahoma.
August 1906	Student, Army Infantry and Cavalry School and Staff College, Fort Leavenworth, Kansas.
March 1907	Promoted to first lieutenant.
June 1908	Appointed instructor, Army Service Schools and Staff College.
June 1911	Inspector-instructor, Massachusetts Volunteer Militia, Boston.
September 1912–June 1913	Duty with Fourth Infantry Regiment, Fort Logan Roots, Arkansas; Fort Snelling, Minnesota; Texas City, Texas.
August 1913–May 1916	Duty in the Philippines; aide de camp to Major General Hunter Liggett.

July 1916	Appointed aide de camp to Major General J. Franklin Bell, San Francisco and New York City.
October 1916	Promoted to captain.
April 1917	United States enters World War I.
June 1917–November 1918	Duty with AEF, France; assistant chief of staff, G-3, First Division; G-3, GHQ; assistant chief of staff, G-3, First Army; temporary promotions to major, lieutenant colonel, and colonel.
November 1918–April 1919	Armistice; chief of staff, Eighth Corps; G-3 duty, GHQ, AEF, France.
May 1919	Appointed aide de camp to General John J. Pershing, France, and Washington, D.C.
July 1920	Promoted to major (permanent).
August 1923	Promoted to lieutenant colonel.
September 1924–May 1927	Duty with Fifteenth Infantry Regiment, Tientsin, China.
July 1927	Duty as instructor, Army War College, Washington, D.C.
15 September 1927	Elizabeth Coles Marshall dies.
October 1927	Appointed assistant commandant, Infantry School, Fort Benning, Georgia.
October 1929	Stock market crash; Great Depression begins.
15 October 1930	Marries Katherine Tupper Brown.
June 1932	Appointed commander, Fort Screven, Georgia, and CCC District F.
June 1933	Appointed commander, Fort Moultrie, South Carolina, and CCC District I.
September 1933	Promoted to colonel.
October 1933	Appointed senior instructor, Illinois National Guard, Chicago.
October 1936	Promoted to brigadier general and appointed commander, Fifth Brigade of Third Division and CCC District, Vancouver Barracks, Washington.

July 1938	Appointed assistant chief of staff, War Plans Division, War Department, Washington, D.C.
October 1938	Appointed deputy chief of staff; Munich crisis.
April 1939	Chosen by Franklin D. Roosevelt as next chief of staff.
1 July 1939	Appointed acting chief of staff.
1 September 1939	Promotion to permanent major general and temporary general on being sworn in as chief of staff; Hitler invades Poland; World War II begins.
April–July 1940	Germany conquers Denmark, Norway, Holland, Belgium, Luxembourg, and France; British evacuate at Dunkirk; Battle of Britain; Roosevelt forms bipartisan cabinet; first billion-dollar defense bills.
September 1940	First peacetime draft; destroyer-bases deal with England; Japan moves into Indochina and signs Tripartite Pact with Germany and Italy; U.S. trade embargo expanded.
November 1940	Roosevelt reelected to third term.
January–April 1941	Lend-Lease, ABC talks, ABC-1, and Rainbow 5.
April–July 1941	Germany invades Balkans and Soviet Union; United States sends troops to Greenland and Iceland and freezes Japanese assets.
August–November 1941	Atlantic Conference; Louisiana maneuvers; undeclared naval war in Atlantic.
7–12 December 1941	Japanese attack Pearl Harbor; U.S. declaration of war; German-Italian-U.S. declarations of war.
December 1941–January 1942	Arcadia Conference and formation of Grand Alliance.
February–July 1942	Axis high tide; Allied strategic debates; U.S. naval victory at Midway.
August–November 1942	Stalingrad, El Alamein, North African, and New Guinea-Guadalcanal counteroffensives.

January 1943	Casablanca Conference and unconditional surrender announcement.
May–September 1943	Trident, Algiers, and Quadrant conferences; invasion of Sicily and Italy; Italy surrenders; Battle of Kursk.
October–December 1943	Moscow-Cairo-Tehran conferences; Overlord reaffirmed with Eisenhower as commander; dual Pacific advance begins.
January 1944	Selected *Time's* Man of the Year.
May 1944	Stepson Allen Tupper Brown dies in Italy.
June 1944	Rome captured; Overlord launched; Marianas islands taken; Battle of Philippine Sea.
July–August 1944	Normandy breakout: Anvil-Dragoon invasion of southern France; Paris liberated.
September 1944	Octagon Conference; Allied European offensive halted.
October 1944	Stilwell recalled from China; invasion of Philippines; Battle of Leyte Gulf.
November 1944	Field Marshal Sir John Dill dies.
December 1944	Appointed general of the army with five stars; German Ardennes offensive.
February 1945	Yalta Conference.
March–April 1945	Conquest of Germany; Soviet-American friction; Iwo Jima invaded; Roosevelt dies.
May 1945	Germany surrenders.
June–September 1945	Okinawa invaded; Potsdam Conference; atomic bomb and Japanese surrender.
November 1945	Retires as chief of staff and is appointed special presidential emissary to China.
January 1947	Recalled from China and appointed secretary of state.
March–April 1947	Moscow Foreign Ministers Conference; Truman Doctrine.
June 1947	Marshall Plan speech at Harvard.
July–September 1947	Wedemeyer mission and report; containment article; Rio Conference and pact; National Security Act.

October–December 1947	European Emergency Aid Bill; last foreign ministers' meeting in London.
January 1948	Second selection as *Time*'s Man of the Year.
February–March 1948	Czech coup; Congress passes European Recovery Program and draft.
March–June 1948	Bogotá Conference and OAS; Brussels Pact; Vandenberg Resolution; Berlin blockade begins.
July–December 1948	Berlin airlift and counterblockade; NATO negotiations; West German constituent assembly meets.
December 1948–January 1949	Undergoes surgery for removal of kidney and resigns as secretary of state.
1949	Appointed head of American Red Cross; Chiang flees China mainland; China White Paper; Soviet atomic bomb.
January 1950	Acheson's defense perimeter speech.
April 1950	NSC-68.
June 1950	Korean War begins.
September 1950	Appointed secretary of defense; MacArthur victories in Korea.
October–December 1950	Thirty-eighth parallel crossed; Chinese intervention and U.S. retreat.
January–March 1951	Decision to limit Korean war objectives to south of thirty-eighth parallel; MacArthur objects.
April–June 1951	Truman relieves MacArthur; Senate hearings; McCarthy's attack on Marshall.
September 1951	Resigns as secretary of defense and retires.
November 1952	Eisenhower elected president.
December 1953	Awarded Nobel Peace Prize.
1954	Senate censures McCarthy.
16 October 1959	Dies at Walter Reed Army Hospital.

NOTES AND REFERENCES

CHAPTER 1

1. Forrest C. Pogue, *George C. Marshall: Statesman, 1945-1959* (New York: Viking Press, 1987), 505–6; CBS, "The General," 1976 television documentary in the American Parade series, George C. Marshall Research Library, Lexington, Va.

2. *George C. Marshall Interviews and Reminiscences for Forrest C. Pogue: Transcripts and Notes, 1956–1957* (Lexington, Va.: Marshall Research Foundation, 1986), 21, 28 February 1957 interviews, 1–68. All of these interviews were conducted by Dr. Pogue.

3. Ibid.

4. Ibid., 22.

5. Ibid., 6 March 1957, 84–85; Robert Payne, *The Marshall Story: A Biography of General George C. Marshall* (New York: Prentice-Hall, 1951), 9.

6. *Marshall Interviews*, 28 February 1957, 51–52; Forrest C. Pogue, *George C. Marshall: Education of a General* (New York: Viking Press, 1963), 35.

7. Larry I. Bland, ed., *The Papers of George Catlett Marshall*, Vol. 1: "*The Soldierly Spirit," December 1880–June 1939* (Baltimore: Johns Hopkins University Press, 1981), 5; Pogue, *Marshall: Education*, 27–28; William Frye, *Marshall: Citizen Soldier* (Indianapolis: Bobbs-Merrill, 1946), 26, 32.

8. Pogue, *Marshall: Education*, 23–24, 28–30; *Marshall Interviews*, 28 February 1957, 42–53.

9. Pogue, *Marshall: Education*, 19.

10. Ibid., 19, 24–25; Frye, *Marshall*, 26, 32–34; *Marshall Interviews*, 21, 28 February 1957, 4, 54.

11. Frye, *Marshall*, 32.

12. Edward M. Coffman, *The Old Army: A Portrait of the American Army in Peacetime* (New York: Oxford University Press, 1986), 328–404.

13. *Marshall Interviews*, 6 March 1957, 69; Pogue, *Marshall: Education*, 39–40; Bland, *Marshall Papers*, 1:7.

14. *Marshall Interviews*, 21 February 1957, 21.

15. Payne, *Marshall Story*, 17.

16. Ibid., 20.

17. *Marshall Interviews*, 6 March 1957, 77–78; Major H. A. DeWeerd, ed., *Selected Speeches and Statements by General of the Army George C. Marshall* (Washington, D.C.: Infantry Journal, 1945), 54–56.

18. *Marshall Interviews*, 6 March 1957, 71, 74; Pogue, *Marshall: Education*, 55–57.

19. Bland, *Marshall Papers*, 1:8–9.

20. Ibid.

21. Ibid., 10.

22. Ibid., 10–11; Pogue, *Marshall: Education*, 62–64; *Marshall Interviews*, 28 February 1957, 66–67.

23. Bland, *Marshall Papers*, 1:10–11, 16; Pogue, *Marshall: Education*, 63–66.

24. Bland, *Marshall Papers*, 1:17–19; Pogue, *Marshall: Education*, 66.

CHAPTER 2

1. *Marshall Interviews*, 13 March 1957, 100–101.

2. Ibid., 101–4: Pogue, *Marshall: Education*, 71–76.

3. Frye, *Marshall*, 75; Pogue, *Marshall: Education*, 77–80; *Marshall Interviews*, 13 March 1957, 111, 121.

4. Pogue, *Marshall: Education*, 77–78; *Marshall Interviews*, 13 March 1957, 119–20.

5. *Marshall Interviews*, 13 March 1957, 123; Pogue, *Marshall: Education*, 89.

6. See Coffman, *The Old Army*.

7. Stephen E. Ambrose, *Upton and the Army* (Baton Rouge: Louisiana State University Press, 1964); Russell F. Weigley, *Towards an American Army: Military Thought from Washington to Marshall* (Westport, Conn.: Greenwood Press, 1962), 100–26, 137–61.

8. Otto L. Nelson, Jr., *National Security and the General Staff* (Washington, D.C.: Infantry Journal Press, 1946), 1–2; Walter Millis, *Arms and Men: A Study in American Military History* (New York: G. P. Putnam's Sons, 1956), 131–210.

9. James L. Abrahamson, *America Arms for a New Century: The Making of a Great Military Power* (New York: Free Press, 1981), 29–60, 105–27, 187–91.

10. Pogue, *Marshall: Education,* 93; Timothy K. Nenninger, *The Leaven-worth Schools and the Old Army: Education, Professionalism, and the Officer Corps of the United States Army, 1881–1918* (Westport, Conn.: Greenwood Press, 1978), 3–8, 34–74, 157.

11. *Marshall Interviews,* 4 April 1957, 134–35.

12. Ibid., 130–38; Bland, *Marshall Papers,* 1:45.

13. Nenninger, *Leavenworth,* 83–99, 129; Frye, *Marshall,* 88.

14. *Marshall Interviews,* 4 April 1957, 138–39; Pogue, *Marshall: Education,* 100.

15. Pogue, *Marshall: Education,* 100–101; *Marshall Interviews,* 4 April 1957, 138.

16. Copy of presentation in George C. Marshall Papers, Pentagon Office File, box 110, folder 5, Marshall Library.

17. Samuel P. Huntington, *The Soldier and the State: The Theory and Politics of Civil-Military Relations* (New York: Random House, 1957), 143–269.

18. John P. Mallan, "Roosevelt, Brooks Adams, and Lea: The Warrior Critique of the Business Civilization," *American Quarterly* 8 (1956): 216–30; William James, "The Moral Equivalent of War," in *Essays on Faith and Morals,* ed. Ralph Barton Perry (Cleveland: World Publishing Co., 1962), 311–28.

19. Frye, *Marshall,* 89, 96.

20. Pogue, *Marshall: Education,* 102–3, 107–8, 115–16.

21. Bland, *Marshall Papers,* 1:74–75.

22. Ibid., 1:76–84.

23. Ibid., 1:92–93; Frye, *Marshall,* 106–11; Pogue, *Marshall: Education,* 120–23; Henry H. Arnold, *Global Mission* (New York: Harper and Brothers, 1949), 44.

24. Bland, *Marshall Papers,* 1:103–4. See also Frye, *Marshall,* 117–20.

25. Bland, *Marshall Papers,* 1:80, and Vol. 2: *"We Cannot Delay,"July 1, 1939–December 6, 1941* (1986), 31–32; Pogue *Marshall: Education,* 124–26.

26. *Marshall Interviews,* 5 April 1957, 193.

27. Bland, *Marshall Papers,* 1:93–95.

28. Ibid., 96.

CHAPTER 3

1. Quotation from Jefferson's 1801 presidential inaugural address in Adrienne Koch and William Peden, eds., *The Life and Selected Writings of Thomas Jefferson* (New York: Modern Library, 1944), 323.

2. Bland, *Marshall Papers,* 1:97; *Marshall Interviews,* 4 April 1957, 155–56; Pogue, *Marshall: Education,* 135–38.

3. George C. Marshall, *Memoirs of My Services in the World War, 1917–1918* (Boston: Houghton Mifflin, 1976), 1–2.

4. Pogue, *Marshall: Education*, 143–46.

5. Ibid., 147; *Marshall Interviews*, 5 April 1957, 168–70; Marshall, *Memoirs*, 7–13; Bland, *Marshall Papers*, 1:646–47, 2:86.

6. *Marshall Interviews*, 4 April 1957, 175–76; Bland, *Marshall Papers*, 1:121–22.

7. *Marshall Interviews*, 4 April 1957, 189; Allan R. Millett, *The General: Robert L. Bullard and Officership in the United States Army, 1881–1925* (Westport, Conn.: Greenwood Press, 1975), 333–34.

8. Bland, *Marshall Papers*, 1:140–41, 144: *Marshall Interviews*, 5 April 1957, 191–93.

9. Payne, *Marshall Story*, 74.

10. Marshall, *Memoirs*, 137–39; *Marshall Interviews*, 11 April 1957, 200.

11. Marshall, *Memoirs*, 149–59; Frye, *Marshall*, 158–59; Pogue, *Marshall: Education*, 161, 174–79.

12. Frye, *Marshall*, 160. See also Pogue, *Marshall: Education*, 179; Payne, *Marshall Story*, 81.

13. Pogue, *Marshall: Education*, 189.

14. Dwight D. Eisenhower, *At Ease: Stories I Tell to Friends* (New York: Doubleday, 1967), 192.

15. *Marshall Interviews* 5 April 1957, 193; Pogue, *Marshall: Education*, 197.

16. Frank E. Vandiver, *Black Jack: The Life and Times of John J. Pershing* (College Station: Texas A&M University Press, 1977), 2:783.

17. *Marshall Interviews*, 6 March 1957, 89–90.

18. Ibid., 88.

19. Pogue, *Marshall: Education*, 314; Bland *Marshall Papers*, 1:259–60.

20. Frye, *Marshall*, 181; Marshall, *Memoirs*, 167, 180.

21. Frye, *Marshall*, 174–79; Weigley, *Towards an American Army*, 226–39; Abrahamson, *America Arms for a New Century*, 181–82; I. B. Holley, Jr., *General John M. Palmer, Citizen Soldiers, and the Army of a Democracy* (Westport, Conn.: Greenwood Press, 1982), 402–63.

22. *Marshall Interviews*, 11 April 1957, 225; Pogue, *Marshall: Education*, 208–9.

23. *Marshall Interviews*, 11 April 1957, 225; Pogue, *Marshall: Education*, 207–8; Bland, *Marshall Papers*, 1:xiii–xiv; Marshall, *Memoirs*, viii.

24. *Marshall Interviews*, 11 April 1957, 228–29.

25. Pogue, *Marshall: Education*, 218–19, 223–24; Vandiver, *Black Jack*, 2:1064.

26. Rose Page Wilson, *General Marshall Remembered* (Englewood Cliffs, N.J.: Prentice-Hall, 1968), 1–133.

27. Bland, *Marshall Papers*, 1:235.

CHAPTER 4

1. Bland, *Marshall Papers*, 1:238.

2. John Braeman, "Power and Diplomacy: The 1920's Reappraised," *Review of Politics* 44 (July 1982): 342–69.

3. Bland, *Marshall Papers*, 1:241; *Marshall Interviews*, 11 April 1957, 230.

4. Bland, *Marshall Papers*, 1:263–64, 270; Pogue, *Marshall: Education*, 1:239–40.

5. Bland, *Marshall Papers*, 1:264–65, 271–72, 277, 294.

6. Ibid, 1:277, 299.

7. Ibid., 1:383.

8. Pogue, *Marshall: Education*, 246; oral history interview with Frank B. Hayne, June 17, 1975, Marshall Papers, box 109.

9. Wilson, *Marshall Remembered*, 159.

10. Bland, *Marshall Papers*, 1:315.

11. Ibid.

12. Ibid., 1:383.

13. Frye, *Marshall*, 210. See also Bland, *Marshall Papers*, 1:334–38, 409–13.

14. Pogue, *Marshall: Education*, 248–59; Bland, *Marshall Papers*, 1:409–15.

15. Wilson, *Marshall Remembered*, 171–84; Pogue, *Marshall: Education*, 261–63; Frye, *Marshall*, 190–91, 208; Payne, *Marshall Story*, 103.

16. Katherine Tupper Marshall, *Together: Annals of an Army Wife* (New York: Tupper and Love, 1946), 2–3; Pogue, *Marshall: Education*, 263–68.

17. Marshall, *Together*, 3–9.

18. Ibid., 12.

19. Bland, *Marshall Papers*, 1:241.

20. Pogue, *Marshall: Education*, 274–79.

21. Ibid., 280, 308; Marshall, *Together*, 13.

22. Bland, *Marshall Papers*, 1:393, 398, 423; Pogue, *Marshall: Education*, 308–11.

23. Bland, *Marshall Papers*, 1:398–99; Pogue, *Marshall: Education*, 282.

24. Marshall, *Together*, 18.

25. Ibid., 18–19; Pogue, *Marshall: Education*, 281; Frye, *Marshall*, 230; Bland, *Marshall Papers*, 1:462–65, 491.

26. Pogue, *Marshall: Education*, 307–8.

27. Bland, *Marshall Papers*, 1:446–47.

28. Ibid., 445–47, 468, 474–75, 481–82, 492, 507–9; Pogue, *Marshall: Education*, 294–98.

29. Marshall, *Together*, 24; Bland, *Marshall Papers*, 1:548.

30. Pogue, *Marshall: Education*, 303–8.

31. Ibid., 302.

32. Frye, *Marshall*, 243; Payne, *Marshall Story*, 110.
33. Marshall, *Together*, 1; Bland, *Marshall Papers*, 1:598.
34. Pogue, *Marshall: Education*, 314–15; Frye, *Marshall*, 246–48.
35. Marshall, *Together*, 41.
36. *Marshall Interviews*, 6 March 1957, 86–87.
37. Ibid.
38. Robert E. Sherwood, *Roosevelt and Hopkins: An Intimate History*, rev. ed. (New York: Grosset & Dunlap), 11, 76, 100–101.
39. Pogue, *Marshall: Education*, 326–29, 408, n. 24; Bland, *Marshall Papers*, 1:641–42.
40. Pogue, *Marshall: Education*, 330.
41. Ibid., 319–20, 338–47.

CHAPTER 5

1. Bland, *Marshall Papers*, 2:47, 59.
2. House Appropriations Committee, *Emergency Supplemental Appropriation Bill for 1940, Hearings* on H.R. 7805, 76th Cong., 3d sess., 29 November 1939, 21.
3. Pogue, *Marshall: Education*, 336–37; Bland, *Marshall Papers*, 1: 654–55, 680, 2:52–54.
4. Draft of speech accepting honorary doctor of science degree from Washington and Jefferson College, 14 October 1939, Marshall Papers, Pentagon Office File, box 110, folder 42; Bland, *Marshall Papers*, 2:110–12, 123–27, 163–64. See also DeWeerd, *Selected Speeches*, 27–34.
5. Bland, *Marshall Papers*, 2:188–90; Forrest C. Pogue, *George C. Marshall: Ordeal and Hope, 1939–1942* (New York: Viking Press, 1966), 16–18, 26–28; Bernard Baruch, *Baruch: The Public Years* (New York: Holt, Rinehart and Winston, 1960), 278; *Marshall Interviews*, 29 October 1956, 574.
6. John Morton Blum, *From The Morgenthau Diaries, Vol. 2: Years of Urgency, 1938–1941* (Boston: Houghton Mifflin, 1965), 138–41.
7. Ibid., 141–44; *Marshall Interviews*, 15 November 1956, 302; 20 February 1957, 480–82; Bland, *Marshall Papers*, 2:231.
8. Bland, *Marshall Papers*, 1:322, 343; Pogue, *Marshall: Ordeal and Hope*, 39–45; Henry L. Stimson and McGeorge Bundy, *On Active Service in Peace and War* (New York: Harper & Brothers, 1947), 330–31.
9. *Marshall Interviews*, 15 January 1957, 259; 11 February 1957, 385; 15 February 1957, 440–41; 13 November 1956, 584–86; Pogue, *Marshall: Education*, 324; Frye, *Marshall*, 310.
10. *Marshall Interviews*, 29 October 1956, 575; Pogue, *Marshall: Ordeal and Hope*, 22.
11. J. Garry Clifford and Samuel R. Spencer, *The First Peacetime Draft* (Lawrence: University Press of Kansas, 1986), 10–11.

12. Pogue, *Marshall: Ordeal and Hope*, 23–24, 34; *Marshall Interviews*, 22 January 1957, 271–74; Blum, *From the Morgenthau Diaries*, 2:150; David G. Haglund, "George C. Marshall and the Question of Military Aid to England, May–June, 1940," *Journal of Contemporary History* 15 (October 1980): 745–60.

13. Mark S. Watson, *Chief of Staff: Prewar Plans and Preparations*, in U.S. Army, *U.S. Army in World War II* (Washington, D.C.: Government Printing Office, 1950), 312; Haglund, "Marshall," 746–47; Pogue, *Marshall: Ordeal and Hope*, 48–53, 64–66; Bland, *Marshall Papers*, 2:237–38, 245–47, 261–62; Blum, *From the Morgenthau Diaries*, 2:162–63.

14. Pogue, *Marshall: Ordeal and Hope*, 64–66; Bland, *Marshall Papers*, 261–62, 348–49; *Marshall Interviews*, 7 December 1957, 241–42; 15 January 1957, 264.

15. Bland, *Marshall Papers*, 2:262–64, 274, 308–13, 323, 355–59. See also DeWeerd, *Selected Speeches*, 60–89, 107; Pogue, *Marshall: Ordeal and Hope*, 56–61; *Marshall Interviews*, 22 January 1957, 276; Clifford, *The First Peacetime Draft*, 48–52, 109–12.

16. Bland, *Marshall Papers*, 2:214–18, 228–30, 704–5; *Marshall Interviews*, 22 January 1957, 271–74; 28 September, 1956, 547.

17. *Marshall Interviews*, 15 November 1956, 303; 7 December 1956, 241–422; 14 February 1957, 399, 408.

18. Eric Larrabee, *Commander in Chief: Franklin Delano Roosevelt, His Lieutenants, and Their War* (New York: Harper & Row, 1987), 98.

19. Forrest C. Pogue, *George C. Marshall: Organizer of Victory, 1943–1945* (New York: Viking Press, 1973), 131–32.

20. Ibid., 131; Bland, *Marshall Papers*, 2:197, 247–49. See also DeWeerd, *Selected Speeches*, 78; Pogue, *Marshall: Ordeal and Hope*, 32–33, 60.

21. Bland, *Marshall Papers*, 2:611; Paul M. Robinett Diary, 30 January 1941, Marshall Library.

22. Frye, *Marshall*, 258.

23. Bland, *Marshall Papers*, 2:395–96, 435–37; *Marshall Interviews*, 22 January 1957, 290.

24. Louis Morton, "Germany First: The Basic Concept of Allied Strategy in World War II," in Kent R. Greenfield, ed., *Command Decisons* (Washington, D.C.: Government Printing Office, 1960), 11.

25. Maurice Matloff and Edwin M. Snell, *Strategic Planning for Coalition Warfare, 1941–1942*, in *U.S. Army in World War II* (1953), 29–30. See also Stetson Conn and Byron Fairchild, *The Framework of Hemispheric Defense* in *U.S. Army in World War II* (1960), and David G. Haglund, *Latin America and the Transformation of U.S. Strategic Thought, 1936–1940* (Albuquerque: University of New Mexico Press, 1984).

26. Watson, *Chief of Staff*, 388–91; Pogue, *Marshall: Ordeal and Hope*, 121–34; Robinett Diary, 16 April 1941.

27. Theodore A. Wilson, *The First Summit: Roosevelt and Churchill at Placentia Bay, 1941* (Boston: Houghton Mifflin, 1969).

28. Watson, *Chief of Staff*, 331–66; Sherwood, *Roosevelt and Hopkins*, 410–18; Albert C. Wedemeyer, *Wedemeyer Reports!* (New York: Henry Holt, 1958), 63–76; Keith E. Eiler, *Wedemeyer on War and Peace* (Stanford, Calif.: Hoover Institution Press, 1987), 10–26.

29. Bland, *Marshall Papers*, 2:705–6.

30. Ibid., 2:572, 588, 591–92; DeWeerd, *Selected Speeches*, 126–67; Payne, *Marshall Story*, 129, 131; Pogue, *Marshall: Ordeal and Hope*, 147–56.

31. Bland, *Marshall Papers*, 2:695–96. See also Pogue, *Marshall: Ordeal and Hope*, 91–101; Larrabee, *Commander in Chief*, 100–102, 116–20; Watson, *Chief of Staff*, 241–69.

32. Pogue, *Marshall: Ordeal and Hope*, 72–79; Bland, *Marshall Papers*, 2:567–70, 581–82, 613–14; Henry L. Stimson Diary, 25, 26 September, 6, 7 October 1941, Stimson Papers, Sterling Library, Yale University, New Haven, Conn.

33. Stimson and Bundy, *On Active Service*, 389.

34. Watson, *Chief of Staff*, 108–9, 434–52, 494–512.

35. Robinett Diary, 21 June 1941; Bland, *Marshall Papers*, 2:627.

36. Quotations from Robinett Diary, 11 April 1941, and Bland, *Marshall Papers*, 2:59, 323. See also Marshall, *Together*, 57–58, 67–68; Pogue, *Marshall: Ordeal and Hope*, 11, 14; Robinett Diary, 5 January 1941; Bland, *Marshall Papers*, 2:275–76.

37. Pogue, *Marshall: Ordeal and Hope*, 12–13; Robinett Diary, 5 January 1941; Marshall, *Together*, 64, 76, 80–84, 114, 118.

38. Bland, *Marshall Papers*, 2:688, 694–95.

39. Marshall, *Together*, 99.

40. Pogue, *Marshall: Ordeal and Hope*, 212, 429–35. See also Gordon Prange et al., *At Dawn We Slept: The Untold Story of Pearl Harbor* and *Pearl Harbor: The Verdict of History* (New York: McGraw-Hill, 1981, 1986); Roberta Wohlstetter, *Pearl Harbor: Warning and Decision* (Stanford: Stanford University Press, 1962); and Martin J. Melosi, *The Shadow of Pearl Harbor: Political Controversy over the Surprise Attack, 1941–1946* (College Station: Texas A&M University Press, 1977).

41. See John Toland, *Infamy: Pearl Harbor and Its Aftermath* (Garden City, N.Y.: Doubleday, 1982); Edwin T. Layton with Roger Pineau and John Costello, *"And I Was There": Pearl Harbor and Midway—Breaking the Secrets* (New York: William Morrow, 1985); Frank P. Mintz, *Revisionism and the Origins of Pearl Harbor* (Lanham, Md: University Press of America, 1985).

42. See sources cited in note 40.

CHAPTER 6

1. Bland, *Marshall Papers*, 2:6–7.

2. *Marshall Interviews*, 21 November 1956, 328; Pogue, *Marshall: Ordeal and Hope*, 280.

3. *Marshall Interviews*, 14 February 1957, 395–97.

4. Larrabee, *Commander in Chief*, 142–43; Ray S. Cline, *Washington Command Post: The Operations Division*, in *U.S. Army in World War II* (1951); Pogue, *Marshall: Ordeal and Hope*, 289–96.

5. Robinett Diary, 29 December 1941.

6. See chapter 5, 82–84.

7. Richard W. Steele, *The First Offensive, 1942: Roosevelt, Marshall and the Making of American Strategy* (Bloomington, Indiana: Indiana University Press, 1973), pp. 76–80; *Marshall Interviews*, 11 February, 1957, 379–80; Alex Danchev, *Very Special Relationship: Field-Marshal Sir John Dill and the Anglo-American Alliance, 1941–44* (London: Pergamon Press, 1986), 18, 56.

8. Thomas B. Buell, *Master of Seapower: A Biography of Fleet Admiral Ernest J. King* (Boston: Little, Brown, 1980), 503–5. See also Matloff and Snell, *Strategic Planning*, 147–156.

9. Stimson Diary, 5–8, 20, 25 March, 1942.

10. Matloff and Snell, *Strategic Planning*, 177–87, 383; J. R. M. Butler and J. M. A. Gwyer, *Grand Strategy, III*, United Kingdom Military Series, J. R. M. Butler, ser. ed., *History of the Second World War* (London: Her Majesty's Stationery Office, 1964), 675–81.

11. Arthur Bryant, *The Turn of the Tide: A History of the War Years Based on the Diaries of Field Marshal Lord Alanbrooke, Chief of the Imperial General Staff* (Garden City, N.Y.: Doubleday, 1957), 285–90.

12. Warren F. Kimball, ed., *Churchill & Roosevelt: The Complete Correspondence* (Princeton: Princeton University Press, 1984), 1:494; Sherwood, *Roosevelt and Hopkins*, 577.

13. U.S. Department of State, *Foreign Relations of the United States: The Conferences at Washington, 1941–1942, and Casablanca, 1943* (Washington, D.C.: Government Printing Office, 1968), 433–36. Hereafter cited as *Foreign Relations* with subtitle and/or year and volume.

14. Kimball, *Churchill & Roosevelt*, 1:520.

15. Stimson Diary, 10 July 1942; Matloff and Snell, *Strategic Planning*, 269.

16. Roosevelt to Marshall, 10–14 July 1942, John L. McCrea Papers, Franklin D. Roosevelt Library, Hyde Park, N.Y.; Matloff and Snell, *Strategic Planning*, 272; Sherwood, *Roosevelt and Hopkins*, 603–5.

17. Marshall to King, memorandum, 15 July 1942, WDCSA 381 War Plans, Folder 1, Record Group 165, National Archives, Washington, D.C.

18. Ibid.; Sherwood, *Roosevelt and Hopkins*, 602–12.

19. *Marshall Interviews*, 5 October, 1956, 557; 13 November 1956, 586.

20. *Foreign Relations: Washington and Casablanca*, 509, 791–98; Wedemeyer, *Wedemeyer Reports!* 192.

21. Mark A. Stoler, *The Politics of the Second Front: American Military Planning and Diplomacy in Coalition Warfare, 1941–1943* (Westport, Conn.: Greenwood Press, 1977), 85–91, 102–6, 116–23.

22. Marshall interview with Col. L. M. Guyer, USAF, and Col. H. C. Donnelly, JCS Historical Section, 11 February 1949, Marshall Papers, Oral History Collection.

23. Sir John Slessor, *The Central Blue: Recollections and Reflections* (London: Cassell, 1956), 358; *Marshall Interviews*, 5 October 1956, 563.

24. JCS 79th meeting, minutes, 10 May 1943, CCS 334 (3-29-43), Record Group 218, National Archives.

25. *Foreign Relations: The Conferences at Washington and Quebec 1943* (1970), 44, 346–63.

26. Stimson Diary, 17, 25, 27 May, 8 June 1943; Bryant, *Turn of the Tide*, 513; Sir Charles Wilson, *Churchill: Taken from the Diaries of Lord Moran: The Struggle for Survival, 1940–1965* (Boston: Houghton Mifflin, 1966), 104; Maurice Matloff, *Strategic Planning for Coalition Warfare, 1943-1944*, in *U.S. Army in World War II* (1959), 152–55.

27. Todd to Assistant Chief of Staff, OPD, memorandum, "Special JCS Meeting of July 26, 1943," OPD Exec. 5, item 11, paper 2, Record Group 165, National Archives; Stimson and Bundy, *On Active Service*, 429–39.

28. *Foreign Relations: Washington and Quebec*, 891, 1024–25, 1037–39, 1121–32; Bryant, *Turn of the Tide*, 574–84; Robert Beitzell, *The Uneasy Alliance: America, Britain and Russia, 1941–1943* (New York: Alfred A. Knopf, 1972), 111–49.

29. *Marshall Interviews*, 29 October 1956, 586. See also Keith Sainsbury, *The Turning Point: Roosevelt, Stalin, Churchill and Chiang Kai-shek, 1943—the Moscow, Cairo and Teheran Conferences* (New York: Oxford University Press, 1985), 123–216.

30. *Foreign Relations: The Conferences at Cairo and Tehran, 1943* (1961), 195, 248–53, 259–60, 477–82, 487–508.

31. Ibid., 487–508, 515–28, 533–52, 565, 576–79, 587, 652. See also Sainsbury, *Turning Point*, 217–80; Beitzell, *Uneasy Alliance*, 303–41; Keith Eubank, *Summit At Teheran* (New York: William Morrow, 1985), 251–348; Paul D. Mayle, *Eureka Summit: Agreement in Principle, and the Big Three at Teheran, 1943* (Newark: University of Delaware Press, 1987).

32. Handwritten Marshall notes, Marshall Papers, Pentagon Office File, box 56, folder 14.

33. Winston S. Churchill, *The Second World War*, vol. 4: *The Hinge of Fate* (Boston: Houghton Mifflin, 1950), 813.

34. Quotation from Elliot Roosevelt, ed., *F.D.R.: His Personal Letters*,

1928–1945 (New York: Duell, Sloan and Pearce, 1950), 2:144–45. See also Pogue, *Marshall: Organizer of Victory*, 262–78.

35. Sherwood, *Roosevelt and Hopkins*, 803.

CHAPTER 7

1. William D. Hassett, *Off the Record with F.D.R., 1942–1945* (New Brunswick: Rutgers University Press, 1958), 249.

2. *Time*, 43 (3 January 1944): 15–18.

3. Marshall, *Together*, 110.

4. Bland, *Marshall Papers*, 2:387–88, 616.

5. Pogue, *Marshall: Ordeal and Hope*, 427. See also Pogue, *Marshall: Organizer of Victory*, 365–66, 483–84; *Marshall Interviews*, 15 November 1956, 307; 14 February 1957, 419–20. On biographies, see Marshall to Surles, memo, 31 March 1944, Marshall Papers, Pentagon Office File, box 68, folder 36; Sexton for Marshall, memo, 9 September, 1942, Sexton Papers, Marshall Library. Congress also awarded five stars to Arnold, Leahy, King, Eisenhower, MacArthur, and Nimitz, and later to Bradley and Halsey.

6. Pogue, *Marshall: Organizer of Victory*, 218–19, 367–69; Payne, *Marshall Story*, 200; Frye, *Marshall*, 338; Edgar F. Puryear, Jr., *19 Stars: A Study in Military Character and Leadership* (Orange, Va.: Green Publishers, 1971), 94.

7. Pogue, *Marshall: Ordeal and Hope*, 321–22.

8. Pogue, *Marshall: Organizer of Victory*, 60; Puryear, *19 Stars*, 82.

9. Marshall, *Together*, 144–45. See also Pogue, *Marshall: Ordeal and Hope*, 301–3; *Organizer of Victory*, 38–68.

10. Puryear, *19 Stars*, 81.

11. Pogue, *Marshall: Organizer of Victory*, 183–87, 370–77, 423–24; Joseph P. Hobbs, *Dear General: Eisenhower's Wartime Letters to Marshall* (Baltimore: Johns Hopkins University Press, 1971), 134–65; Harry C. Butcher, *My Three Years with Eisenhower* (New York: Simon & Schuster, 1946), 247.

12. Trumbull Higgins, *Soft Underbelly: The Anglo-American Controversy over the Italian Campaign, 1939–1945* (New York: Macmillan, 1968), 137–53.

13. Kimball, *Churchill & Roosevelt*, 3:221–23; Pogue, *Marshall: Organizer of Victory*, 405–20; Maurice Matloff, "The ANVIL Decision: Crossroads of Strategy," in Greenfield, *Command Decisions*, 383–400; Winston S. Churchill, *The Second World War*, vol. 6: *Triumph and Tragedy* (Boston: Houghton Mifflin, 1953), 57–71.

14. Hobbes, *Dear General*, 216; Alfred D. Chandler, ed., *The Papers of Dwight David Eisenhower. The War Years*, vol. 4 (Baltimore: Johns Hopkins University Press, 1970): 2521. See also Russell F. Weigley, *Eisenhower's Lieutenants: The Campaigns of France and Germany, 1944–1945* (Bloomington: Indiana University Press, 1981), 77–319; David Eisenhower, *Eisenhower: At War, 1943–1945* (New York: Random House, 1986), 260–553.

15. Bland, *Marshall Papers*, 2:411–13.

16. Larrabee, *Commander in Chief*, 155; *Marshall Interviews*, 14 February 1957, 399–400; Pogue, *Marshall: Ordeal and Hope*, 372. See also Ernest J. King and Walter M. Whitehill, *Fleet Admiral King: A Naval Record* (New York: W. W. Norton, 1952); Thomas B. Buell, *Master of Seapower: A Biography of Admiral Ernest J. King* (Boston: Little, Brown, 1980); Robert William Love, Jr., "Ernest Joseph King," in Love, ed., *The Chiefs of Naval Operations* (Annapolis, Md.: Naval Institute Press, 1980), 137–79.

17. Love, "King," 162–63.

18. Steele, *The First Offensive*, 81–93; Robert Dallek, *Franklin D. Roosevelt and American Foreign Policy, 1932–1945* (New York: Oxford University Press, 1979), 331–34; Christopher Thorne, *Allies of a Kind: The United States, Britain and the War against Japan, 1941–1945* (New York: Oxford University Press, 1978), 156, 261–63, 368; D. Clayton James, *The Years of MacArthur*, vols. 1, 2 (Boston: Houghton Mifflin, 1970–75), esp. 2:83–88, 137–41, 248–53, 361–63, 403–40.

19. *Marshall Interviews*, 21 November 1956, 347; 11 April 1957, 221–22; Pogue, *Marshall: Ordeal and Hope*, 373–75.

20. Matloff, *Strategic Planning, 1943–1944*, 88–105, 185–95, 307–21, 451–59, 479–89, 512–13; Louis Morton, *Strategy and Command: The First Two Years*, in *U.S. Army in World War II* (Washington, D.C.: U.S. Government Printing Office, 1962); Robert Ross Smith, "Luzon vs. Formosa," in Greenfield, *Command Decisions*, 461–77.

21. *Foreign Relations: The Conference at Quebec, 1944* (1972), 313, passim; Matloff, *Strategic Planning, 1943–1944*, 508–31.

22. *Marshall Interviews*, 19 November 1956, 494; Pogue, *Marshall: Organizer of Victory*, 101; Pogue, *George C. Marshall: Global Commander*, Harmon Memorial Lecture 10 (Colorado: U.S. Air Force Academy, 1968), 18.

23. Bland, *Marshall Papers*, 2:602–3; "Notes on General Marshall," 19 April 1961, Reginald MacDonald Buchanan Papers, Marshall Library; Danchev, *Very Special Relationship*, 1, 3, 48–55.

24. Danchev, *Very Special Relationship*, 145–46 and passim. See also Pogue, *Organizer of Victory*, 337, 481–83; *Marshall Interviews*, 11 February 1957, 379–80; Payne, *Marshall Story*, 133, 222, 232.

25. Bland, *Marshall Papers*, 2:336; Pogue, *Marshall: Organizer of Victory*, 96–99, 103–14; Pogue, *Marshall: Statesman*, 430–36.

26. Pogue, *Marshall: Organizer of Victory*, 349–50, 471–73; Frye, *Marshall*, 351–52.

27. Matloff, *Strategic Planning, 1943–44*, 39–42, 428–32; Raymond G. O'Connor, *Diplomacy for Victory: FDR and Unconditional Surrender* (New York: Norton, 1971), 46–61, 84–95, 101–2; Dallek, *Roosevelt*, 373–76.

28. Warren Kimball, *Swords or Ploughshares? The Morgenthau Plan for De-*

feated Nazi Germany, 1943–1946 (New York: Lippincott, 1976); Pogue, *Marshall: Organizer of Victory*, 458–59.

29. See chapter 8, 142–44; Holley, *Palmer*, 620–79; Michael Sherry, *Preparing for the Next War: American Plans for Postwar Defense, 1941–1945* (New Haven: Yale University Press, 1977), 1–119.

30. *Foreign Relations: The Conferences at Malta and Yalta, 1945* (1955), 975–84.

31. See, for example, Hanson W. Baldwin, *Great Mistakes of the War* (New York: Harper and Brothers, 1949); Chester Wilmot, *The Struggle for Europe* (New York: Harper, 1952); Huntington, *Soldier and the State*, 315–44.

32. See, for example, O'Connor, *Diplomacy for Victory*, 39, 50, 63–68, 79–81, 103–4; Dallek, *Roosevelt*, 506–22, 533-34; John L. Gaddis, *Strategies of Containment: A Critical Appraisal of Postwar American National Security Policy* (New York: Oxford University Press, 1982), 3–15.

33. *Marshall Interviews*, 11 February 1957, 381–82; Pogue, *Marshall: Organizer of Victory*, 315; handwritten notes by Marshall in Marshall Papers, Pentagon Office File, box 56, folder 14; Danchev, *Very Special Relationship*, 37.

34. *Foreign Relations*, 1944, 1 (1966):699–703.

35. Notes for Off-the-Record Talk to Overseas Press Club in New York City, 1 March 1945, Marshall Papers, Pentagon Office File, box 111, folder 49. See also John L. Snell, *The Meaning of Yalta: Big Three Diplomacy and the New Balance of Power* (Baton Rouge: Louisiana State University Press, 1956), and *Illusion and Necessity: The Diplomacy of Global War, 1939–1945* (Boston: Houghton Mifflin, 1963); Diane Shaver Clemens, *Yalta* (New York: Oxford University Press, 1970).

36. U.S.S.R. Ministry of Foreign Affairs, *Russia: Correspondence between the Chairman of the Council of Ministers of the U.S.S.R. and the Presidents of the U.S.A. and the Prime Ministers of Great Britain during the Great Patriotic War of 1941–45* (Moscow: Foreign Languages Publishing House, 1957), 2:204–8. Hereafter cited as *Stalin's Correspondence*.

37. Pogue, *Marshall: Organizer of Victory*, 573–78; Stephen E. Ambrose, *Eisenhower and Berlin: The Decision to Halt at the Elbe* (New York: W. W. Norton, 1967).

38. Pogue, *Marshall: Organizer of Victory*, 585.

39. Marshall to Wilson for Churchill, 3 April 1945, Marshall Papers, Pentagon Office File, box 61, folder 9.

40. *Time*, 43 (5 January 1944): 16; *Churchill from the Diaries of Lord Moran*, 597.

41. Pogue, *Marshall: Organizer of Victory*, 584–85.

42. Stimson, *On Active Service*, 664; Marshall, *Together*, 251–52.

43. *Churchill from the Diaries of Lord Moran*, 292; Anthony Sampson, *Macmillan: A Study in Ambiguity* (London: Penguin Press, 1967), 61.

CHAPTER 8

1. James L. Baughman, *Henry R. Luce and the Rise of the American News Media* (Boston: Twayne Publishers, 1987), 130–33.

2. Roosevelt to Marshall, memorandum, 15 October 1943, Roosevelt Papers, PSF, box 109, Marshall folder.

3. Baughman, *Luce*, 139–40; *Time*, 31 (3 January 1938): 12–16; Dallek, *Roosevelt*, 328–29; Michael Schaller, *The U.S. Crusade in China, 1938–1945* (New York: Columbia University Press, 1979), 1–100.

4. Barbara Tuchman, *Stilwell and the American Experience in China, 1911–1945* (New York: Macmillan, 1970), 9–200; Charles F. Romanus and Riley Sunderland, *Stilwell's Mission to China*, in *U.S. Army in World War II* (1953), 63–80; Pogue, *Marshall: Ordeal and Hope*, 355–60.

5. Pogue, *Marshall: Ordeal and Hope*, 366.

6. Tuchman, *Stilwell*, 283, 321, 461–66; Joseph W. Stilwell, *The Stilwell Papers*, arr. and ed. Theodore White (New York: William Sloane Associates, 1948); Schaller, *U.S. Crusade in China*, 168, 177–90.

7. Jack Belden, *Retreat with Stilwell* (New York: Alfred A. Knopf, 1943), 32; Danchev, *Very Special Relationship*, 73.

8. From unpublished Stilwell diaries, Stilwell Papers, Hoover Institute, Stanford, California, quoted in Danchev, *Very Special Relationship*, 73.

9. Schaller, *U.S. Crusade in China*, 65–85, 132–36; Tuchman, *Stilwell*, 215–20, 335–40, 358–62; Romanus and Sunderland, *Stilwell's Mission*, 313–89; Herbert Feis, *The China Tangle: The American Effort in China from Pearl Harbor to the Marshall Mission* (Princeton, N.J.: Princeton University Press, 1953).

10. *Stilwell Papers*, 245.

11. Ibid., 333; *Foreign Relations*, 1944, 6 (1967):147–48, 157–58.

12. *Foreign Relations*, 1944, 6:165–66; Schaller, *U.S. Crusade in China*, 164–75; Tuchman, *Stilwell*, 455–509; Charles F. Romanus and Riley Sunderland, *Stilwell's Command Problems*, in *U.S. Army in World War II* (1956), 297–472.

13. *Foreign Relations*, 1945, 5 (1965):253, 256–58; Harry S. Truman, *Memoirs*, Vol 1: *Year of Decisions* (Garden City, N.Y.: Doubleday, 1955), 82.

14. Deane to Marshall, 2 December 1944, Marshall Papers, Pentagon Office File, box 63, folder 1, reprinted in John R. Deane, *The Strange Alliance: The Story of Our Efforts at Wartime Cooperation with Russia* (New York: Viking Press, 1947), 84–86.

15. Marshall to Stimson, memorandum, 21 December 1944, Marshall Papers, Pentagon Office File, box 63, folder 32; Stimson to Roosevelt, memorandum, 3 January 1945, Roosevelt Papers, PSF SAFE: Russia file; *Stalin's Correspondence*, 2:207–8; *Foreign Relations*, 1945, 5:253–54.

16. *Foreign Relations, Malta and Yalta*, 106–8, and *1944*, 1:699–703.

17. Truman, *Memoirs*, 1:10–11.

18. Martin J. Sherwin, *A World Destroyed: The Atomic Bomb and the Grand Alliance* (New York: Alfred A. Knopf, 1975), 167–70, 200–19.

19. P. M. S. Blackett, *Fear, War and the Bomb: Military and Political Consequences of Atomic Energy* (New York: Whittlesey House, 1949); Gar Alperowitz, *Atomic Diplomacy: Hiroshima and Potsdam* (New York: Random House, 1965).

20. Sherwin, *A World Destroyed*; Barton J. Bernstein, "Roosevelt, Truman and the Atomic Bomb, 1941–1945: A Reinterpretation," *Political Science Quarterly* 90 (Spring 1975): 23–69.

21. Pogue, *Marshall: Statesman*, 17–19, 550–51 n. 30.

22. Ibid., 20–21; Stimson Diary, 23–24 July 1945.

23. *Foreign Relations: The Conference of Berlin* (1960), 2:378–79; Truman, *Memoirs*, 1:416; Sherwin, *A World Destroyed*, 227.

24. Robert Butow, *Japan's Decision to Surrender* (Stanford: Stanford University Press, 1954), 112–233.

25. Stimson press conference statement, 19 September 1945, John McAuley Palmer Papers, box 1, folder 1, Marshall Library, partially reprinted in Stimson, *On Active Service*, 662–64; Pogue, *Marshall: Statesman*, 1.

26. Holley, *Palmer*, 631–91; Sherry, *Preparing for the Next War*, 58–73; Weigley, *Towards an American Army*, 241–46.

27. *Biennial Report of the Chief of Staff of the United States Army, July 1, 1943 to June 30, 1945, to the Secretary of War* (Washington, D.C.: Government Printing Office, 1945), 117–23.

28. Ibid., 290; outline for speech to Illinois Manufacturers Association, 12 December 1944, Marshall Papers, Pentagon Office File, box 111, folder 45. See also addresses in folders 47, 56, and 62, and Sherry, *Preparing for the Next War*, 199–205.

29. 29 October 1945 address to *Herald Tribune Forum*, Marshall Papers, Pentagon Office File, box 111, folder 72; Sherry, *Preparing for the Next War*, 217–26; Weigley, *Towards an American Army*, 247–53.

30. Pogue, *Marshall: Statesman*, 2–3.

31. Thomas Paterson, *Soviet-American Confrontation: Postwar Reconstruction and the Origins of the Cold War* (Baltimore: Johns Hopkins University Press, 1973), 1–14.

32. Pogue, *Marshall: Statesman*, 3, 26; Marshall, *Together*, 282.

33. Schaller, *U.S. Crusade in China*, 177–229, 251–89.

34. Steven I. Levine, "A New Look at American Mediation in the Chinese Civil War: The Marshall Mission and Manchuria," *Diplomatic History* 3 (Fall 1979): 349–63, and *Anvil of Victory: The Communist Revolution in Manchuria, 1945–1948* (New York: Columbia University Press, 1987), 26–53.

35. Walter Bedell Smith, *My Three Years in Moscow* (Philadelphia: Lippincott, 1950), 216.

36. Pogue, *Marshall: Statesman*, 29–30.
37. Ibid., 66.
38. *Foreign Relations*, 1945, 7(1969):767–70.
39. Eiler, *Wedemeyer*, 161.
40. Ibid.; *Marshall Interviews*, 5 April 1957, 188.
41. *Foreign Relations*, 1946, 9(1972):950–53, 1099–1101; Pogue, *Marshall: Statesman*, 108–117.
42. Marshall to Eisenhower, 17 September 1946, Marshall Papers, China Mission File, box 122, folder 32; *Foreign Relations*, 1946, 10(1972):447; Pogue, *Marshall: Statesman*, 121–43; Payne, *Marshall Story*, 284.
43. 7 January 1947 statement in Department of State *Bulletin*, 19 January 1947, 83–85, reprinted in *Marshall's Mission to China* (Arlington, Va.: University Publications of America, 1976), 2:516–21.
44. Eric Goldman, *The Crucial Decade—and After: America, 1945–1960* (New York: Random House, 1960), 116.
45. John Melby, *The Mandate of Heaven: Record of a Civil War, China 1945–49* (Toronto: University of Toronto Press, 1968), 172; Tuchman, *Stilwell*, 531.

CHAPTER 9

1. Truman, *Memoirs*, 1:551–52; Daniel Yergin, *Shattered Peace: The Origins of the Cold War and the National Security State* (Boston: Houghton Mifflin, 1977), 151–62, 223–23, 259–61.
2. Pogue, *Marshall: Statesman*, 113, 139–141.
3. *Foreign Relations*, 1946, 10:681.
4. Pogue, *Marshall: Statesman*, 144–46.
5. Robert H. Ferrell, *George C. Marshall*, vol. 15 in Samuel Flagg Bemis and Robert H. Ferrell, eds., *The American Secretaries of State and Their Diplomacy* (New York: Cooper Square, 1966), 37, 53–54.
6. *Marshall Interviews*, 20 November 1956, 525–26.
7. Pogue, *Marshall: Statesman*, 146–51: Joseph Marion Jones, *The Fifteen Weeks* (New York: Harcourt, Brace & World, 1955), 106–7.
8. Walter Isaacson and Evan Thomas, *The Wise Men: Six Friends and the World They Made: Acheson, Bohlen, Harriman, Kennan, Lovett, McCloy* (New York: Simon and Schuster, 1986); Dean Acheson, *Present at the Creation: My Years in the State Department* (New York: W. W. Norton, 1969).
9. Charles Bohlen, *Witness to History, 1929–1969* (New York: W. W. Norton, 1973), 259, 268; Acheson, *Present at the Creation*, 140–42, 213, and *Sketches from Life of Men I Have Known* (New York: Harper & Brothers, 1959), 147, 163–64.
10. Pogue, *Marshall: Statesman*, 149–50; Acheson, *Sketches*, 154, 160–61; T. Michael Ruddy, *The Cautious Diplomat: Charles E. Bohlen and the Soviet*

Union, 1927–1969 (Kent, Ohio: Kent State University Press, 1986), 70; George F. Kennan, *Memoirs, 1925–1950* (Boston: Little, Brown, 1967), 345–46.

11. Kennan, *Memoirs*, 346–47; Bohlen, *Witness*, 270.

12. Reprinted in Pogue, *Marshall: Statesman*, 523–25.

13. *Foreign Relations*, 1946, 4 (1970): 696–709; Kennan, *Memoirs*, 271–97.

14. X, "The Sources of Soviet Conduct," *Foreign Affairs* 25 (July 1947): 566–82; Kennan, *Memoirs*, 354–67; Gaddis, *Strategies of Containment*, 25–53; Thomas H. Etzold and John Lewis Gaddis, eds., *Containment: Documents on American Policy and Strategy, 1945–1950* (New York: Columbia University Press, 1978), 25–37.

15. Pogue, *Marshall: Statesman*, 152, 154; John Morton Blum, ed., *The Price of Vision: The Diary of Henry A. Wallace, 1942–1946* (Boston: Houghton Mifflin, 1973), 522; Yergin, *Shattered Peace*, 10–11, 245–64.

16. See p. 158; *Foreign Relations*, 1947, 5 (1971): 32–37; Jones, *The Fifteen Weeks*, 7.

17. *Foreign Relations*, 1947, 5:60–62.

18. Acheson, *Present at the Creation*, 219; Jones, *The Fifteen Weeks*, 139–41.

19. Richard M. Freeland, *The Truman Doctrine and the Origins of McCarthyism: Foreign Policy, Domestic Politics, and Internal Security, 1946–1948* (New York: Alfred A. Knopf, 1975), 89; Acheson, *Present at the Creation*, 219; Jones, *The Fifteen Weeks*, 141–42, 151–54, 269–74.

20. Ferrell, *Marshall*, 72–73; Kennan, *Memoirs*, 313–24; Bohlen, *Witness to History*, 261; Pogue, *Marshall: Statesman*, 165–67.

21. Yergin, *Shattered Peace*, 299–300; *Foreign Relations*, 1947, 2 (1972): 337–44.

22. Kennan, *Memoirs*, 325–26; Bohlen, *Witness to History*, 263; State Department *Bulletin*, 16 (11 May 1947): 924.

23. *Foreign Relations*, 1947, 3 (1972): 220–30; Kennan, *Memoirs*, 326–36; Gaddis, *Strategies of Containment*, 34–38.

24. Michael J. Hogan, *The Marshall Plan: America, Britain, and the Reconstruction of Western Europe, 1947–1952* (Cambridge: Cambridge University Press, 1987), 1–45; John Gimbel, *The Origins of the Marshall Plan* (Stanford: Stanford University Press, 1976).

25. Jones, *The Fifteen Weeks*, 24–30, 199–205, 226–29, 246–49, 274–81; Acheson, *Present at the Creation*, 226–32; State Department *Bulletin*, 16 (18 May 1947): 991–94; *Foreign Relations*, 1947, 3:204–19, 230–32.

26. Bohlen, *Witness to History*, 263–65; Kennan, *Memoirs*, 336–43; *Foreign Relations*, 1947, 3:224–30.

27. *Marshall Interviews*, 20 November 1956, 522–24; Pogue, *Marshall: Statesman*, 208–13.

28. State Department *Bulletin*, 16 (15 June 1947): 1159–60.

29. Isaacson and Thomas, *The Wise Men*, 424; *Marshall Interviews*, 19, 20 November 1956, 491, 520–22.

30. Pogue, *Marshall, Statesman*, 237–49; Ferrell, *Marshall*, 128–30.

31. Gimbel, *Origins of the Marshall Plan*, 273.

32. Pogue, *Marshall: Statesman*, 236.

33. *Marshall Interviews*, 19 November 1956, 491.

34. *Time*, 51 (5 January 1948): 18–21.

35. *Foreign Relations*, 1947, 1 (1973): 770–77 and 1948, 3 (1974): 283–88; Gaddis, *Strategies of Containment*, 72–74; Walter Millis, ed., *The Forrestal Diaries* (New York: Viking Press, 1951), 340.

36. *Foreign Relations*, 1947, 1:772–73, and 1948, 2 (1973): 1177–78.

37. See Etzold and Gaddis, *Containment*, 135–44; Gaddis, *Strategies of Containment*, 74–79; and below chap. 10.

38. William Stueck, *The Wedemeyer Mission* (Athens, Ga.: University of Georgia Press, 1984), 29–53, 74–79.

39. *Foreign Relations*, 1948, 7 (1972): 838–48; Etzold and Gaddis, *Containment*, 236–47; Melvyn P. Leffler, "The American Conception of National Security and the Beginnings of the Cold War, 1945–1948," *American Historical Review*, 89 (April 1984):346–81.

40. *Foreign Relations*, 1947, 3:229–30; Etzold and Gaddis, *Containment*, 225–51; Gaddis, *Strategies of Containment*, 27–33, 41–46.

41. *Marshall's Mission to China*, 1: xxxiii.

42. Stueck, *The Wedemeyer Mission*, 86–91; Tang Tsou, *America's Failure in China* (Chicago: University of Chicago Press, 1963), 470–77.

43. David Wyman, *The Abandonment of the Jews: America and the Holocaust, 1941–1945* (New York: Random House, 1984).

44. George T. Mazuzan, *Warren R. Austin at the U.N., 1946–1953* (Kent, Ohio: Kent State University Press, 1977), 98–99.

45. Ferrell, *Marshall*, 190; *Foreign Relations*, 1948, 5, pt. 2 (1976):972–75; John Snetsinger, *Truman, the Jewish Vote, and the Creation of Israel* (Stanford, Calif.: Hoover Institution Press, 1974); Zvi Ganin, *Truman, American Jewry, and Israel* (New York: Holmes and Meier, 1974); Peter Grose, *Israel in the Mind of America* (New York: Alfred A. Knopf, 1983).

46. Pogue, *Marshall: Statesman*, 371–77, 408, 413; Payne, *The Marshall Story*, 311; Marshall to Charlotte B. Coles, Marshall Papers, Pentagon Office File, box 61, folder 35; Yergin, *Shattered Peace*, 262.

47. Acheson to Marshall, 10 January 1949, Marshall Papers, Pentagon Office File, box 56, folder 4.

CHAPTER 10

1. Demetrios Caraley, *The Politics of Military Unification* (New York: Columbia University Press, 1966); Douglas Kinnard, *The Secretary of Defense* (Lexington: University Press of Kentucky, 1980), 8–43;

2. Paul Y. Hammond, "Super Carriers and B-36 Bombers: Appropriations, Strategy and Politics," in Harold Stein, ed., *American Civil-Military Decisions: A Book of Case Studies* (Birmingham: University of Alabama Press, 1963), 465–564.

3. *Foreign Relations*, 1948, 1, pt. 2 (1976): 652–55.

4. Department of State, *United States Relations with China with Special Reference to the Period 1944–1949* (Washington, D.C.: Government Printing Office, 1949).

5. Ibid.; State Department *Bulletin*, 22 (23 January 1950): 111–18.

6. John Spanier, *The Truman-MacArthur Controversy and the Korean War* (New York: W. W. Norton, 1965), 41–61.

7. Gaddis, *Strategies of Containment*, 83–88; Leffler, "American Conception of National Security," 346–81; Lloyd C. Gardner, *Architects of Illusion: Men and Ideas in American Foreign Policy, 1941–1949* (Chicago: Quadrangle Books, 1970), 270–300.

8. Text in *Foreign Relations*, 1950, 1 (1977): 234–92. For further discussion, see Gaddis, *Strategies of Containment*, 89–109; Paul Y. Hammond, "NSC-68: Prologue to Rearmament," in Warner R. Schilling, Paul Y. Hammond, and Glenn H. Snyder, *Strategy, Politics and Defense Budgets* (New York: Columbia University Press, 1962), 267–378.

9. Etzold and Gaddis, *Strategies of Containment*, 383–85.

10. Pogue, *Marshall: Statesman*, xvii–xviii.

11. *Congressional Record*, 81st Cong., 2d sess., 15 September 1950, 96, pt. 11, 14913–17.

12. Senate, Armed Services Committee, Hearing, "Nomination of General of the Army George C. Marshall to be Secretary of Defense," 19 September 1950, 81st Cong., 2d sess., 22–23.

13. Ibid., 20–26; Pogue, *Marshall: Statesman*, 424–26.

14. *Marshall Interviews*, 5 April 1957, 183; Payne, *The Marshall Story*, 315.

15. Pogue, *Marshall: Statesman*, 437–38.

16. D. Clayton James, *The Years of MacArthur*, vol. 3: *Triumph and Disaster 1945–1964* (Boston: Houghton Mifflin, 1985), 487–536.

17. James F. Schnabel and Robert J. Watson, *The History of the Joint Chiefs of Staff: The Joint Chiefs of Staff and National Policy*, vol. 3: *The Korean War* (Wilmington, Del.: Michael Glazier, 1979), pt. 1, 394–468; Burton I. Kaufman, *The Korean War: Challenges in Crisis, Credibility, and Command* (New York: Alfred A. Knopf, 1986), 144–51.

18. Kaufman, *Korean War*, 157–62; James, *Years of MacArthur*, 3: 560–90; Spanier, *Truman-MacArthur Controversy*, 187–207.

19. Merle Miller, *Plain Speaking: An Oral Biography of Harry S. Truman* (New York: Berkeley Publishing Corp., 1973), 287.

20. Ibid., 304.

21. Schnabel and Watson, *History of the Joint Chiefs of Staff*, 3:534–46; James, *Years of MacArthur*, 3:591–97. For criticism of Marshall's previous caution, see Isaacson and Thomas, *The Wise Men*, 533–40.

22. Spanier, *Truman-MacArthur Controversy*, 211–13.

23. Ibid., 213; Thomas C. Reeves, *The Life and Times of Joe McCarthy: A Biography* (New York: Stein and Day, 1982), 372.

24. Hearings before the Senate Committee on Armed Services and Committee on Foreign Relations, *Military Situation in the Far East*, 1951, 82d Cong., 1st sess., pt. 1, 3–320.

25. Ibid., 323–724, 732, summarized in Spanier, *Truman-MacArthur Controversy*, 214–54.

26. *Congressional Record*, 82d Cong., 1st sess., 14 June 1951, 6556–6603; Senator Joseph R. McCarthy, *America's Retreat from Victory: The Story of George Catlett Marshall* (New York: Devin-Adair Company, 1951); Reeves, *McCarthy*, 371–74.

27. Marshall to Spencer L. Carter, 14 June 1948, Marshall papers, Pentagon Office File, box 60, folder 19.

28. Pogue, *Marshall: Statesman*, 496.

29. Stephen E. Ambrose, *Eisenhower: Soldier, General of the Army, President-Elect, 1890–1952* (New York: Simon and Schuster, 1983), 548, 562–67; Reeves, *McCarthy*, 437–40.

30. Wilson, *General Marshall Remembered*, 371.

31. Pogue, *Marshall: Statesman*, 497–98.

32. Gaddis, *Strategies of Containment*, 127–97; Herbert S. Parmet, *Eisenhower and the American Crusades* (New York: Macmillan, 1972), 574–75; Fred I. Greenstein, *The Hidden-Hand Presidency: Eisenhower as Leader* (New York: Basic Books, 1982), 155–227.

33. Pogue, *Marshall: Statesman*, 501–7.

34. Ibid., 495, 507–9; interview with Cols. L. M. Guyer and H. C. Donnelly, JCS Historical Section, 11 February 1949, Marshall Papers, Oral History Collection; *New York Times Book Review*, 28 June 1987, 3.

35. Marshall to Bradley, 9 January 1948, Marshall papers, Pentagon Office File, box 58, folder 11.

36. Pogue, *Marshall: Statesman*, 508–11; Wilson, *General Marshall Remembered*, 386–97.

37. For an insightful comparison of the two men, see Don Higginbotham, *George Washington and the American Military Tradition* (Athens: University of Georgia Press, 1985), 106–38.

BIBLIOGRAPHIC ESSAY

Biographies, Papers, and Memoirs

The major published source for information on Marshall is the magisterial, four-volume biography by Forrest C. Pogue, *George C. Marshall: Education of a General, 1880–1939; Ordeal and Hope, 1939–1942; Organizer of Victory, 1943–1945*; and *Statesman, 1945–1959* (New York: Viking Press, 1963–86). The result of more than thirty years of research and writing, this work makes extensive use of Marshall's personal papers and a series of interviews he granted the author, as well as government documents, memoirs, and secondary works. Totaling more than 2,000 pages, it stands as a monument to its author, as well as its subject.

Three single-volume "popular" biographies of Marshall have been published. Although the earliest and therefore incomplete, William Frye's *Marshall: Citizen Soldier* (New York: Bobbs, Merrill, 1947) remains the best of these on Marshall up to 1945. The most recent and complete, Leonard Mosley's *Marshall: Hero for Our Times* (New York: Hearst Books, 1982), is without any doubt the worst and should be avoided at all costs because of its factual errors and interpretive fantasies. In between these two in terms of quality as well as publication date is Robert Payne's *The Marshall Story: A Biography of General George C. Marshall* (New York: Prentice-Hall, 1951). See also Robert Ferrell's *George C. Marshall*, volume 15 in Samuel Flagg Bemis and Robert H. Ferrell, eds., *The American Secretaries of State and Their Diplomacy* (New York: Cooper Square, 1966), a solid, comprehensive study of Marshall's two years as secretary of state but one written before the declassification of much archival material.

Interesting biographical essays on different aspects of Marshall's character and career can be found in Edgar F. Puryear, Jr., *Nineteen Stars: A Study of Military Character and Leadership* (Orange, Va.: Green Publishers, 1971); Forrest C. Pogue, *George C. Marshall: Global Commander*, Harmon Memorial Lectures in Military History Number 10 (Colorado Springs: U.S. Air Force Academy,

1968); Larry I. Bland, *"Fully the Equal of the Best"*: George C. Marshall and the *Virginia Military Institute* (Lexington, Va.: George C. Marshall Foundation, 1987); Josiah Bunting III, "George C. Marshall: A Study in Character," in Henry S. Bausum, ed., *The John Biggs Cincinnati Lectures in Military Leadership and Command, 1986* (Lexington, Va.: VMI Foundation, 1986), 109–16; Alexander DeConde, "George C. Marshall, 1947–1949," in Norman A. Graebner, ed., *An Uncertain Tradition: American Secretaries of State in the Twentieth Century* (New York: McGraw-Hill, 1961). Don Higginbotham analyzes similarities between Washington and Marshall in the last chapter of *George Washington and the American Military Tradition* (Athens: University of Georgia Press, 1985), 106–38.

Marshall's papers are housed in the George C. Marshall Foundation Research Library and Museum adjoining the VMI campus in Lexington, Virginia. Two volumes of these papers have already been published under the outstanding editorship of Larry I. Bland as *The Papers of George Catlett Marshall, vol. 1: "The Soldierly Spirit," December 1880–June 1939*; and vol. 2: *"We Cannot Delay," July 1, 1939–December 6, 1941* (Baltimore: Johns Hopkins University Press, 1981–86). Four additional volumes are scheduled for publication. The library also holds the papers of many of Marshall's friends and associates and printed copies of his oral history interviews, *George C. Marshall Interviews and Reminiscences for Forrest C. Pogue: Transcripts and Notes, 1956–1957* (Lexington, Va.: Marshall Research Foundation, 1986). Many of Marshall's official papers after 1938 have also been published, as noted under the appropriate headings in this essay.

Throughout his lifetime Marshall refused to publish any memoirs. He did write a manuscript about his World War I experience but then tried to destroy it. His stepdaughter discovered a remaining copy after his death and published it in 1976 as *Memoirs of My Services in the World War, 1917–1918* (Boston: Houghton Mifflin, 1976). Numerous insights into his personality and life from 1929 to 1945 can be found in the memoirs of his second wife, Katherine Tupper Marshall, *Together: Annals of an Army Wife* (New York: Tupper and Love, 1946). The memoirs of goddaughter Rose Page Wilson, *General Marshall Remembered* (Englewood Cliffs, N.J.: Prentice-Hall, 1968) are also useful, especially for the 1920s. The numerous memoirs of his professional associates from 1917 to 1951 are listed under the appropriate headings.

General Works and Guides

The literature on the rise of the United States to world power during Marshall's lifetime is enormous. The best starting place is the comprehensive and annotated bibliography edited by Richard Dean Burns for the Society for Historians of American Foreign Relations, *Guide to American Foreign Relations since*

1700 (Santa Barbara, Calif: ABC-CLIO, 1983). Particularly valuable for this volume are chapters 19–28 covering the years 1914–53 and chapter 40 on the armed forces, strategy, and foreign policy.

For U.S. military history and thought in general, see Russell Weigley, *Towards an American Army: Military Thought from Washington to Marshall* (New York: Columbia University Press, 1962), *History of the United States Army*, expanded ed. (Bloomington: Indiana University Press, 1984), and *The American Way of War: A History of United States Military Strategy and Policy* (New York: Macmillan, 1973). The most up-to-date textbook in the field is Alan R. Millett and Peter Maslowski, *For the Common Defense: A Military History of the United States of America* (New York: Free Press, 1984). Dated but still valuable are Walter Millis's interpretive historical essay, *Arms and Men: A Study in American Military History* (New York: Putnam, 1956), and Samuel P. Huntington's *The Soldier and the State: The Theory and Politics of Civil-Military Relations* (New York: Random House, 1957).

Army Expansion and Reform

For VMI see William Couper, *One Hundred Years at V.M.I.*, 4 vols. (Richmond, Va.: Garrett and Massie, 1939); and Henry A. Wise, *Drawing Out the Man: The V.M.I. Story* (Charlottesville: University Press of Virginia, 1978). The pre-1898 army is comprehensively analyzed in Edward M. Coffman's, *The Old Army: A Portrait of the American Army in Peacetime, 1784–1898* (New York: Oxford University Press, 1986). For the army's role in the Spanish-American War and the Philippine insurrection, see David Trask, *The War with Spain in 1898* (New York: Macmillan, 1981); Graham Cosmas, *An Army for Empire: The United States Army in the Spanish-American War* (Columbia: University of Missouri Press, 1971); John Morgan Gates, *Schoolbooks and Krags: The United States Army in the Philippines* (Westport, Conn.: Greenwood Press, 1973); and Stuart C. Miller, *"Benevolent Assimilation": The American Conquest of the Philippines, 1899–1903* (New Haven: Yale University Press, 1982). Marshall believed that the work by one of his subordinates, William T. Sexton, *Soldiers in the Sun: An Adventure in Imperialism* (Harrisburg, Pa.: Military Service Publishing Co., 1939), described the army experience in the Philippines as he had known it. See also David H. Bain, *Sitting in Darkness: Americans in the Philippines* (Boston: Houghton Mifflin, 1984).

Army professionalization and progressive reform are analyzed in Stephen E. Ambrose, *Upton and the Army* (Baton Rouge: Louisiana State University Press, 1964); James L. Abrahamson, *America Arms for a New Century: The Making of a Great Military Power* (New York: Free Press, 1981); Timothy K. Nenninger, *The Leavenworth Schools and the Old Army: Education, Professionalism, and the Officer Corps of the United States Army, 1881–1918* (Westport, Conn.: Greenwood Press, 1978); Peter Karsten, "Armed Progressives: The Military Reorganizes for the American Century," in Jerry Israel, ed., *Building the Organizational Society* (New York: Free Press, 1972); and Jack C. Lane, *Armed Progressive: General Leonard Wood* (San Rafael, Calif.: Presidio, 1978). For the general staff and army organization, see Otto L. Nelson, Jr., *National Security and the General Staff* (Washington, D.C.: Infantry Journal, 1946); James E. Hewes, Jr., *From Root to McNamara: Army Organization and Administration, 1900–1963* (Washington, D.C.: Government Printing Office, 1963); and Paul Y. Hammond, *Organizing for Defense: The American Military Establishment in the Twentieth Century* (Princeton: Princeton University Press, 1961). For early efforts to coordinate strategic planning with foreign policy, see Richard Challener, *Admirals, Generals and American Foreign Policy, 1898–1914* (Princeton: Princeton University Press, 1973), and John A. S. Grenville and George B. Young, *Politics, Strategy and American Diplomacy, 1873–1917* (New Haven: Yale University Press, 1967). The arguments and struggle for preparedness and a citizen-soldier army are carefully analyzed in I. B. Holley, Jr., *General John M. Palmer, Citizen Soldiers, and the Army of a Democracy* (Westport, Conn.: Greenwood Press, 1982), as well as in Palmer's numerous publications, in J. Garry Clifford's *The Citizen Soldiers: The Plattsburg Training Camp Movement, 1913–1920* (Lexington: University of Kentucky Press, 1972), and in John Patrick Finnegan's *Against the Spectre of a Dragon: The Campaign for American Military Preparedness, 1914–1917* (Westport, Conn.: Greenwood Press, 1974).

World War I and Interwar Years

Ross Gregory's *The Origins of American Intervention in the First World War* (New York: Norton, 1971) is a brief and informative introduction. The best study of the U.S. armed forces in the war is Edward M. Coffman's *The War to End All Wars: The American Military Experience in World War I* (New York: Oxford University Press, 1968). See also Harvey A. DeWeerd, *President Wilson Fights His War: World War I and the American Intervention* (New York: Macmillan, 1968). David F. Trask's *The United States in the Supreme War Council: American War Aims and Inter-Allied Strategy, 1917–1918* (Middletown, Conn.: Wesleyan University Press, 1961) and *Captains & Cabinets: Anglo-American Naval Relations, 1917–1918* (Columbia: University of Missouri Press, 1972) analyze Allied politico-military relationships. For wartime mobilization, see Daniel R. Beaver, *Newton D. Baker and the American War Effort, 1917–1919* (Lincoln: University of Nebraska Press, 1966); Edward M. Coffman, *The Hilt of the Sword: The Career of Peyton C. March* (Madison: University of Wisconsin Press, 1966); David M. Kennedy, *Over Here: The First World War and American Society* (New York: Oxford University Press, 1980), and Robert D. Cuff, *The War Industries Board:*

Business-Government Relations during World War I (Baltimore: Johns Hopkins University Press, 1973). A comprehensive and recent study of the entire U.S. experience in World War I is Robert H. Ferrell, *Woodrow Wilson and World War I, 1917–1921* (New York: Harper & Row, 1985).

Marshall's previously cited memoirs describe his own experiences during the war. See also memoirs by John J. Pershing, *My Experiences in the World War,* 2 vols. (New York: Stokes, 1931); James G. Harbord, *The American Army in France, 1917–1919* (Boston: Little, Brown, 1936); Hunter Liggett, *Commanding an American Army: Recollections of the World War* (Boston: Houghton Mifflin, 1925); and Robert L. Bullard, *Personalities and Reminiscences of the War* (Garden City, N.Y.: Doubleday, Page, 1925). The best biographies of Pershing are the two-volume studies by Frank G. Vandiver, *Black Jack: The Life and Times of John J. Pershing,* 2 vols. (College Station: Texas A&M Press, 1977), and by Donald W. Smythe, *Guerrilla Warrior: The Early Life of John J. Pershing* (New York: Scribner's, 1973) and *Pershing: General of the Armies* (Bloomington: Indiana University Press, 1986). See also Allan R. Millett's *The General: Robert L. Bullard and Officership in the United States Army, 1881–1925* (Westport, Conn.: Greenwood Press, 1975).

U.S. foreign and naval policies during the interwar years have been intensely studied and dramatically reappraised during the last two decades, but complementary studies of the army and national security policy in general are not as plentiful. See John Braeman, "Power and Diplomacy: The 1920's Reappraised," *Review of Politics* 44 (July 1982): 342–69, for a provocative general reassessment, as well as Fred Greene, "The Military View of American National Policy, 1904–1940," *American Historical Review* 66 (January 1961): 354–77; Lester H. Brune, *The Origins of American National Security Policy: Sea Power, Air Power and Foreign Policy, 1900–1941* (Manhattan, Kans.: MA/AH Publishing, 1981); and Keith D. McFarland, *Harry H. Woodring: A Political Biography of FDR's Controversial Secretary of War* (Lawrence: University Press of Kansas, 1975). Warren I. Cohen, *Empire without Tears: America's Foreign Relations, 1921–1933* (New York: Knopf, 1987), and Thomas H. Buckley and Edwin B. Strong, Jr., *American Foreign and National Security Policies, 1914–1945* (Knoxville: University of Tennessee Press, 1987), offer brief and informative surveys based on the most recent literature. See also David G. Haglund, *Latin America and the Transformation of U.S. Strategic Thought, 1936–1940* (Albuquerque: University of New Mexico Press, 1984); Michael K. Doyle, "The U.S. Navy and War Plan Orange, 1933–1940: Making Necessity of a Virtue," *Naval War College Review* 32 (May–June 1980): 49–63; and Louis Morton, "Army and Marines on the China Station: A Study in Military and Political Rivalry," *Pacific Historical Review* 29 (February 1960); 51–73; "War Plan ORANGE: Evolution of a Strategy," *World Politics* 11 (January 1959): 221–50; and "National Policy and Military Strategy," *Virginia Quarterly Review* 36 (Winter 1960): 1–17.

World War II: General

The starting place for any serious research into Marshall and the U.S. Army during the World War II years is the enormous eighty-volume official history, *U.S. Army in World War II*. Particularly valuable for this work were Mark S. Watson's *Chief of Staff: Prewar Plans and Preparations*; Maurice Matloff and Edwin Snell, *Strategic Planning for Coalition Warfare, 1941–1942*; Maurice Matloff, *Strategic Planning for Coalition Warfare, 1943–1944*; Ray S. Cline, *Washington Command Post: The Operations Division*; Richard M. Leighton and Robert W. Coakley, *Global Logistics and Strategy*, 2 vols.; and the individual theater studies. Two useful collections of summary essays can be found in Kent R. Greenfield's *Command Decisions* (Washington, D.C.: Government Printing Office, 1960) and *American Strategy in World War II: A Reconsideration* (Baltimore: Johns Hopkins University Press, 1963). One should also consult the navy and air force official multivolume histories, Samuel Eliot Morison's *History of United States Naval Operations in World War II*, 15 vols. (Boston: Little, Brown, 1947–62), and Wesley Frank Craven and James Lea Cate, eds., *The Army Air Forces in World War II*, 7 vols. (Chicago: University of Chicago Press, 1948–58), as well as the official British history, particularly the six-volume *History of the Second World War: Grand Strategy* series edited by J. R. M. Butler. See also Vernon E. Davis, "The History of the Joint Chiefs of Staff During World War II: Organizational Development," 2 vols., Record Group 218, National Archives, Washington, D.C., available on microfilm, and Grace Person Hayes, *The History of the Joint Chiefs of Staff in World War II: The War against Japan* (Annapolis, Md.: Naval Institute Press, 1953, 1982).

For Marshall's public statements during the war, see Major H. A. De-Weerd, ed., *Selected Speeches and Statements of General of the Army George C. Marshall* (Washington, D.C.: Infantry Journal, 1945). His three biennial reports during the war were published individually by the Government Printing Office in 1941, 1943, and 1945, and then together with those of his JCS colleagues as *The War Reports of General of the Army George C. Marshall, Chief of Staff, General of the Army H. H. Arnold, Commanding General, Army Air Forces, and Fleet Admiral Ernest J. King, Commander-in-Chief of the United States Fleet and Chief of Naval Operations* (Philadelphia: Lippincott, 1947). For documents and minutes of the wartime summit conferences in which Marshall participated, see the special conference volumes in the State Department's *Foreign Relations of the United States* series, (*Washington, 1941–1942* and *Casablanca, 1943*; *Washington and Quebec, 1943*; *Cairo and Tehran, 1943*; *Quebec, 1944*; *Malta and Yalta, 1945*; and *Berlin, 1945*). Marshall also participated in the drafting of many of Roosevelt's letters to Allied leaders. Some of these are in *Foreign Relations*, but the definitive collection of the extensive Churchill-Roosevelt correspondence with outstanding, detailed commentary is Warren Kimball, ed., *Churchill & Roose-*

velt: *The Complete Correspondence*, 3 vols. (Princeton: Princeton University Press, 1984). For correspondence with Stalin, see U.S.S.R. Ministry of Foreign Affairs, *Russia: Correspondence between the Chairman of the Council of Ministers of the U.S.S.R. and the Presidents of the U.S.A. and the Prime Ministers of Great Britain during the Great Patriotic War of 1941–1945*, 2 vols. (Moscow: Foreign Languages Publishing House, 1957).

The most important published memoirs and diaries of Marshall's wartime associates are Henry H. Arnold, *Global Mission* (New York: Harper & Brothers, 1949); Ernest J. King and Walter M. Whitehill, *Fleet Admiral King: A Naval Record* (New York: Norton, 1952); William D. Leahy, *I Was There* (New York: Whittlesey House, 1950); Henry L. Stimson and McGeorge Bundy, *On Active Service in Peace and War* (New York: Harper & Brothers, 1947); John M. Blum, *From the Morgenthau Diaries*, 3 vols. (Boston: Houghton Mifflin, 1959–67); Cordell Hull, *The Memoirs of Cordell Hull*, 2 vols. (New York: Macmillan, 1948); and W. Averell Harriman, *Special Envoy to Churchill and Stalin, 1941–1946* (New York: Random House, 1975). On the British side, see Winston S. Churchill's incomparable *The Second World War* (Boston: Houghton Mifflin, 1948–53), as well as Arthur Bryant, *The Turn of the Tide* and *Triumph in the West: A History of the War Years Based on the Diaries of Field-Marshal Lord Alanbrooke, Chief of the Imperial General Staff* (Garden City, N.Y.: Doubleday, 1957–59); Sir Charles Wilson, *Churchill Taken from the Diaries of Lord Moran: The Struggle for Survival, 1940–1965* (Boston: Houghton Mifflin, 1966); Anthony Eden, *The Memoirs of Anthony Eden, Earl of Avon: The Reckoning* (Boston: Houghton Mifflin, 1965); Sir Hastings Ismay, *The Memoirs of General Lord Ismay* (New York: Viking, 1960); and Sir John Kennedy, *The Business of War* (London: Hutchinson, 1957). For memoirs and letters of key U.S. generals, see Dwight D. Eisenhower, *Crusade in Europe* (New York: Doubleday, 1948) and *At Ease: Stories I Tell to Friends* (New York: Doubleday, 1967); Alfred D. Chandler, Jr., *The Papers of Dwight David Eisenhower: The War Years*, 5 vols (Baltimore: Johns Hopkins University Press, 1970); Joseph P. Hobbs, *Dear General: Eisenhower's Wartime Letters to Marshall* (Baltimore: Johns Hopkins University Press, 1971); Omar N. Bradley, *A Soldier's Story* (New York: Holt, 1951) and with Clay Blair *A General's Life: An Autobiography* (New York: Simon & Schuster, 1983); Mark Clark, *Calculated Risk* (New York: Harper & Brothers, 1950); John R. Deane, *The Strange Alliance: The Story of Our Efforts at Wartime Cooperation with Russia* (New York: Viking, 1947); Douglas MacArthur, *Reminiscences* (New York: McGraw-Hill, 1964); Martin Blumenson, *The Patton Papers*, 2 vols. (Boston: Houghton Mifflin, 1972–74); Albert C. Wedemeyer, *Wedemeyer Reports!* (New York: Henry Holt, 1958); Keith E. Eiler ed. *Wedemeyer on War and Peace* (Stanford, Calif.: Hoover Institution Press, 1987); and Theodore H. White, ed., *The Stilwell Papers* (New York: William Sloan Associates, 1948).

The most recent and valuable biographical analyses of Marshall's wartime associates include Alex Danchev, *Very Special Relationship: Field-Marshall Sir John*

Dill and the Anglo-American Alliance, 1941–1944 (London: Pergamon, 1986); Thomas M. Coffey, *HAP: The Story of the U.S. Air Force and the Man Who Built It, General Henry H. "Hap" Arnold* (New York: Viking, 1982); Thomas B. Buell, *Master of Seapower: A Biography of Fleet Admiral Ernest J. King* (Boston: Little, Brown, 1980); Robert William Love, Jr., ed., *The Chiefs of Naval Operations* (Annapolis, Md.: Naval Institute Press, 1980); Henry H. Adams, *Witness to Power: The Life of Fleet Admiral William D. Leahy* (Annapolis, Md.: Naval Institute Press, 1985); Martin Gilbert, *Winston S. Churchill*, vols. 6, 7 (Boston: Houghton Mifflin, 1983–86); David Fraser, *Alanbrooke* (New York: Atheneum, 1982); Stephen E. Ambrose, *Eisenhower*, 2 vols. (New York: Simon & Schuster, 1983–84) and *The Supreme Commander: The War Years of General Dwight D. Eisenhower* (New York: Doubleday, 1969); D. Clayton James, *The Years of MacArthur*, 3 vols. (Boston: Houghton Mifflin, 1970–85); Barbara Tuchman, *Stilwell and the American Experience in China, 1911–1945* (New York: Macmillan, 1970); and Russell A. Gugeler, "George Marshall and Orlando Ward, 1939–1941," *Parameters* 13 (March 1983): 28–42. Robert Sherwood's *Roosevelt and Hopkins: An Intimate History*, rev. ed. (New York: Grosset & Dunlap, 1950), remains valuable despite its age but should be supplemented with three more recent works: Henry H. Adams, *Harry Hopkins: A Biography* (New York: G. P. Putnam's Sons, 1977); George McJimsey, *Harry Hopkins: Ally of the Poor and Defender of Democracy* (Cambridge: Harvard University Press, 1987); and Dwight W. Tuttle, *Harry L. Hopkins and Anglo-American Soviet Relations, 1941–1945* (New York: Garland, 1983).

The best analyses of Marshall's wartime commander in chief are Robert Dallek's *Franklin D. Roosevelt and American Foreign Policy, 1933–1945* (New York: Oxford University Press, 1979) and James MacGregor Burns, *Roosevelt: The Soldier of Freedom, 1940–1945* (New York: Harcourt Brace Jovanovich, 1970). See also Robert Divine, *Roosevelt and World War II* (Baltimore, Md.: Johns Hopkins University Press, 1969). Eric Larrabee, *Commander in Chief: Franklin Delano Roosevelt, His Lieutenants, and Their War* (New York: Harper & Row, 1987), is a solid popular history with long chapters on Marshall and Roosevelt, as well as other members of the JCS and numerous theater commanders. D. Clayton James, *A Time for Giants: The Politics of the American High Command in World War II* (New York: Franklin Watts, 1987) offers much briefer biographical sketches.

Gaddis Smith, *American Diplomacy During the Second World War*, rev. ed. (New York: Knopf, 1985) is a comprehensive yet brief and up-to-date survey. See also Herbert Feis, *Churchill, Roosevelt and Stalin: The War They Waged and the Peace They Sought*, 2d ed. (Princeton: Princeton University Press, 1967); William H. McNeil, *America, Britain and Russia: Their Cooperation and Conflict, 1941–1946* (London: Oxford University Press, 1953); and John L. Snell, *Illusion and Necessity: The Diplomacy of Global War, 1939–1945* (Boston: Houghton Mifflin, 1963). Dated but typical of the early attacks on U.S. strategy and diplomacy during the war are Hanson Baldwin's *Great Mistakes of the War* (New York: Harper & Brothers, 1950) and Chester Wilmot, *The Struggle for Europe* (New York: Harper & Brothers, 1952). Gabriel Kolko's *The Politics of War: The World and United States Foreign Policy, 1943–1945* (New York: Random House, 1968) is sharply critical from an opposing leftist perspective. For Soviet foreign policy, see Vojtech Mastny, *Russia's Road to the Cold War: Diplomacy, Warfare, and the Politics of Communism, 1941–1945* (New York: Columbia University Press, 1979).

World War II: Specific Issues

For U.S. entry see Robert Divine, *The Reluctant Belligerent: American Entry into World War II*, 2d ed. (New York: Wiley, 1979); Arnold A. Offner, *The Origins of the Second World War* (New York: Praeger, 1975); and William L. Langer and S. Everett Gleason, *The Challenge to Isolation, 1937–1940* and *The Undeclared War, 1940–1941* (New York: Harper & Brothers, 1952–53). More specialized works include J. Garry Clifford and Samuel R. Spencer, Jr., *The First Peacetime Draft* (Lawrence: University Press of Kansas, 1986); David Reynolds, *The Creation of the Anglo-American Alliance, 1937–1941: A Study in Competitive Cooperation* (Chapel Hill: University of North Carolina Press, 1982); David G. Haglund, "George C. Marshall and the Question of Aid to England, May–June, 1940," *Journal of Contemporary History* 15 (October 1980): 745–60; Mark M. Lowenthal, "Roosevelt and the Coming of the War: The Search for United States Policy, 1937–1942," *Journal of Contemporary History* 16 (July 1981): 413–40; Joseph P. Lash, *Roosevelt and Churchill, 1939–1941: The Partnership That Saved the West* (New York: Norton, 1976); Theodore A. Wilson, *The First Summit: Roosevelt and Churchill at Placentia Bay, 1941* (Boston: Houghton Mifflin, 1969); James R. Leutze, *Bargaining for Supremacy: Anglo-American Naval Collaboration, 1937–1941* (Chapel Hill: University of North Carolina Press, 1977); and Warren F. Kimball, *The Most Unsordid Act: Lend-Lease, 1939–1941* (Baltimore: Johns Hopkins University Press, 1969). For German-American relations, see James V. Compton, *The Swastika and the Eagle: Hitler, the United States and the Origins of World War II* (Boston: Houghton Mifflin, 1967); Saul Friedlander, *Prelude to Downfall: Hitler and the United States, 1939–1941* (New York: Knopf, 1967); Patrick Abbazia, *Mr. Roosevelt's Navy: The Private War of the U.S. Atlantic Fleet, 1939–1942* (Annapolis, Md.: Naval Institute Press, 1975); Thomas A. Bailey and Paul B. Ryan, *Hitler vs. Roosevelt: The Undeclared Naval War* (New York: Free Press, 1979); and Waldo Heinrichs, "President Franklin D. Roosevelt's Intervention in the Battle of the Atlantic," *Diplomatic History* 10 (Fall 1986): 311–32.

Japanese-American relations and the coming of war in the Pacific are analyzed in Dorothy Borg and Shumpei Okamoto, eds., *Pearl Harbor as History:*

Japanese-American Relations, 1931–1941 (New York: Columbia University Press, 1973); Herbert Feis, *The Road to Pearl Harbor: The Coming of the War between the United States and Japan* (Princeton: Princeton University Press, 1950); Jonathan G. Utley, *Going to War with Japan, 1937–1941* (Knoxville: University of Tennessee Press, 1985); Akira Iriye, *Across the Pacific: An Inner History of American-East Asian Relations* (New York: Harcourt, Brace & World, 1967); Richard D. Burns and Edward M. Bennett, eds., *Diplomats in Crisis: United States–Chinese–Japanese Relations, 1919–1941* (Santa Barbara, Calif.: ABC-Clio, 1974); and Paul W. Schroeder, *The Axis Alliance and Japanese-American Relations, 1941* (Ithaca, N.Y.: Cornell University Press, 1958). The best analyses of the Pearl Harbor attack are Roberta Wohlstetter, *Pearl Harbor: Warning and Decision* (Stanford: Stanford University Press, 1962), and Gordon Prange, *At Dawn We Slept: The Untold Story of Pearl Harbor,* and *Pearl Harbor: The Verdict of History* (New York: McGraw-Hill, 1981, 1986). For the ensuing political debate over responsibility, see Martin Melosi, *The Shadow of Pearl Harbor: Political Controversy over the Surprise Attack, 1941–1946* (College Station: Texas A&M University Press, 1977). For the conspiracy thesis, see Frank P. Mintz, *Revisionism and the Origins of Pearl Harbor* (Lanham, Md.: University Press of America, 1985).

The 1941–43 Allied debate over global and European strategy is analyzed in Trumbull Higgins, *Winston Churchill and the Second Front, 1940–1943* (New York: Oxford University Press, 1957), *Soft Underbelly: The Anglo-American Controversy over the Italian Campaign, 1939–1945* (New York: Macmillan, 1968), and "The Anglo-American Historians' War in the Mediterranean, 1942–1945," *Military Affairs* 34 (October 1970): 84–88; Richard M. Leighton, "OVERLORD Revisited: An Interpretation of American Strategy in the European War, 1942–1944," *American Historical Review* 68 (July 1963): 919–37; Michael Howard, *The Mediterranean Strategy in the Second World War* (London: Weidenfeld Nicolson, 1968); Richard W. Steele, *The First Offensive, 1942: Roosevelt, Marshall, and the Making of American Strategy* (Bloomington: Indiana University Press, 1973); Mark A. Stoler, *The Politics of the Second Front: American Military Planning and Diplomacy in Coalition Warfare, 1941–1943* (Westport, Conn.: Greenwood Press, 1977); Joseph L. Strange, "The British Rejection of Operation SLEDGE-HAMMER: An Alternative Motive," *Military Affairs* 46 (February 1982): 6–13; Walter Scott Dunn, *Second Front Now 1943* (University: University of Alabama Press, 1980); and John Grigg, *1943: The Victory That Never Was* (New York: Hill & Wang, 1980). For the numerous Allied conferences during these years, see Robert Beitzell, *The Uneasy Alliance: America, Britain and Russia, 1941–1943* (New York: Knopf, 1972); Keith Eubank, *Summit at Teheran* (New York: William Morrow, 1985); Paul D. Mayle, *Eureka Summit: Agreement in Principle and the Big Three at Tehran, 1943* (Newark: University of Delaware Press, 1987); and Keith Sainsbury, *The Turning Point: Roosevelt, Stalin, Churchill and Chiang-Kai-Shek, 1943—the Moscow, Cairo and Teheran Conferences* (New York: Oxford University Press, 1985). For additional background on the North African campaign, see Arthur Layton Funk, *The Politics of TORCH: The Allied Landings and the Algiers Putsch, 1942* (Lawrence: University Press of Kansas, 1974), and Keith Sainsbury, *The North African Landings, 1942* (Newark: University of Delaware Press, 1979). For Normandy and the European campaign, see Eisenhower Foundation, *D-Day: The Normandy Invasion in Retrospect* (Lawrence: University Press of Kansas, 1971), and Russell F. Weigley, *Eisenhower's Lieutenants: The Campaigns of France and Germany, 1944–1945* (Bloomington: Indiana University Press, 1981). John S. D. Eisenhower, *Allies: Pearl Harbor to D-Day* (New York: Doubleday, 1982), and David Eisenhower, *Eisenhower: At War, 1943–1945* (New York: Random House, 1986), are perceptive works by Ike's son and grandson, respectively.

For the breaking and use of Axis secret codes, see Ronald Lewin, *Ultra Goes to War* (New York: McGraw-Hill, 1978) and *The American Magic: Codes, Ciphers and the Defeat of Japan* (New York: Farrar, Straus and Giroux, 1982). The home front is analyzed in John M. Blum, *V Was for Victory: Politics and American Culture During the World War II* (New York: Harcourt Brace Jovanovich, 1976); and Richard Polenberg, *War and Society: The United States, 1941–1945* (Philadelphia: Lippincott, 1976). For unconditional surrender, Raymond G. O'Connor's *Diplomacy for Victory: FDR and Unconditional Surrender* (New York: Norton, 1971) provides a brief interpretive and historiographical analysis. Stephen E. Ambrose's *Eisenhower and Berlin: The Decision to Halt at the Elbe, 1945* (New York: Norton, 1967) performs a similar service for this controversial episode. For analyses of the equally controversial Yalta Conference, see Richard Fenno, ed., *The Yalta Conference*, 2d ed. (Lexington, Mass.: D. C. Heath, 1972); John L. Snell, ed., *The Meaning of Yalta: Big Three Diplomacy and the New Balance of Power* (Baton Rouge: Louisiana State University Press, 1956); Diane Shaver Clemens, *Yalta* (New York: Oxford University Press, 1970); Alan G. Theoharis, *The Yalta Myths: An Issue in U.S. Politics, 1945–1955* (Columbia: University of Missouri Press, 1970); and Russell D. Buhite, *Decisions at Yalta: An Appraisal of Summit Diplomacy* (Wilmington, Del.: Scholarly Resources, 1986). See also George C. Herring, *Aid to Russia, 1941–1946: Strategy, Diplomacy and the Origins of the Cold War* (New York: Columbia University Press, 1973). Army planning for the postwar era is analyzed in Michael Sherry, *Preparing for the Next War: American Plans for Postwar Defense, 1941–1945* (New Haven: Yale University Press, 1977). For other services and departments, see Harley Notter, *Postwar Foreign Policy Preparation, 1943–1945* (Washington, D.C.: Government Printing Office, 1950); Vincent Davis, *Postwar Defense Policy and the U.S. Navy, 1943–1946* (Chapel Hill: University of North Carolina Press, 1962); Perry McCoy Smith, *The Air Force Plans for Peace, 1943–1945* (Baltimore: Johns Hopkins University Press, 1970); and Herman S. Wolk, *Planning and Organizing the Postwar Air Force, 1943–1947* (Washington, D.C.: Office of Air Force History, 1984). See also Warren Kimball, *Swords or Ploughshares?*

The Morgenthau Plan for Defeated Nazi Germany, 1943–1946 (Philadelphia: Lippincott, 1976).

The Pacific and Asia

For the war against Japan, see Christopher Thorne's outstanding *Allies of a Kind: The United States, Britain and the War against Japan, 1941–1945* (New York: Oxford University Press, 1978); Ronald H. Spector, *Eagle against the Sun: The American War with Japan* (New York: Random House, 1984); Akira Iriye, *Power and Culture: The Japanese-American War, 1941–1945* (Cambridge: Harvard University Press, 1981); H. P. Willmott, *Empires in the Balance: Japanese and Allied Pacific Strategies to April 1942* (Annapolis, Md.: Naval Institute Press, 1982); and John W. Dower, *War without Mercy: Race and Power in the Pacific War* (New York: Pantheon, 1986). For the atomic bomb and Japan's surrender, see Richard Hewlett and Oscar Anderson, *The New World, 1939–1946*, vol. 1 in the official *A History of the United States Atomic Energy Commission* (University Park, Pa.: Pennsylvania State University Press, 1962), as well as Martin Sherwin, *A World Destroyed: The Atomic Bomb and the Grand Alliance* (New York: Knopf, 1975); and Barton J. Bernstein, ed., *The Atomic Bomb: The Critical Issues* (Boston: Little, Brown, 1976). See also Brian L. Villa, "The U.S. Army, Unconditional Surrender, and the Potsdam Declaration," *Journal of American History* 63 (June 1976): 66–92 and "The Atomic Bomb and the Normandy Invasion," *Perspectives in American History* 11 (1977–78): 463–502. For the Potsdam conference, see Herbert Feis, *Between War and Peace: The Potsdam Conference* (Princeton: Princeton University Press, 1960), and Charles L. Mee, Jr., *Meeting at Potsdam* (New York: Evans, 1975).

Wartime and postwar relations with China are analyzed in Michael Schaller, *The U.S. Crusade in China, 1938–1945* (New York: Columbia University Press, 1978); Herbert Feis, *The China Tangle: The American Effort in China from Pearl Harbor to the Marshall Mission* (Princeton: Princeton University Press, 1953); Tang Tsou, *America's Failure in China, 1941–50* (Chicago: University of Chicago Press, 1963); Yonosuki Nagai and Akire Iriye, eds., *The Origins of the Cold War in Asia* (New York: Columbia University Press, 1977); and Russell D. Buhite, *Patrick J. Hurley and American Foreign Policy* (Ithaca, N.Y.: Cornell University Press, 1973). For Stilwell's mission, see Riley Sunderland and Charles F. Romanus, eds., *Stilwell's Personal File: China, Burma, India, 1942–1944*, 5 vols. (Wilmington, Del.: Scholarly Resources, 1976), as well as the volumes by these authors in *U.S. Army in World War II* and the Tuchman biography.

Documents relating to the Marshall mission to China are in the State Department's White Paper, *United States Relations with China with Special Reference to the Period 1944–1949* (Washington, D.C.: Government Printing Office,

1949), and its *Foreign Relations* series volumes for 1945 and 1946. See also *Marshall's Mission to China, December 1945–January 1947: The Report and Appended Documents*, 2 vols. (Arlington, Va.: University Publications of America, 1976). For memoirs relating to the mission, see John Robinson Beal, *Marshall in China* (Garden City, N.Y.: Doubleday, 1970), and John F. Melby, *The Mandate of Heaven: Record of a Civil War, China, 1945–49* (Toronto: University of Toronto Press, 1968). No book-length secondary account of the mission has yet been written, although Steven I. Levine analyzes it extensively in "A New Look at American Mediation in the Chinese Civil War: The Marshall Mission and Manchuria," *Diplomatic History* 3 (Fall 1979): 349–75, and his recent *Anvil of Victory: The Communist Revolution in Manchuria, 1945–1948* (New York: Columbia University Press, 1987).

The State Department and Cold War

The massive historiographical debate over the origins of the cold war is explained and analyzed in J. Samuel Walker, "Historians and Cold War Origins: The New Consensus," in Gerald K. Haines and J. Samuel Walker, eds., *American Foreign Relations: A Historiographical Review* (Westport, Conn.: Greenwood Press, 1981). For general histories of the conflict and its origins from differing perspectives, see Stephen Ambrose, *Rise to Globalism: American Foreign Policy since 1938*, 4th rev. ed. (New York: Penguin, 1985); Barton J. Bernstein, ed., *Politics and Policies of the Truman Administration* (Chicago: Quadrangle, 1970); Herbert Feis, *From Trust to Terror: The Onset of the Cold War, 1945–1950* (New York: Norton, 1970); John L. Gaddis, *The United States and the Origins of the Cold War, 1941–1947* (New York: Columbia University Press, 1972); Joyce Kolko and Gabriel Kolko, *The Limits of Power: The World and United States Foreign Policy, 1945–1954* (New York: Harper & Row, 1972); Walter LaFeber, *America, Russia and the Cold War, 1945–1984* (New York: Knopf, 1985); Thomas G. Paterson, *On Every Front: The Making of the Cold War* (New York: Norton, 1979); Adam Ulam, *The Rivals: America and Russia since World War II* (New York: Viking, 1971); and Daniel Yergin, *Shattered Peace: The Origins of the Cold War and the National Security State* (Boston: Houghton Mifflin, 1977).

The key document collection is once again the State Department's *Foreign Relations* series. The 1947–48 volumes cover all the conferences Marshall attended as secretary of state, as well as regular diplomatic correspondence. For Marshall's public statements, see the State Department *Bulletin* and the microfilm typescript, *Press Conferences of the Secretary of State, 1922–1974* (Wilmington, Del.: Scholarly Resources). See also Thomas H. Etzold and John L. Gaddis, eds., *Containment: Documents on American Policy and Strategy, 1945–1950* (New York: Columbia University Press, 1978); and Anna K. Nelson, ed., *The State Department Policy Planning Staff Papers*, 3 vols. (New York: Garland, 1983).

Key memoirs, diaries, and paper collections for this time period include Harry S. Truman, *Memoirs*, 2 vols. (Garden City, N.Y.: Doubleday, 1955–56); Robert H. Ferrell, ed., *Off the Record: The Private Papers of Harry S. Truman* (New York: Harper & Row, 1980); Dean Acheson, *Present at the Creation: My Years in the State Department* (New York: Norton, 1969), and *Sketches from Life of Men I Have Known* (New York: Harper & Brothers, 1959); Charles Bohlen, *Witness to History, 1929–1969* (New York: Norton, 1973); Joseph M. Jones, *The Fifteen Weeks* (New York: Harcourt, Brace & World, 1955); Walter Millis, ed., *The Forrestal Diaries* (New York: Viking, 1951); George F. Kennan, *Memoirs*, 2 vols. (Boston: Little, Brown, 1967–72); William L. Clayton, "GATT, the Marshall Plan, and OECD," *Political Science Quarterly* 78 (December 1963): 493–503; Frederick J. Dabney, *Selected Papers of Will Clayton* (Baltimore: Johns Hopkins University Press, 1971); and Arthur H. Vandenberg, Jr., ed., *The Private Papers of Senator Vandenberg* (Boston: Houghton Mifflin, 1952). See also John Morton Blum, ed., *The Price of Vision: The Diary of Henry A. Wallace, 1942–1946* (Boston: Houghton Mifflin, 1973); Walter Bedell Smith, *My Three Years in Moscow* (Philadelphia: Lippincott, 1950); Lucius D. Clay, *Decision in Germany* (Garden City, N.Y.: Doubleday, 1950); and Jean Edward Smith, ed., *The Papers of General Lucius D. Clay: Germany, 1945–1949*, 2 vols. (Bloomington: Indiana University Press, 1974).

For relevant biographical studies of President Truman, see Robert J. Donovan, *Conflict and Crisis: The Presidency of Harry S. Truman, 1945–1948* (New York: Norton, 1977); and Richard F. Haynes, *The Awesome Power: Harry S. Truman as Commander in Chief* (Baton Rouge: Louisiana State University Press, 1973). While very entertaining, Merle Miller's *Plain Speaking: An Oral Biography of Harry S. Truman* (New York: Berkely, 1973) must be used with caution. For other biographies, see Gaddis Smith's *Dean Acheson*, the volume 16 companion to the Ferrell Study of Marshall cited at the beginning of this essay, in Samuel F. Bemis and Robert H. Ferrell, eds., *The American Secretaries of State and Their Diplomacy* (New York: Cooper Square, 1972); David S. McLellan, *Dean Acheson: The State Department Years* (New York: Dodd, Mead, 1976); T. Michael Ruddy, *The Cautious Diplomat: Charles E. Bohlen and the Soviet Union, 1927–1969* (Kent, Ohio: Kent State University Press, 1986); George T. Mazuzan, *Warren R. Austin at the U.N., 1946–1953* (Kent, Ohio: Kent State University Press, 1977); John H. Backer, *Winds of History: The German Years of Lucius DuBignon Clay* (New York: Van Nostrand Reinhold, 1983); Lloyd C. Gardner, *Architects of Illusion: Men and Ideas in American Foreign Policy, 1941–1949* (Chicago: Quadrangle, 1970); and Walter Isaacson and Evan Thomas, *The Wise Men: Six Friends and the World They Made; Acheson, Bohlen, Harriman, Kennan, Lovett, McCloy* (New York: Simon and Schuster, 1986).

Michael J. Hogan's *The Marshall Plan: America, Britain and the Reconstruction of Western Europe, 1947–1952* (Cambridge: Cambridge University Press, 1987) is the most recent and comprehensive treatment of the European Recovery Program. See also Alan S. Milward, *The Reconstruction of Western Europe, 1945–1951* (London: Methuen, 1984); John Gimbel, *The Origins of the Marshall Plan* (Stanford, Calif.: Stanford University Press, 1976); Harry B. Price's official history, *The Marshall Plan and Its Meaning* (Ithaca, N.Y.: Cornell University Press, 1955); Charles L. Mee, Jr., *The Marshall Plan: The Launching of the Pax Americana* (New York: Simon & Schuster, 1984); Theodore Wilson, *The Marshall Plan, 1947–1951* (New York: Foreign Policy Association, 1977); Hadley Arkes, *Bureaucracy, the Marshall Plan, and the National Interest* (Princeton: Princeton University Press, 1973); Thomas G. Paterson, *Soviet-American Confrontation: Postwar Reconstruction and the Origins of the Cold War* (Baltimore: Johns Hopkins University Press, 1973); Thomas A. Bailey, *The Marshall Plan Summer: An Eyewitness Report on Europe and the Russians in 1947* (Stanford, Calif.: Hoover Institution Press, 1977); Harold L.. Hitchens, "Influences on the Congressional Decision to Pass the Marshall Plan," *Western Political Quarterly* 21 (March 1968): 51–68; and Scott Jackson, "Prologue to the Marshall Plan: The Origins of the American Commitment for a European Recovery Program," *Journal of American History* 65 (March 1979): 1043–68.

Containment and national security policy are cogently and perceptively analyzed in John L. Gaddis, *Strategies of Containment: A Critical Appraisal of Postwar American National Security Policy* (New York: Oxford University Press, 1982); and Melvyn P. Leffler, "The American Conception of National Security and the Beginnings of the Cold War, 1945–1948," *American Historical Review* 89 (April 1984): 364–81. See also Thomas G. Paterson, ed., *Containment and the Cold War: American Foreign Policy Since 1945* (Reading, Mass: Addison-Wesley, 1973); Charles Gati, ed., *Caging the Bear: Containment and the Cold War* (Indianapolis: Bobbs-Merrill, 1972); Lloyd Gardner, "James V. Forrestal and George F. Kennan: Will the Real 'Mr. X' Please Stand Up?" in his previously cited *Architects of Illusion;* C. Ben Wright, "Mr. X and Containment," *Slavic Review* 35 (1976): 1–36; the exchange of views on containment in *Foreign Affairs* 55 and 56 (1977–78): 873–87, 430–31; and the exchange in *International Studies Quarterly* 15 (December 1971): 526–43 and 17 (June 1973): 205–26. For the Truman Doctrine, see Richard M. Freeland, *The Truman Doctrine and the Origins of McCarthyism: Foreign Policy, Domestic Politics, and Internal Security, 1946–1948* (New York: Knopf, 1972); Bruce R. Kuniholm, *The Origins of the Cold War in the Near East: Great Power Conflict and Diplomacy in Iran, Turkey and Greece* (Princeton: Princeton University Press, 1980); and Lawrence S. Wittner, *American Intervention in Greece, 1943–1949* (New York: Columbia University Press, 1982).

For Germany, see John Gimbel, *The American Occupation of Germany: Politics and the Military, 1945–49* (Stanford, Calif.: Stanford University Press, 1968); Edward N. Peterson, *The American Occupation of Germany: Retreat to Victory* (Detroit: Wayne State University Press, 1978); John H. Backer, *The*

Decision to Divide Germany: American Foreign Policy in Transition (Durham, N.C.: Duke University Press, 1978). The Berlin crisis is analyzed in Avi Shlaim, *The United States and the Berlin Blockade, 1948–1949: A Study in Crisis Decision Making* (Berkeley: University of California Press, 1983); W. Phillips Davison, *The Berlin Blockade: A Study in Cold War Politics* (Princeton: Princeton University Press, 1958); Manuel F. Gottlieb, *The German Peace Settlement and the Berlin Crisis* (New York: Paine-Whitman, 1960); and Jean Edward Smith, *The Defense of Berlin* (Baltimore: Johns Hopkins University Press, 1963). For NATO see Lawrence S. Kaplan, *The United States and NATO: The Formative Years* (Lexington: University of Kentucky Press, 1984); Timothy P. Ireland, *Creating the Entangling Alliance: The Origins of the North Atlantic Treaty Organization* (Westport, Conn.: Greenwood Press, 1981); Escott M. Reid, *Time of Fear and Hope: The Making of the North Atlantic Treaty, 1947–1949* (Toronto: McClelland and Stewart, 1977); and Robert Osgood, *NATO: The Entangling Alliance* (Chicago: University of Chicago Press, 1962).

For U.S. policy toward China from 1947 to 1950, see the works cited above on wartime and postwar relations with China and the Marshall mission, as well as William Stueck, *The Wedemeyer Mission: American Politics and Foreign Policy during the Cold War* (Athens: University of Georgia Press, 1984); Nancy Bernkopf Tucker, *Patterns in the Dust: Chinese-American Relations and the Recognition Controversy, 1949–1950* (New York: Columbia University Press, 1983); Ernest R. May, *The Truman Administration and China, 1945–1949* (Philadelphia: Lippincott, 1975); Lewis M. Purifoy, *Harry Truman's China Policy: McCarthyism and the Diplomacy of Hysteria, 1947–1951* (New York: New Viewpoints, 1976); and Dorothy Borg and Waldo Heinrichs, eds., *Uncertain Years: Chinese-American Relations, 1947–1950* (New York: Columbia University Press, 1980). Peter Grose, *Israel in the Mind of America* (New York: Knopf, 1983), offers a brief, popular, and perceptive account of Palestine partition and Israeli recognition issues. For more detailed studies, see John Snetsinger, *Truman, the Jewish Vote and the Creation of Israel* (Stanford, Calif.: Hoover Institution Press, 1974); Zvi Ganin, *Truman, American Jewry and Israel, 1945–1948* (New York: Holmes and Meier, 1979); William Roger Louis, *The British Empire in the Middle East, 1945–1951: Arab Nationalism, the United States, and Postwar Imperalism* (New York: Oxford University Press, 1984); Kenneth R. Bain, *The March to Zion: United States Policy and the Founding of Israel* (College Station, Tx.: Texas A&M University Press, 1979); Michael J. Cohen, *Palestine and the Great Powers, 1945–1948* (Princeton: Princeton University Press, 1982); and Evan M. Wilson, *Decision on Palestine: How the United States Came to Recognize Israel* (Stanford, Calif.: Hoover Institute Press, 1979).

The Defense Department and the Korean War

For the establishment and early history of the Defense Department and Joint Chiefs of Staff, see Demetrios Caraley, *The Politics of Military Unification* (New York: Columbia University Press, 1966); Alice C. Cole et al., eds., *The Department of Defense: Documents on Establishment and Organization, 1944–1978* (Washington, D.C.: Government Printing Office, 1979); Warner R. Schilling, Paul Y. Hammond, and Glenn H. Snyder, *Strategy, Politics and Defense Budgets* (New York: Columbia University Press, 1962); Douglas Kinnard, *The Secretaries of Defense* (Lexington: University of Kentucky Press, 1980); Paul Y. Hammond, "Super Carriers and B-36 Bombers: Appropriations, Strategy and Politics," in Harold Stein, ed., *American Civil-Military Deicisons: A Book of Case Studies* (Birmingham: University of Alabama Press, 1963); the series of articles on the services and unification in *Prologue* 7 (Spring 1975): 6–31; Paul R. Schratz, ed., *Evolution of the American Military Establishment since World War II* (Lexington, Va.: George C. Marshall Research Foundation, 1977); Lawrence J. Korb, *The Joint Chiefs of Staff: The First Twenty-five Years* (Bloomington: Indiana University Press, 1976); Richard K. Betts, *Soldiers, Statesmen and Cold War Crises* (Cambridge: Harvard University Press, 1977); and the official history by James F. Schnabel and Robert J. Watson, *The History of the Joint Chiefs of Staff: The Joint Chiefs of Staff and National Policy*, 4 vols. (Wilmington, Del.: Michael Glazier, 1979).

For nuclear strategy, see Gregg Herken, *The Winning Weapon: The Atomic Bomb in the Cold War, 1945–1950* (New York: Knopf, 1980); Harry R. Borowski, *A Hollow Threat: Strategic Air Power and Containment before Korea* (Westport, Conn.: Greenwood Press, 1982); and David A. Rosenberg, "American Atomic Strategy and the Hydrogen Bomb Decision," *Journal of American History* 66 (June 1979): 62–87. For early war plans, see the Etzold and Gaddis collection of containment documents cited above. NSC-68 is analyzed in previously cited works by Gaddis on containment and Hammond on defense budgets. See also Joseph M. Siracusa, "NSC-68: A Reappraisal," *Naval War College Review* 33, (November–December 1980): 4–14; Sam Postbrief, "Departure from Incrementalism in U.S. Strategic Planning: The Origins of NSC-68," *Naval War College Review* 32 (March–April 1980): 34–57; Samuel F. Wells, Jr., "Sounding the Tocsin: NSC 68 and the Soviet Threat," *International Security* 4 (Fall 1979): 116–58; and the rejoinders by Gaddis and Paul Nitze in the 1980 volume, 164–76.

The most recent studies of the Korean conflict are Bruce Cumings, *The Origins of the Korean War: Liberation and the Emergence of Separate Regimes, 1945–1947* (Princeton: Princeton University Press, 1981); William W. Stueck, Jr., *The Road to Confrontation: American Policy toward China and Korea, 1947–1950* (Chapel Hill: University of North Carolina Press, 1981); Charles M. Dobbs, *The Unwanted Symbol: American Foreign Policy, the Cold War and Korea, 1945–*

1950 (Kent, Ohio: Kent State University Press, 1981); and Burton I. Kaufman, *The Korean War: Challenges in Crisis, Credibility and Command* (New York: Knopf, 1986). For popular accounts, see Joseph C. Goulden, *Korea: The Untold Story of the War* (New York: Times Books, 1982); David Rees, *Korea: The Limited War* (New York: St. Martin's Press, 1964); and Thomas R. Fehrenbach, *This Kind of War* (New York: Macmillan, 1963). See also Ronald J. Caridi, *The Korean War and American Politics: The Republican Party as a Case Study* (Philadelphia: University of Pennsylvania Press, 1968); and Francis H. Heller, comp., *The Korean War: A 25 Year Perspective* (Lawrence: Regents Press of Kansas, 1977). Official studies include the JCS history by Schnabel and Watson cited above, as well as *United States Army in the Korean War*, 3 vols. (Washington, D.C.: Government Printing Office, 1961–72); Robert F. Futrell, *The United States Air Force in Korea, 1950–1953* (New York: Duell, Sloan and Pearce, 1961); and James A. Field, *History of United States Naval Operations in Korea* (Washington, D.C.: Government Printing Office, 1962). For documents, see the appropriate volumes of *Foreign Relations*, as well as the collections cited above.

The Truman-MacArthur controversy is analyzed in previously cited relevant biographies and histories, as well as Trumbull Higgins, *Korea and the Fall of MacArthur: A Precis in Limited War* (New York: Oxford University Press, 1960); and John Spanier, *The Truman-MacArthur Controversy and the Korean War* (New York: Norton, 1965). The congressional hearings on MacArthur's relief should also be consulted. Matthew B. Ridgway's *The Korean War* (New York: Doubleday, 1967) and J. Lawton Collins's *War in Peacetime: The History and Lessons of Korea* (Boston: Houghton Mifflin, 1969) are important military memoirs. For McCarthyism, see Thomas C. Reeves, *The Life and Times of Joe McCarthy: A Biography* (New York: Stein & Day, 1982); David Caute, *The Great Fear: The Anti-Communist Purge under Truman and Eisenhower* (New York: Simon & Schuster, 1978); Robert Griffith, *The Politics of Fear: Joseph R. McCarthy and the Senate* (Lexington: University of Kentucky Press, 1970); and Michael P. Rogin, *The Intellectuals and McCarthy: The Radical Specter* (Cambridge: MIT Press, 1967).

INDEX

ABOUT THE AUTHOR

Mark A. Stoler is professor of history at the University of Vermont in Burlington, specializing in twentieth-century U.S. diplomatic and military history. He received his B.A. from the City College of New York and his M.A. and Ph.D. from the University of Wisconsin–Madison. He is the author of *The Politics of the Second Front* and, with Marshall True, *Explorations in American History*. His other publications include an edited collection of documents on the origins of the cold war and numerous articles on World War II strategy, diplomacy, and historiography; the Vietnam War; and the teaching of U.S. history. He has been a visiting professor in the Strategy Department of the Naval War College in Newport, Rhode Island, a Fulbright lecturer at the University of Haifa in Israel, and a recipient of the University of Vermont's George V. Kidder Outstanding Faculty Award.